Statewatch*ing* the new Europe
a handbook on the European state

Statewatching the new Europe
a handbook on the European state

Edited by Tony Bunyan

Written by

Tony Bunyan
Michael Farrell
Liz Fekete
Paddy Hillyard
Peter Klerks
Mike Tomlinson
Frances Webber

with an overview by
A Sivanandan

and help and advice from Trevor Hemmings, Ann Singleton and Hilary Arnott. Cover by Louise Trewavas.

and financial support from Unison, the European Commission, Ajahma Trust and the Silbury Fund.

Printed by
Russell Press
Radford Mill
Norton Street
Nottingham NG7 3HN
UK

ISBN 1 874481 02 4

CONTENTS

Contributors

Tony Bunyan is editor of *Statewatch* bulletin and specialises in issues concerning Europe and civil liberties. He is author of The Political Police in Britain, 1976. He previously worked for *State Research* (1977-1981) and from 1982-1991 as head of police monitoring units, including that of the Greater London Council.

Michael Farrell is a former leader of the Northern Ireland civil rights movement, who has written extensively about the history of the conflict there. He is now a lawyer practising in Dublin and Vice-Chairperson of the Irish Council for Civil Liberties (his paper is written in a personal capacity).

Liz Fekete is a researcher at the Institute of Race Relations, presently working on the European Race Audit. She is active in the anti-racist movement and is a member of the Campaign Against Racism and Fascism

Paddy Hillyard is a Senior Lecturer in Social Policy at Bristol University. His books include the recently published: Suspect Community: Peoples' experience of the Prevention of Terrorism Acts in Britain, and the Coercive State. He is a former chair of Liberty and a long-standing member of its Executive Committee.

Peter Klerks of Leiden University has been working on policing, security and intelligence and human rights issues for ten years.

Mike Tomlinson is a Lecturer in Social Policy at Queens University, Belfast. His books include: Northern Ireland: Between civil rights and civil war; Whose Law and Order: Aspects of Crime and Social Control in Ireland; and Unemployment in West Belfast. He is on the editorial board of the Irish Reporter and is a founder member of the West Belfast Economic Forum.

A Sivanandan is editor of *Race & Class*, director of the Institute of Race Relations, and is active in the black movement. He is author of A Different Hunger (Pluto, 1982) and Communities of Resistance: writings on Black Struggles for Socialism (Verso, 1990).

Frances Webber is a barrister specialising in immigration law, who writes for the Institute of Race Relations European Race Audit and is a member of the Campaign Against Racism and Fascism.

Preface

This handbook looks at the European state, linking the developments on immigration and asylum policy, the Trevi and Schengen groups, Europol and the European Information System. Much of the information about the new state is inaccessible and shrouded in secrecy and has not been open to discussion in parliaments (national and European). The handbook is intended to try and remedy this by bringing together the available information and placing in an analytical framework.

Information is also given for each of the EC and EFTA (EEA) states on policing, internal security services, immigration and asylum policies, and racist and fascist groups.

Some obvious areas have not been covered, for example, prisons and data protection because we did not feel able to deal with them adequately in this edition.

Revisions, comments and contributions

It is intended to prepare a revised and up-dated second edition of the handbook for publication in 1995, and therefore comments and suggestions and offers to contribute on specific subject areas or countries are invited.

To keep in touch with on-going developments you can subscribe to the *Statewatch* bulletin, which is published six times a year. The bulletin covers the state in the UK and Europe and contains: news, features, listings of new books, reports and articles, and of debates in the UK and European Parliaments. New contributors to the bulletin are welcomed.

The subscription to the bulletin in the UK and Europe is: £8 per year (students and unemployed); £10 (individuals); £15 (groups); £20 (institutions). Payment from outside the UK should be by Eurocheque, international money order or a sterling cheque drawn on a UK bank.

If you would like to comment on this handbook, subscribe and/or contribute to the bulletin please contact:

Statewatch, PO Box 1516,
London N16 0EW, UK

Tel: 081 802 1882 Fax: 081 880 1727
GEO2: Statewatch-off Greennet: ecstatewatch.

Beyond state-watching

A Sivanandan[1]

State-watching Europe is a futile business - unless you are going to do something about it. They watch us, we watch them - that's no big deal. Getting to know what the new Euro-state is up to, or even why and how, does not stop it from doing whatever it wants to do.

We have known about the secret goings on, the clandestine meetings from as far back as 10, 15 years ago. We have known about Trevi and Schengen and the Ad Hoc Committee on Immigration and the Dublin Convention. We have even known about the secret proposals, made at the prime ministerial meeting at Edinburgh last year. But Trevi and Schengen and all that informal network is now being formalised into a new Euro-state, a new Eurobureaucracy, unaccountable to the European parliament, unaccountable to us, the people. And we have not been able to make a dent in their plans.

Why? Firstly, because our counter-information services, pressure groups, operate in a vacuum. There is no movement any more, no working-class movement, no Left movement, to contextualise them in a larger politics, to give them a larger frame of reference than their particular concern, afford them a larger area of support, translate their thinking into doing, make them effective, give them clout. In fact, Statewatch (State Research as it then was), the National Council for Civil Liberties (which now fondly calls itself 'Liberty') and the present Institute of Race Relations came out of the political movement of its times - the first in order to stop state infringement of the rights of Agee and Hosenball who had blown the whistle on the counter-insurgency operations of the CIA, the second to defend the right to demonstrate on the part of the hunger marchers of 1934, and the third to invigilate the rise of state racism and the fillip it gave to popular racism and fascism.

In the second place, there is no political culture today which informs and coheres the various aspects and strands of our struggles against the state. Instead, we have what the pseudo-marxists term cultural politics - the enclosed, ad hoc, one issue politics of the so-called new social forces. But then the pseuds deny that there is any such thing as a state, only power blocs.

Thirdly, there is no overall climate of political analysis, which allows the work of organisations like Statewatch to become grist in the mills of activists - against racism, sexism, the poll tax, whatever. There is, that is, no understanding of where the state fits in into each one of our struggles - and therefore no concerted attack on the state. In the event, the state is able to repel or buy off each one of our struggles individually.

What we have today in the place of political analysis is political commentary,

---

1. This is the text of a talk given to the 'Statewatching the new Europe' Conference, London, 27 March 1993.

political 'discourse', a discussion of political ideas qua ideas - and even then, the emphasis is not on the ideas themselves, but on how they should be dressed up, on their presentation. Representation is all. And, according to the pseudo-marxists, reality itself is a matter of interpretation, construction, presentation - of words, ideas, images. 'Philosophers', they might have said with a nod to Marx, 'have interpreted the world; our task is to change the interpretation'.

Fourthly, there is no Labour Party, or its equivalent in Europe, which is answerable to a labour movement, and is therefore centrally concerned with the poor and the powerless and the disempowered. It has become, instead, a free-floating entity with no loyalty, no commitment, no values - and has turned the Parliamentary Labour Party into a despicable bunch of tired opportunists in weary search of the Holy Grail of Power - for what purpose, when their policies are no different from the Tories, I do not know.

Finally, there is no Left - to speak to our changing times, to catch history on the wing. Instead, they have either let themselves become fossilised in some troglodyte past or taken refuge in the navel-gazing single issue politics of the new social forces.

So what should we do? What should Statewatch do - more? What should those of us gathered here today - anti-racists, anti-fascists, anti-statists, students, do? How do we come together after this conference to develop a concerted struggle against the encroachments of an increasingly authoritarian Euro-state? (For that I see as the burden of my talk here today.) What are the things that unite us? What are the things that connect us to each other? It is not enough to understand that racism and fascism are connected, that racism and imperialism are connected, that fascism and state authoritarianism are connected, without also understanding the ways in which they are connected today, and how much more formidable those connections have become - and how much more invisible.

What are the changes that have taken place in the world since we last had a movement? And how do we, in understanding those changes, go some way towards creating a movement which moves with the times and is, therefore, effective?

We are caught in a trough between two eras. The era of industrial capitalism, with its thousand factories and 10,000 workers, all assembled under the same roof, is over, and we are moving into an era where industrial manufacture is based not so much on living labour as on the brains of dead labour, fed into robots and computers and other micro-electronic gadgetry - like CAD (computer aided design) and CAM (computer aided manufacture) and who knows what tomorrow.

Where once muscle power was replaced by steam power and then by electricity, and so instigated the industrial revolution, today electronics replaces the brain. That is the size of the technological revolution of our times. And look at the implications.

(a) Firstly, Capital (I expect that the term is still in fashion) is no longer captive to Labour. Not only can it do with less labour, but also with less variety of labour, with the unskilled or semi-skilled at one end of the production process and the highly-skilled at the other. The skills have been taken into the machines, leaving it to the highly skilled to programme them and the unskilled to operate them.

The heavy labour-intensive industries of the period of industrial capitalism - iron, steel, ship-building - are dead or dying, or have passed on to the so-called Newly Industrialising Countries where labour is still cheap and plentiful or could be made to be so. Coal is a-dying. Industries which employed thousands of workers on the factory floor and in the pits and bound them in communities of resistance to capital are gone or going - and traditional labour organisations rendered ineffectual and effete.

Thatcher's war against the unions was not won by genius or guile or sheer bloody-mindedness, but by changes in the production process which were already making the craft or industry-based union a thing of the past.

(b) Secondly, Capital is no longer fixed to one place. It can take up its plant and walk to wherever labour is cheap and captive, and that is invariably in the Third World. It can move from free trade zone to free trade zone in Malaysia, Taiwan, Brazil, Sri Lanka, from one reserve pool of cheap, captive labour to another extracting maximum profit, discarding each when done.

The factories themselves can now be broken down into smaller units and scattered all over the world, in global assembly lines, stretching (in the microelectronics industry, for instance) from Silicon Valley in California or Silicon Glen in Scotland to the free trade zones of the Third World.

And the countries of the Third World, for their part, enter into a Dutch auction with each other to offer transnational corporations cheaper and cheaper labour, deunionised, captive labour, rightless, female labour and child labour, tax incentives, and unencumbered land rights and mineral rights and rights to raw materials.

But what keeps the labour cheap and captive and takes the land away from the peasants and hands it over to agri-business, and the natural resources to mining companies, is the installation and/or maintenance in Third World countries of military regimes and/or parliamentary dictatorships by the western powers.

Trade no longer follows the flag; the flag follows trade. Capital has broken its national bonds, technology allows it, and the governments of the west must follow in capital's wake to set up the political and social orders within which it can safely and profitably operate.

Not necessarily this time by force of arms, but by the force of an economic logic preached by the World Bank, sustained by the International Monetary Fund, worked by Structural Adjustment Programmes, and mediated by the General Agreement on Tariffs and Trade.

These are the new agents of imperialist plunder. These are the new conquistadors who lay waste the Third World and move whole populations from countryside to urban wastelands and from urban wastelands to the inner cities of Europe - there to do the shit work of silicon age capitalism as cleaners and porters, house-maids and waiters, sweat-shop workers and piece-workers, and the peripheral, peripatetic, hire-and-fire-at-will workers of manufacturing industry. These are not economic refugees looking for a better life in western economies. These are political refugees fleeing from the devastation that western economies have caused in their countries. It is your economics that makes our politics that makes us refugees in your economies.

Hence, the distinction that European governments continue to make between economic and political refugees is meaningless, false - statutory lies. But you and I don't have to believe them; the refugees and asylum seekers thrown up on Europe's shores are our responsibility, and the responsibility, particularly, of black people, of Third World people, who were once refugees and asylum seekers themselves. For to have the experience and forget the meaning is to lie against oneself.

The fight against racism, therefore, must be centrally concerned with the right of entry for refugees - and the right, at least, to a fair and impartial hearing, and time to hear it in. I am not interested in the fight against racism - in the Asylum Bill, for instance - at the level of whether or not visitors from Third World countries are allowed to visit their families, when there's a deeper, more profound racism which keeps refugees out. I am not interested in the fight against racism at the middle-class level of equal opportunities (or equal opportunism as I prefer to call it), I am interested in the fight against racism at the level of the unhoused, the unemployed, the unrefuged. I am interested, above all, in the fight against racism at the level of life and death - and that includes racial attacks, murders on the street, deaths in custody, and sending off of refugees back to their countries of death.

And these are not issues 'out there', which concern only 'them', 'their' rights and their freedoms. These are issues that are of vital concern to all of us, and affect our rights and our freedoms, because the clandestine non-accountable, hush-hush way in which policies on these issues are being decided by the European community augurs ill for democracy.

You have heard of the secret goings on at Trevi (which, as Tony Bunyan has pointed out, does not refer to the fountain in Rome but is an acronym for terrorism, radicalism, extremism and violence) and the Ad Hoc Group on Immigration. And you know about the inter-governmental deals made under the Schengen Accord - and the Dublin Convention. You probably know about the leaked draft resolution (presented at the Inter-Prime Ministers' meeting in Edinburgh last October) which required that those who feared human rights violations should 'stay in their own country and seek protection or redress from their own authorities'. Refugee status, it added, should not be granted in Europe, 'merely because levels of security, economic opportunity or individual liberty are below ours'!

But apart from the fact that these meetings and resolutions are setting the basis for an international code of institutional racism, which defines all Third World people as immigrants and refugees, and all immigrants and refugees as terrorists and drug-runners and cannot tell a citizen from an immigrant or an immigrant from a refugee, let alone one black from another - for, as I've said before, we all carry our passports on our faces - apart from all that, what should be of the greatest concern to all of us is the steady, silent growth of an European state apparatus which has no legislative mandate, no mechanism to make it accountable, and no due processes by way of law to protect the interests of its citizens against it. And that signals the first steps in the establishment of an authoritarian European state.

But such a drift was on the cards already, because transnational corporations need to transgress national boundaries and set up a transnational state, a Euro-state, which serves their interests rather than the interests of the governed, on the basis that only through serving business interests does one serve the interests of the economy as a whole and, therefore, of the people, thereby lifting unemployment! That is the new economic orthodoxy, right across Europe, and no one challenges it, least of all the so-called 'Socialists'.

Where, in other words, the nation state was the political expression of industrial capitalism, the Euro-state is the political expression of post-industrial capitalism. But where in industrial capitalism, there was a working-class movement to challenge the depredations of Capital and keep it from establishing an authoritarian state - all the so-called bourgeois freedoms such as freedom of speech, of assembly, the right to withhold one's labour, universal suffrage, even the welfare state sprang not from bourgeois benefice but from working class struggles - today, there is no organised opposition to Capital in sight.

But that lack of opposition stems partly from the lack of information, of investigative journalism, of whistle-blowing, of the suppression of news items, documentaries, programmes that are not conducive to the authority of the state, that are not palatable to the government, or to the controllers of the communication industry. And that control is being concentrated, more and more, in fewer and fewer hands. A handful of transnational corporations like IBM and a handful of mega-media moguls, like Murdoch and Springer, own and/or control the means of mass communication. And they decide, through the two minute TV and the three minute tabloid, what information we should have, or, more precisely, what disinformation we should be fed, what thoughts we should think, what values we should uphold, what commodities we should consume, what lives we should lead.

In a word, they shape the dominant culture of our times. Thatcher did not create the individualist, consumer-oriented, dog-eat-dog society we live in. They did. She was their willing instrument. And the thrust of such a culture is to weaken the social fabric, fragment society (was it any wonder that Mrs Thatcher should declare that there was no such thing as society), break up community, destroy collectivity, and dissipate opposition. Conversely, to reverse that culture we must return to the values of community and the collective interest.

Let me come at it from another angle. The post-industrial society has been correctly termed the Information Society. But we have to understand information in two ways. Firstly, as I've said before, as data used in the labour and production process, as the 'brains of the dead' fed into robots and computers. Secondly, as data fed to you and me through the mass media, as brains for the dead, to create popular culture. Information fed into software to programme robots, computers, etc and information fed into the communication process to programme popular culture. Information, that is, is the raw material both of the production process and the cultural process. And the people who control the one, control the other. The control and/or ownership of both are concentrated in the same hands, and those same hands shape not only the economy and popular culture but the governments of the day. It is no accident that ministers in our governments often came from giant corporations and/or go back to giant corporations or into industry that they have helped to privatise while in government: water, gas, electricity, transport. In a word, the hands that shape the information, shape our economy, shape our culture, shape our politics.

And it is that concentration of power that we have got to address ourselves to - by concentrating our own efforts, by unifying our own struggles. The objective connections are there, as I hope I have shown. And, in sum, what they mean is that:

(a) Anti-statists must understand the changing nature of post-industrial society and go beyond investigating the state apparatus to see how the state operates in the interstices of civil society.

(b) Anti-racists must have an understanding of imperialism in order to understand the political reasons for taking up the cause of refugees and asylum seekers: if they come for us in the morning, they will come for you that night.

(c) Anti-fascists must have an understanding of how the state itself is veering towards authoritarianism by using the Right as a ploy to bolster its own authority - as Kohl's use of the Nazis to revoke Clause 16 of the Constitution (and so close the gates on refugees) shows. Or the numbers argument of the British government's Asylum Bill, which holds that less refugees means less fascism (which carried to its logical conclusion leads to the 'final solution').

We have not only to connect our different struggles but open out to each others struggles, learn from each others' struggles - not making our particular struggle the gauge of other peoples' struggles, our commitment the measure of everybody else's - and so create not coalitions and alliances but a growing, organic unity.

On the practical level, we need to enunciate programmes that will bring us together and politicise the public, enlarge our constituency right across Europe. That is why, for instance, *CARF* and *Race & Class* and the Berlin Anti-Racist Initiative put out a set of 15 proposals as part of an anti-racist policy programme addressed to the European governments. Not because we expected those governments to take them up, but to challenge them on basic rights - such as the reform of clause 116 of the German constitution which bases citizenship on blood - and so broaden our struggle, unifying our different strands, and strengthen the hand of long-time foreign residents in Germany, for instance, in the fight against racism and fascism.

At the grassroots level, we need to take up the cases in our local communities - turn cases into issues, issues into causes, causes into a movement. And we can begin here, now, today - with the case of Omasase Lumumba, the nephew of Patrice Lumumba, the great Zairean revolutionary who was murdered over 30 years ago by the Belgian government. Omasase Lumumba was tortured in Zaire, sought refuge in Switzerland where he lived for 10 years, lost his residential rights through the break-up of his marriage, fled to England to seek political asylum, and died in custody in Pentonville prison.

Thank you.

A SIVANANDAN

Trevi, Europol and the European state

Tony Bunyan

Introduction

This Chapter charts the development of a series of ad hoc groups under the umbrella of *intergovernmental* cooperation between the 12 EC states since 1975. It shows that under the Maastricht Treaty these ad hoc groups, covering immigration, asylum, policing and law, are to be replaced by permanent structures under the auspices of the Council of Ministers. These groups which have been meeting in secret will continue to do so outside the scrutiny of parliaments (European and national) and people - they will be largely unaccountable and undemocratic.

The period of ad hoccery lasted from 1976 to 1988, when the EC states began the process of formalising its work.[1] The appointment of the Coordinators' Group in 1988 and the adoption of the 'Palma Document' in 1989 marked the beginning of the *transformation* from ad hoc inter-state mechanisms to a permanent European state.

The new structure will under the control of the K4 Coordinating Committee, a group of senior officials from Interior Ministries, accountable only to the Council of (Interior) Ministers. The K4 Coordinating Committee will also oversee the setting up of the European Information System (EIS) which will hold intelligence and information on immigration, asylum, policing and drugs. Both the ad hoc and new structures give officials (Interior Ministry, police, immigration, customs, and security services) unprecedented access to decision-making. A senior officer at Scotland Yard described the process:

> Once you get your proposal agreed around the individual working groups, you will get a ministerial policy decision at the end of the current six months. You must remember that the largest club in the world is Law Enforcement - and in Trevi you have that *plus* ministerial muscle.[2]

1993/4 will be a period of transition, waiting on the implementation of the Maastricht Treaty, thereafter the European state will be in place.

This Chapter is divided into three parts: I: the history and role of the Trevi group; II: the emergence of Europol in the post-Maastricht era; III: the emergence of the European state. It includes detailed descriptions of the main developments as this information has been taken from reports and documents which are not readily available.

I: The Trevi group

The Trevi group was set up in 1976 by the 12 EC states to counter terrorism and to coordinate policing in the EC.[3] The group's work is based on intergovernmental cooperation between the 12 states, a process which excludes the main EC institutions - the European Commission and the European Parliament.

The creation of the Trevi group was preceded by a number of intergovernmental meetings on terrorism in 1971 and 1972. At a Council of Ministers meeting in Rome in December 1975 UK Foreign Secretary James Callaghan proposed, and the Minsters agreed, to set up a special working group to combat terrorism in the EC.[4] This proposal was formalised in Luxembourg on 29 June 1976 at a meeting in EC Interior Ministers. The decision meant that, in future, Ministers were accompanied by senior police and security service officials at these meetings.

Five working groups were set up in 1976, reporting to the *Trevi Senior Officials* group, who in turn presented reports initially annually to meetings of the *Trevi Ministers*, the 12 Interior Ministers of the EC. The *Trevi 'troika'* is comprised of three sets of senior officials from the current EC Presidency, the last Presidency and the next one (so, for example, in the second half of 1992 it was comprised of Portugal, the UK and Denmark). The job of the 'troika' is to assist and brief the current Presidency and its officials.

Structure
Trevi thus works at three levels: Ministerial (through now six-monthly meetings of Interior Ministers), the Trevi Senior Officials group (which also meets six-monthly) and the working parties (on which sit Interior/Home Ministry officials, senior police officers, immigration and customs officials, and internal security service representatives). The structure of the Trevi group looks like this:

> *Ministers*: meet every June and December
> *Trevi Senior Officials*: meet every May and November[5]
> *Trevi 'troika'*: meet immediately prior to each Trevi working group and the Trevi Senior Officials meetings (eg: Trevi Senior Officials Troika)
> *Working Groups*: Interior Ministry officials, police officers, and security services.

Later a number of countries outside the EC were given observer status. They do not actually take part in the discussion but are briefed by the 'troika' officials after the meeting. This group called *Friends of Trevi*, is comprised of: Sweden, Austria, Morocco, Norway, Switzerland, Finland, Canada and the USA. Two other countries are 'briefed' - Spain (Argentina) and Germany (Hungary).[6]

Trevi working groups
The five working groups set up after the EC Interior Ministers meeting in Luxembourg in 1976 were:

> *Working group 1* (known as Trevi 1): responsible for measures to combat terrorism; it continues today in this role.
> *Working group 2* (Trevi 2): scientific and technical knowledge and police training; the work of this group later expanded to embrace public order and football hooliganism.
> *Working group 3* (Trevi 3): set up to deal with security procedures for civilian air travel; this work was later taken over by Trevi 1.

On 21 June 1985 at a Trevi Ministers meeting in Rome the role of Trevi

3 was redefined to look at organised crime at a strategic, tactical and technical level and drug trafficking.[7] This group prepared the way for the creation of the European Drugs Unit.

Working group 4 (Trevi 4): safety and security at nuclear installations and transport.

Working group 5 (Trevi 5): contingency measures to deal with emergencies (disasters, fire prevention and fire fighting).

Of the original five working parties only two were active - Trevi 1 and Trevi 2. Trevi 3, 4 and 5 never met; Trevi 3 was given a new role in 1985 (see above).

At the second meeting of EC Interior Ministers on Trevi in London in May 1977 it was reported that: *Group 1: Terrorism*: Agreed that the EC states would: (i) produce reports outlining the experience gained from the handling of any major terrorist incident; (ii) exchange information on their arrangements for handling major terrorist incidents, particularly at government level, to enhance cooperation in the event of an incident involving more than one country; (iii) establish central contact points for the exchange of information on international terrorism matters. And that:

> In the UK the Security Service was designated as the central contact point on intelligence matters and the Metropolitan Police European Liaison Section as the central contact point on policing matters.

Group 2: Police technical matters and police training: It was agreed to provide information on the present level of technical and training arrangements and to promote the exchange of information.[8]

In April 1989 the *Trevi 92* working group was set up to specifically consider the 'policing and security implications of the Single European Market' and to improve cooperation to 'compensate for the consequent losses to security and law enforcement' in the EC.[9] Trevi 92 worked with the customs group MAG 92 and the Ad Hoc Working Group on Immigration to give: 'early attention to the study of a possible computerised information system for law enforcement purposes' (the European Information System (EIS)). This group was disbanded at the end of 1992 and its work redistributed (see below).

The *Ad Hoc Group on Europol* was set up after a meeting in Luxembourg in June 1992. This followed the report on 'The Development of Europol' was agreed in Maastricht in December 1991. Finally, the *Ad Hoc Group on Organised Crime* was set up in 1992.

The working groups: Working group 1 (Trevi 1)

This working group is concerned with combatting terrorism and is the only one with an operational role (as distinct from one of coordination). One of its main tasks has been to produce:

> a regular joint analysis of the terrorist threat from both within and outside the Community, providing an overview to inform strategy and tactics in countering terrorist groups which operate internationally, and enabling member states to draw one another's attention to features of the threat in

relation to which co-operation may be needed.[10]

Following a series of terrorist attacks in France, Karachi and Istanbul, there was an emergency meeting of Trevi/Interior Ministers in London on 25-26 September 1986.[11] It was decided to set up a secure, dedicated fax system, based in the European Liaison Section (ELS) of the Metropolitan Police Special Branch, to provide an immediate system of gathering and exchanging information between the 12 EC police forces. The meeting also asked the Trevi 'troika' to be responsible for collating and analysing the information gathered and to maintain contact with countries outside the EC.[12]

At the meeting of Trevi Ministers (Interior Ministers) in London on 1 December 1992 the Trevi Senior Official group reported that Trevi 1 had agreed a 'full Terrorist Threat Assessment Document' reporting that: 'There had been no significant change to the overall threat from terrorism in the last six months'.[13] For the first time the assessment included a report on 'future' threats.[14]

In 1992 the UK hosted seminars on gathering intelligence on terrorist incidents and on bomb scene management. Later the group endorsed a set of 'good practice guidelines' and agreed to compile a list of key contacts on counter-terrorism. Work on investigating terrorist funding and laws in each country is being undertaken by the Judicial Cooperation Working Group.

The growing volume of communications between Trevi officials in the 12 EC states has created problems for the TREVI Secure Fax Network (TSFN). This question is now being considered in the longer-term under the 'third pillar' of the Maastricht Treaty, covering justice and home affairs. This will require a new, secure communications system for the 'third pillar':

> the Coordinators' Group was now focusing on a communications system for the third pillar as a whole, including the Commission and Council Secretariat.[15]

The Trevi Senior Officials group also submitted a report to the Coordinators' Group 'on future police cooperation structures'.

Working group 2 (Trevi 2)
There are no formal terms of reference for Trevi 2, which is termed by some the 'ways and means' group. It is concerned with police cooperation and the exchange of information on: (1) police equipment, including computers and communications; (2) public order and football hooliganism; (3) police training, including language training; (4)forensic science, including proposals for creating central collections of information on drugs, explosives, fingerprints and Arab documents; (5) other scientific or technical matters, such as exchange of information on research programmes.[16]

The working group also analyses Trevi specialist seminars and makes recommendations to the Trevi Senior Officials group. For example, in April 1990 a seminar was held in London on DNA genetic fingerprinting and another one in 1991 for firearms and ballistics experts. During the UK Presidency in 1987 the working group took the lead in setting up 'a system of Trevi permanent correspondents for the exchange of information between EC countries in relation to the international movement of football supporters'. [17]

The report on Trevi 2, presented to the Trevi Ministers at their meeting on 1 December 1992, showed that it is working on: (1) the policing of road traffic; (2) cryptology, the legal position on the interception of communications being undertaken by Belgium and the Netherlands;[18] (3) police training including the production of a European directory on police training; (4) police communications on an EC-wide level, with agreement needed between Schengen and non-Schengen countries.

Working group 3 (Trevi 3)

Working group 3 did not start work until 1985 when it was given the job of dealing with serious organised international crime. Its principal area of activity has been with drug trafficking.[19] The group decided on the need for posting Drugs Liaison Officers (DLO's) to countries outside the EC on 28 April 1987 (initially in the USA, India, Finland, Canada, Norway and Sweden). It was agreed that these officers would liaise if posted to the same country and that the information gathered would be shared. The Home Office reported to the Home Affairs Select Committee in 1989 that the group had agreed that all member states should set up National Drugs Intelligence Unit and that consideration was being given to the need for a European Drugs Intelligence Unit.

Trevi 3 also works on armed robbery, stolen vehicles, the protection of witnesses, the illegal use of non-cash payment, the protection of cultural property and training to combat violent organised crime. In addition, this group was dealing with immigration controls at borders until the Trevi 92 working group took over in 1989.

Reporting to the Trevi Senior Officials group in November 1992 Trevi 3 said that it is tackling money-laundering, crime analysis, agreeing common terminologies, methods and techniques. The common definitions agreed include 'terrorism' as: 'the use and attempt to use violence by a structured group to obtain political objectives' and 'organised crime' as: 'an uninterrupted series of criminal activities committed by a group of individuals with the intention of obtaining benefits, influence or power'.

Trevi 92

The Trevi 92 working group was set up in 1989. Its main work has been on the Programme of Action agreed in June 1990. At the meeting of Trevi Ministers in London on 1 December 1992, it was agreed that:

> Trevi Ministers note and agree the Trevi 1992 Working Group report on the level of implementation of the Programme of Action. They take the view that police cooperation needs to be monitored and coordinated *in the transitional period until the implementation of new structures.* Senior Officials will take on this task; at the same time they will see to it that there is general coordination at national level. All unallocated items of work which have not been completed in the Trevi 92 Working Group will be considered by Working Group III. Working Group III may request that Senior Officials redistribute any such items, should it emerge they sit better in a different working group.[20]

The European Commission took part in Trevi 92 from the beginning of 1991.[21] The Trevi 92 working group has now ended with its responsibilities being taken over by the Trevi Senior Officials group and the detailed work by Trevi 3.

Ad Hoc Group on Europol

The Ad Hoc Group on Europol was set up in June 1992 and has now taken over part of Trevi 92 and Trevi 3's work. The working group agreed the provisions for the European Drugs Unit (EDU) and drafted the text of the Ministerial agreement on Europol - agreed on 1 December 1992. This is intended to legitimise Europol until a Convention has been drafted and then agreed in each country's parliament. In the meantime, control of Europol's development will lie with the Trevi Senior Officials group, with the Ad Hoc group on Europol undertaking the detailed work. The UK continues to provide the chair of this group.

Ad Hoc Group on Organised Crime

The Ad Hoc Group on Organised Crime was set up in September 1992 and held two meetings, 18 September and 28 October. Further meetings were held during the Danish Presidency (January - June 1993). The group is undertaking a survey of organised crime in each state.

Police Working Group on Terrorism (PWGOT)

After the shooting of Sir Richard Dykes, the UK Ambassador to the Netherlands, and his Dutch footman in the Hague in March 1979, the head of the Dutch criminal bureau called a meeting of Special Branches from the Belgium Gendarmerie, the Germany BKA and the Metropolitan Police Special Branch (MPSB). From this meeting the Police Working Group on Terrorism, comprising of Special Branches and internal security services, was formed with the 12 EC countries plus Finland, Norway, Sweden and Austria. It meets every six months in different capital cities. It value was described by a officer of the European Liaison Section of the Metropolitan Police Special Branch:

> I cannot stress too much the importance of the police working group across the whole field of terrorism in Western Europe, including Northern Ireland. We know these people, they are our personal friends, they come here to the Yard when they happen to be in London. We make contact with them when we go abroad, regardless of what we are going for. It has become a very solid group of working colleagues. We trust each other implicitly and pass information to each other without question.[22]

In evidence to the Home Affairs Select Committee, the Metropolitan Police Special Branch said that PWGOT has 'promoted co-operation at a more operational level' than the Trevi working groups.[23]

In 1986 'with the backing of Trevi, the Police Working Group began installing its own coded facsimile system' and it was fully operational by 1988. It:

> is now in daily use, enabling written or graphic material to be transmitted speedily and securely throughout the fifteen country network. Responsibility

for the distribution of its facsimile codes rests with MPSB. It is perhaps worth mentioning that the Police Working Group Facsimile Communication System has been so successful that TREVI has decided to install the same equipment throughout its network.[24]

It is this fax system which is now reported to be overloaded and they are looking to the new European Information System to replace the TSFN providing a secure interface is made available.[25]

Trevi: declarations
There are four substantial documents published on Trevi's work: the 'Palma Document' (Madrid, June 1989); the 'Declaration of Trevi Group Ministers' (Paris, 15 December 1989); the 'Programme of Action' (Dublin, June 1990); and the Coordinators report on the progress on the Palma Document (Edinburgh, December 1992). Summaries of the four reports are given at the end of this Chapter.

The 'Palma Document', agreed at the EC Council meeting in Madrid in 1989, was a report drawn up by the Coordinators' Group. For the first time Trevi's work was put in the overall context of the emerging policies on policing, law, immigration and asylum, and legal systems which underpin the European state. The tasks set for Trevi led to the Programme of Action (see below) which developed the projects of the European Information System (EIS) and the European Drugs Intelligence Unit (the first initiative of Europol).[26]

The Declaration of Trevi Ministers, agreed in December 1989, speaks of the 'new requirements' with the creation of a 'European area without internal borders' and the need to cooperate on: fighting terrorism, international crime, narcotics and illegal trafficking of every sort' (para 1).

The 'Programme of Action' agreed by the Trevi Ministers in Dublin in June 1990 is defined as a 'synthesis of the arrangements ... between police and security services' for consideration by the Trevi working groups in relation to 'terrorism, drug trafficking or any forms of crime including organised illegal immigration'.[27]

The three documents show the often repetitive yet progressive development of policies on terrorism, policing, drug trafficking, and the interface between policing and immigration controls. A year later, in December 1991 at Maastricht, it was agreed to create Trevi's successor 'Europol'. Trevi Ministers presented a report to the EP Council on the *Development of Europol* and Europol was entrenched in the Maastricht Treaty (Article K, see below).

However, it is the Coordinators' Group report on the Palma document, to the European Council in December 1992, which shows the progress they made towards preparing the ground for the new structures, and illustrates the inter-relationships established between police, customs, immigration and security services agencies.[28]

Trevi and the UK
The UK government has been an enthusiastic supporter of the Trevi group because of its intergovernmental basis which excludes the Commission and the European Parliament. In its view: Trevi's distinctive strength lies in the informal, spontaneous and practical character of its discussions.[29]

The UK participation in Trevi is as follows: *Trevi Secretariat* in the Home Office;

Trevi working groups: Association of Chief Police Officers (ACPO) and MI5, the Security Service (see below); *European Liaison Section* of the Metropolitan Police Special Branch (see below) - contact point on terrorism; *National Criminal Intelligence Service* (NCIS) - the contact point for policing and criminal investigations [30]; *Metropolitan Police: European Unit (MS18)*, many other police forces are setting up similar units; and *MI5*, the Security Service.

The evidence from the Metropolitan Police Special Branch to the Home Affairs Select Committee inquiry in 1990 was extremely coy when referring to the Trevi group. It says that: '* * * Home Office Police Department is the lead British agency and it co-ordinates all UK Trevi arrangements..'[31] The * * * reference is repeated several times, when clearly referring to MI5. It goes on to set out the UK participation:

> *Senior Officials*: (policy and overseeing/tasking of working groups): Home Office officials (F4), * * * , and Police;
> *Working group I*: (terrorism): Home Office (F4), * * * and Police;
> *Working group II*: (technical forum; specialised aspects of countering terrorism; police training, equipment etc): Home Office, Scientific Research & Development Branch and Police as required;
> *Working group III*: (serious and organised international crime and drugs): Home Office (F3), Police.
> *Trevi 1992*: (all aspects of '1992' including compensatory measures): Home Office (F4), Police and other agencies as required.

* * * is also referred to in the context of meetings with EC counterparts in relation to the IRA.[32]

The European Liaison Section (ELS)

The European Liaison Section (ELS) of the Metropolitan Police Special Branch was set up in January 1976 and, in 1977, was given the responsibility of liaising with Special Branch equivalents and security services in other EC countries. In evidence to the Home Affairs Select Committee the Home Office states that it 'has grown substantially, particularly in recent years'.[33] The Anti-Terrorist Branch, based at Scotland Yard which was already investigating international terrorist incidents in London found that there was no easy mechanism for contact with other EC police forces: 'It was decided then to set up a dedicated unit, staffed by linguists, which could liaise directly with Special Branch or equivalent agencies on the continental mainland, in order to obtain speedy responses to anti-terrorist matters'.[34]

When Trevi was formally set up in 1976 the ELS was already established 'with its own independent European network' and the ELS became 'an integral part of the United Kingdom TREVI machinery'.[35] The ELS 'maintain daily contact with their European counterparts'. The ELS network includes the other 11 EC countries plus Austria, Gibraltar, Finland, Iceland, Malta, Norway, Sweden and Switzerland.

The ELS has two communications system, one a secure 24 hour telecommunications system for emergencies, the other an encoded facsimile link which enables correspondence, photographs and fingerprints to be transmitted speedily and securely.[36] The requests received by the ELS for information may be a 'simple name checks in records to more complicated enquiries requiring several hours or even days to complete'. The number of communications they have handled has risen from 935 (1987) to 1,193 (1988), to 1,969 (1989).[37]

Accountability

The European Commission is not involved in the Trevi structure, as the 'EC has no direct police competence'.[38] The line of accountability for Trevi is not to the Commission but to the Council of Ministers structure (which represents governments). Trevi is seen by the Home Office as a 'forum for discussion' and co-operation between the member states of the EC:

> Trevi is essentially an informal body whose objective is to advance co-operation on the ground. Police matters are outside Community competence and so Trevi is independent of the European Community's institutional structure, and the EC Commission is not represented at any of its meetings.[39]

The sleight of hand is well described by a Home Office official who spoke of:

> the shuffling of chairs - if I can so describe it - so that at a ministerial immigration meeting when the Interior and Justice Ministers are present and the Commission is present, during the coffee break the chairs are shuffled and the Commission disappears and when they meet in their Trevi mode after coffee the Commission has gone. [40]

The work of the Trevi group since its formation in 1976 has been shrouded in secrecy. It was not until 1989 that the first communique for public use was made available in the UK.[41] This has been followed by a six-monthly written answer to a 'planted' parliamentary question after each of the meetings of the Interior Ministers.[42]

The deliberations of Trevi and its Working Groups may be beyond the reach of democratic questioning and debate but they are open to and determined by state officials, police officers, security and intelligence agencies. This is presented as a means of these officials and officers 'contributing their professional views'.

The Home Secretary described his view as to whether there were sufficient democratic controls and safeguards as follows:

> It does not need any safeguards. You have to remember what Trevi is. Trevi is merely a gathering together of the Ministers of the Interior of the EC countries to give, hopefully, political impetus to various plans or closer policing co-operation. That is all it is. It is not an executive body. Therefore, accountability is from the individual Ministers of the Interior to their own governments, and there is no need for the body as a whole to be thought of as responsible to any other organisation.[43]

Thus state officials present their reports to Ministers who, in turn, report to governments. National parliaments may or not be informed depending on each country's practice but they have no powers over what is decided, nor does the European Parliament.

II: From Trevi to Europol

In the late 1980s the idea of a European-style FBI was put forward by a number of police chiefs in the UK, Germany and elsewhere. The first stage of Europol is not going to be an 'FBI' as it will not have operational powers of arrest, charge or prosecute suspects (this may come when it is reviewed in 1994). There was also the question of the relationship between the idea of Europol and Interpol. The then UK Home Secretary, Mr Waddington, told the Home Affairs Select Committee that Interpol: 'can be no more than a channel of communication'.[44] Interpol's recent overhaul, and the addition of new computer facilities (eg: Automatic Search Facility, ASF) has not deflected the development of Europol. [45]

The creation of a EC-level policing body to be known as 'Europol' was formally put forward by the German delegation to the European Council meeting in Luxembourg in June 1991. The Council meeting noted the German proposal and asked for them to be incorporated into the Maastricht Treaty draft.[46] The Masstricht Treaty sets out a 'commitment to full establishment of a Central European Criminal Investigation Office ("Europol")' to cover drug trafficking and organised crime by the end of 1993. Initially it would undertake the 'exchange of information and experience' and but in the second phase, the 'power to act within the Member States would be granted'.

This was followed by a report from the Trevi Ministers on Europol at their meeting in Maastricht on 3 December 1991:

> Following the Palma document of 1989, Trevi Ministers decided on a detailed Programme of Action, out of which a number of items have been developed or are under detailed study eg: European Information System (EIS), the coordination of Drug Liaison Officers; collections of data for drugs, explosive substances and fingerprints; recommendations on police cooperation in general and specific measures for cooperation in frontier zones, on transborder observation and pursuit. A far-reaching Trevi decision (Dublin 1990) was to establish a European Drugs Intelligence Unit.[47]

The purpose of Europol is set out as the need for:

> a central organisation to facilitate the exchange and coordination of criminal information, and the development of intelligence between Member States in respect of crime extending across the borders of Member States, whether originating outside Europe or not.

The report said that in the meantime: 'Member states [can] proceed with the development of the national criminal intelligence units which are essential to support the central organisation'.

One aspect of Trevi's work which was not mentioned in this report is terrorism. This was one of the first indications that Trevi 1's work might remain outside the new structures. It was also agreed that contact points should be set up in each country for the maintenance of public order in member states 'so that contact can be made at an early stage if specific disturbances of public order acquire an international dimension ... The Ministers emphasised in this regard the fundamental right to demonstrate.'[48] This decision to set up Europol was confirmed at the EC Council meeting in Maastricht on 9-10 December 1991.

Between the Luxembourg meeting in 1991 and the report on Europol presented to the European Council in Maastricht, the European Drugs Intelligence Unit became a part of the 'European Drugs Unit', and Europol is defined in the Maastricht Treaty not as the European Criminal Investigation Office but as the 'European Police Office'. These changes suggests that a wider remit is envisaged.

Title K of the Maastricht Treaty covers: 'Provisions on cooperation in the fields of justice and home affairs'. Article K.1 of this Title says that members states regard police cooperation as a matter of common interest (together with immigration and third country nationals; fraud; judicial cooperation in civil and criminal matters; customs). 'Police cooperation' is set out as: 'preventing and combating terrorism, unlawful drug trafficking and other serious forms of international crime, including if necessary certain aspects of customs cooperation, in connection with the organisation of a Union-wide system for exchanging information with a European Police Office (Europol)'.[49]

The Declaration on Police Cooperation, appended to the Treaty, says that on the basis of the work programme and timetable drawn up by the Luxembourg EC Summit they were going to proceed with the exchange of information and experience in the following functions: (a) support for national criminal investigation and security authorities, in particular in the coordination of investigations and search operations; (b) creation of databases; (c) central analysis and assessment of information in order to take stock of the situation and identify investigative approaches; (d) collection and analysis of national prevention programmes for forwarding to Member States and for drawing up Europe-wide prevention strategies; (e) measures relating to further training, research, forensic matters and criminal records departments.[50]

The Declaration ends by saying that Member States would consider, at the latest during 1994, whether 'the scope of such cooperation should be extended'. The final statement at the Maastricht meeting said that the initial function of Europol would be to organise the exchange of information on drugs, and that the European Council had instructed Trevi Ministers (Home or Internal Affairs Ministers) to expedite the creation of Europol.[51] Europol will be formalised through an inter-governmental Convention. UK Prime Minister John Major made explicit his support for the development of Europol outside the formal structures of the EC. The creation of Europol he said is: 'a classic case for intergovernmental cooperation between the countries of the Community rather than for co-operation within the framework of Community law'.[52]

Europol

The functions set out for Europol mirror those currently being undertaken by the Trevi group. The preparatory work is being undertaken by the Ad Hoc Group on Europol, set up in 1992, which currently comes under the auspices of the Trevi

Senior Officials who report to the Trevi Ministers' six-monthly meetings. This K4 Committee is currently shadowing the work of Trevi, including Europol, pending the ratification of the Maastricht Treaty. When the work of the Trevi group is subsumed under this Committee, probably in 1994, it is not yet clear whether all of its functions will be undertaken by Europol, or in the case of anti-terrorist work, by another new group. In time the Trevi group may well be seen as the precursor of Europol, a fully-fledged EC-wide police force.

Nearly two years later, in April 1993, there was a small working party, based in a Portacabin in Strasbourg, engaged on the creation of the first Europol initiative, the European Drugs Unit (EDU).[53] Their permanent base has not been decided, there are no computer links, data protection provisions are still to be discussed, and there are few back-up staff. It might be thought that the Europol 'idea' is still-born.

However, when the Maastricht Treaty is ratified Europol will move onto an entirely different footing - a convention to formally set it up is being discussed by governments and will presented for each national parliament to ratify in late 1993, funding from the European Community budget will be provided, and its base - either in the Hague or Rome - will be confirmed. The remit and powers of Europol therefore pose basic questions for democratic accountability and the relations between the European state and the citizen.

In its first stage, up to 1994, Europol is to exchange information initially relating to drugs between the 12 national states. A host of questions arise. Is a distinction to be made between *information* and *intelligence* (which may be hearsay or based on speculation)? How will the subjects of 'information' be able to challenge what is being held on them? What is the line between *intelligence* and *operations/investigations* - information and intelligence largely determine the direction of operations. Will the governments decide in 1994 to extend Europol's role from *information/intelligence* to a body with *investigative* powers as well? Will there be a European Public Prosecutor's Office to determine the charges to be brought? And where will these charges be heard - in which court?

Mr Peter Lloyd, Minister of State at the Home Office, confirmed that the computer network being set up for the EDU is being considered as one 'capable of expansion to cover all aspects of Europol as the organisation develops'.[54] He also confirmed that, in relation to Europol, the UK refused to accept two articles of the Council of Europe's Recommendation R (87) 15 on the use of personal data in the police sector.[55] The first, Article 2.2 of this Recommendation, would ensure that individuals are informed that information recorded without their knowledge is still held on file. The second, Article 2.4, also rejected by the UK, states that:

> The collection of data on individuals solely on the basis that they have a particular racial origin, particular religious convictions, sexual behaviour or political opinions or belong to particular movements or organisations which are not proscribed by law should be prohibited. The collection of data concerning these factors may only be carried out if absolutely necessary for the purposes of a particular enquiry.

In a report adopted by the European Parliament at the end of 1992 the Belgian Socialist MEP Lode van Outrive sets out some of the possibilities. The report suggests that the exchange of information could follow the model set down by the Schengen Information System (see Appendix 5). It asks what the role of liaison officers working for the EDU will be and who will monitor them? Several EC countries now have liaison officers not just within the EC but also in Asia and Latin America.[56]

At its meeting on 23 October 1992 the Coordinators' Group agreed a report to be presented to the Trevi Ministers meeting on 1 December suggesting a broad framework for 'the future organisation of European police cooperation'. Further, it was agreed that Trevi Senior Officials and their national coordinators (who together form the Coordinators Group at EC level) should keep in close touch on the future structures for policing (including the need for 'a secure communication system for the interior and justice pillar' and guidelines on links with third countries).

The European Drugs Unit (EDU)
The embryonic office and staff of Europol has been set up in Strasbourg. The office has been set provisionally on the same site as the Schengen Information System. The fifteen staff of the EDU, the working party, is comprised of 3 representatives from the UK, 3 from France, 3 from Germany, 2 from the Netherlands, 1 from Spain, 1 from Denmark, 1 from Ireland, and 1 from Italy. Belgium and Luxembourg are not currently represented. The group is headed by Mr Storbeck (Germany), with a deputy from Belgium, Colonel Bruggeman. The competition for the permanent site of Europol is between the Hague (Netherlands), Strasbourg (France) and Rome (Italy).

When the EDU is up and running, each officer will have two computer screens: one providing a link to their national computer, the other running an EC-wide information system. Each officer will have to decide what information to pass onto the common system without breaking the data protection laws of their country.

The future of Europol
The stages in the development of a EC-wide police and security role can be set out as follows: *Stage 1:* The Trevi group: created in 1976 as an ad hoc intergovernmental series of working groups. *Stage 2:* implementing the Maastricht policy by providing:

a) central gathering of information and intelligence;
b) training and techniques for policing and public order;
c) the incorporation of a number of legal conventions, such as the transfer of prisoners;
d) a common computerised information system, the European Information System (EIS), covering laws, criminal information and intelligence, immigration and asylum and other matters;
e) the European Drugs Unit (EDU) as the first of a number of specialist units;
f) overall supervision under K4 Committee and its sub-groups.

This structure may well not include the work of Trevi working group 1 on terrorism and the associated networks, which already have a direct operational role.

Stage 3: After the review date of 1994 laid down in the Maastricht Treaty to discuss whether co-operation in this field should be extended. This could lead to the development of Europol as an EC-wide police force limited to inter-state questions but with operational powers. This shift would require the following additional features: a) new European laws and the extension of present Conventions; b) Europol being given the powers of arrest; c) a European Prosecutors Office - to make charges and appear in court; d) a defined European court, for example, the existing EC Court of Justice; e) and finally, a European-wide police complaints system.

III: The European state

The construction of the European state is now moving apace. The ad hoc arrangements, such as the Trevi group and the Ad Hoc Group on Immigration (started in 1986) and their myriad of working groups and sub-groups, are to be taken over by new, permanent structures over the next two or three years.

The process of formalisation began in December 1988 with the appointment of the Coordinators' Group at the Rhodes EC Council meeting.[57] The group's official title is the 'Coordinators of Free Movement', which is misleading when the scope of their work is examined. It is comprised of 12 senior officials from the Interior Ministries of the 12 EC states, a chairman, and the Vice-President of the European Commission responsible for the internal market. The group meets monthly and prepares six-monthly reports to the EC Council meetings at the end of each Presidency. Its work is structured as follows:

National meetings: monthly meetings prior to Coordinators' Group meetings are held in each country of the relevant departments eg: police, immigration, customs and internal security service officials).

Coordinators' Group meeting: monthly, at which it considers reports from all the working groups (Trevi, Ad Hoc Group on Immigration etc) and decides which matters should be reported and which require decisions at governmental level (eg: where there is no agreement on, say, the location of Europol).

Report to EC Council: six-monthly. The Coordinators' Group reports to the EC Council meetings, within its remit, on the activities of the following groups:

- the Council of the European Communities (the organisation working on behalf of the 12 EC governments/states based in Brussels);
- the Trevi group and its working parties;
- the Ad Hoc Group on Immigration and its working parties;
- the Mutual Assistance Group (MAG 92, customs officers);
- the working groups on judicial cooperation in criminal matters.

The Coordinators' Group is an intergovernmental group, it is not accountable to the European Parliament. Its remit is to look at the measures needed to 'compensate' for the removal of internal border controls. The issues it has therefore brought together are related to strengthening external borders controls, immigration and asylum policies, measures against terrorism, international crime, drug trafficking, police and judicial cooperation, and the exchange of information and intelligence in the above fields.

The substantive report from the Coordinators' Group, known as the 'Palma Document', set out the *essential* measures needed to 'compensate' for the removal of internal border controls, and the *transitional* measures needed prior to the creation of permanent structures. One aspect of this report was the coordination of police, security service and legal work across the EC and the formulation of the remit and structures needed at the next stage of the development of the EC spelt out in the Maastricht Treaty.

The Coordinators' Group, like the Trevi Group and the Ad Hoc Group on Immigration, will be replaced by permanent structures, based in the Council (not the Commission) when the Maastricht Treaty and a number of Conventions are ratified. While the Coordinators' Group may disappear, its officials will not as they will form the membership of the K4 Committee.

The Schengen Agreement

Alongside the development of the new structures has been the example of the Schengen Agreement (see Appendix 5). The original five members of the Schengen Agreement - France, Germany, Netherlands, Belgium and Luxembourg - were later joined by Italy, Spain, Portugal and Greece. Three of the 12 EC states, Denmark, Ireland and the UK, have not joined because of the disagreement over the abolition of border controls. When, and if, this issue is resolved, there will be little to divide the Schengen and non-Schengen countries. Denmark is committed to removing its controls when two Conventions - the Dublin Convention and the External Borders Convention - have been implemented and the European Information System is in place.

The Schengen countries are proceeding with the abolition of internal border controls and a series of agreements on 'hot pursuit' and legal problems. They have also moved in advance of 'the 12' states by signing an agreement with Poland allowing for 'illegal' entrants to be returned (March 1993). This was followed by an agreement in May 1993 between Germany and Poland on the same issue. The Schengen countries have also opened negotiations with the EFTA countries to join them when their entry to the EC is finalised.

On the whole the practical issues taken up by the Schengen countries - policing, immigration and asylum, drug trafficking, and external border controls - mirror most of those undertaken by the Trevi Group and the Ad Hoc Group on Immigration. Although the Schengen system of committees, working parties and sub-committees will coexist with the new post-Maastricht K4 structure it has now been decided that the agreement establishing the Schengen Information System (SIS) is to be used for the European Information System as well (EIS, see below). With the Schengen Information System due to go on line in December 1993 it is unlikely that two separate computer networks will be set up.[58]

The effect of the Maastricht Treaty

The mechanism for overseeing the new structure is set out in Title K of the Maastricht Treaty (Justice and Home Affairs). A Coordinating Committee of senior officials from each EC state is to be set up (Article K.4).[59] The text of Articles K.3 and K.4 suggest that the Commission has a role to play, but Jacques Delors, in reply to a question in the European Parliament, said in November 1992 that the new arrangement will work as follows: 'Member states will inform and consult each other within the Council. The Council may adopt joint positions, decide on joint operations and draw up conventions; the Commission has no power of initiative in this area'.[60] The finance for the new set-up will come from the EC budget.

The Commission's power of initiative is limited to two areas of immigration policy related to visas. In the drawing up of Conventions, for adoption by each Member State, the Commission has the power of initiative together with the Council and any Member State.[61] But in the areas of 'judicial cooperation in criminal matters, customs cooperation and police cooperation, the Member States alone have the right of initiative (Article K.3)'.[62]

The Home Office in evidence to the Home Affairs Select Committee said that the Maastricht Treaty places work on immigration:

> together with that of the Trevi work on police co-operation in a wider context and on a more formal basis. Thus Interior Minsters will in future meet as the Council of Ministers and will have a new Treaty base for their work; and the Treaty establishes a Coordinating Committee of senior officials to support the Council on justice and home affairs matters...[with the exception of two visa matters] the new arrangements leave these matters outside the Treaty of Rome, and therefore outside Community competence and wholly under national control.[63]

These areas are therefore to remain intergovernmental.

The K4 Coordinating Committee
One of the major tasks undertaken by the Coordinators Group during the UK Presidency in the second half of 1992 was the 'preparation of the infrastructure arrangements to underpin Title VI (ie, interior and justice matters)'.[64] They proposed, and it was agreed, that all the current ad hoc groups would to be taken over by the new K4 Committee responsible for justice and home affairs.

The K4 Committee will have a member from each EC state and one from the Commission. The Committee will have three 'senior steering groups', each with a number of working groups:

1) *Immigration and asylum* (Article K1 (1,2,3 and Article 100c);

a) asylum; b) immigration policy; c) the control of external frontiers; d) visas; e) clearing houses on asylum and immigration (CIREA and CIREFI).

2) *Security and law enforcement, police and Customs cooperation* (Article K1 (4,5,8,9);[65]

a) counter terrorism; b) public order, training, scientific and technical work; c) combatting serious crime (in cooperation with experts in judicial cooperation); d) Europol; e) Customs; f) Drugs.

3) *Judicial cooperation* (article K1 (6,7).

a) criminal judicial cooperation; b) civil judicial cooperation.

The Coordinators Group report at the end of 1992 said that they had not yet considered: the steps needed for the additional support required from the Council Secretariat, 'communications and security of information; contacts with third countries'. The report sees the structure of these new steering groups and the *consequent operational units (eg: Europol)* being initially set by the findings of existing ad hoc groups ('Trevi, the Ad Hoc Group on Immigration, etc').

The Coordinators are also concerned with 'the necessary level of security protection' for 'certain classes' of work 'currently carried out in the Trevi system' and that covered by the MAG system (customs cooperation). They are assessing the 'volume of sensitive material' and 'the degree of security protection that it justifies' and see this concern with security extending to 'the organisation *and recruitment* of the Secretariat by the Secretary-General of the Council'. In the light of the withdrawal of the Commission's proposal on secrecy regulations (dealing with information and the vetting of employees) a separate initiative or convention will have to be agreed (see Chapter 2). The Coordinators are also considering the creation of a permanent *communications* system to cover all the activities of the K4 Committee. At present there are two systems: the Trevi TSFN and the COREU system used for judicial cooperation under the umbrella of European Political Cooperation (known as EPC, and coming under the Council).

European Information System
The idea of creating a 'common information system' has been part of the agenda of the Trevi/Ad hoc Working Group on Immigration for several years.[66] The evidence to the Home Affairs Select Committee in 1990 from the Home Office stated: 'The three principal groups, Trevi, the customs group MAG 92, and the EC Ad Hoc Working Group on Immigration, have decided to give early attention to the study of a possible computerised information system for law enforcement purposes which would operate for the benefit of all EC member states'.[67]

The evidence notes that the Schengen countries had already started to develop the Schengen Information System (SIS). The development of the EIS is 'under the direct aegis of the Horizontal Group'. The Coordinators Group is concerned with the 'juridical basis for an instrument at the level of the Twelve on the EIS'.[68] And the EIS was 'being studied for policing by the Trevi 1992 Group and for customs by the Mutual Assistance Group 1992'.[69]

The creation of the EIS represents a major step forward in the creation of the European state infrastructure: 'The creation of the European Information System is universally accepted as one of the most important of the measures that have been identified as being essential in the context of the implementation of Article 8a of the Treaty of Rome'.[70]

The EIS would, initially, hold the computerised list of non-admissible persons described in Articles 10 and 13 of the External Borders Convention and include the data protection provisions currently being discussed (Article 13).[71] And it is seen as: 'representing a further stage of police co-operation and judicial co-operation'.

The meeting of the EC Prime Ministers at the Council meeting in Maastricht in 1991 formally endorsed the setting up of the EIS. The Coordinators Group considered a report from the Horizontal Group at its meeting on 26-27 May 1992 which looked at the constitution of the Schengen Information System, its scope and location.[72] It agreed on: 'the need to set up a single information system *based on the Convention applying the Schengen Agreement'*.

By the summer of 1993 negotiations were underway on drawing up a Convention on the EIS which is exactly the same as the Schengen Information System in every detail. The Schengen countries are insisting that there must be no changes because they do not want to have to renegotiate its provisions (strong objections to the SIS were lodged in France and in the Netherlands). This places the non-Schengen countries, Denmark, Ireland and the UK, in the position that they have to accept the whole scheme without amendment (so too do the countries about to join the EC, Austria, Finland, Norway and Sweden).

The EIS is not just intended to cover external borders and immigration but *all the areas of intergovernmental work covered in Titles IV (EC Atomic Energy Authority) and VI (Justice and Home Affairs)*. The formal creation of the EIS will require an intergovernmental Convention (along the lines of the Dublin Convention, the External Borders Convention and the Europol Convention).

The K4 Committee, its steering groups (and working parties), the support staff from the Secretariat of the Council, the new EC-wide organisations to be set up (such as Europol), the new secure communications system, and the European Information System (EIS) are going to provide the core of the European state.

Conclusion

Two key features of modern states are: 1) mechanisms for the maintenance of law and order through the law (the courts and judiciary) and its enforcers (the police); and 2) a system of internal security to take over when the 'normal' rule of law is unable to contain opposition. It therefore comes as no surprise that, as the economic project of the Community reaches the stage of intrinsic interdependence it also becomes imperative to ensure its base is secure from internal 'subversion' and external 'threats'. The Maastricht Treaty takes, for the first time, the economic and political dimensions together - economic and financial policy, military and foreign policy, immigration and law and order - the so-called three 'pillars'.

This qualitative shift cannot be attributed simply to being features of 'supranational' or 'transnational' cooperation. The move from ad hoc cooperation to permanent institutions and agencies - to the creation of a European state - is a quite logical development. But this state is different to those of the national states of the EC. The usual tenets of 'liberal democracy' cannot be applied to the new European state. The idea of the 'separation of powers' between the executive, the legislature - backed by an independent civil service - and the judiciary does not apply. This state has been conceived by governments, honed by state officials, and passed back to governments to agree - only then have national parliaments been asked to ratify the whole package. Although national parliaments are asked to ratify the Conventions, the Conventions are not open to amendment. *Resolutions* and *agreements* between the EC states, which set out new policies, do not even require parliamentary approval. The effect of these Conventions, 'resolutions' and 'agreements' is in almost every instance to diminish peoples' rights. No democratic accountability or due process of law to protect the citizen is built in (after all, people and parliaments played no part in framing the new structures).

The legitimacy of any state depends on it being seen as 'neutral', independent of sectional bias, and acting in the interests of all. The legitimacy of this new state is therefore open to question. It is limited to having the approval of governments and state officials, who have justified it to themselves on the grounds of pooling expertise to ensure greater efficiency in combating the perceived threats to internal order. Take for example the issue of data protection. West German lawyer Thilo Weichert, observes: 'What is amazing on the European level is that data protection is articulated less as a matter of concern of civil rights groups, but as that of enlightened bureaucrats afraid about the whole apparatus being accepted by EC citizens'.[73]

States also acquire legitimacy by protecting society and citizens from commonly perceived 'enemies'. The ending of the Cold War, with its 'threat' of nuclear war and communist subversion, removed the rationale for much internal security planning. In its place is the ideology that the removal of frontiers presents common 'problems' to the EC. This shift left many agencies casting around for new roles, and they have found them in the perceived external 'threats' from terrorism, drugs and immigration. Internal opposition is portrayed as acting against the interests of all with the internal security services and police defining new 'threats' to be ideologically marginalised and targeted for surveillance.[74]

Taken together with the policies on immigration and asylum (Chapter 8), the culture of secrecy (Chapter 2) and the backdrop of rising racism and fascism the European state institutionalises the 'cordon sanitaire' at its external borders and sets up draconian mechanisms for internal control which will affect the whole community. It has all the hallmarks of an authoritarian state in which power resides in the hands of officials with no democratic or legal mechanisms to call them to account. An unaccountable and secret state, removed as it is from democratic pressures, public debate and legal restraints, operates in an arbitrary and authoritarian manner. The lack of public awareness is not just due to the secrecy with which this state has been created. It has been aided by the collusion of the media which has failed to invigilate on behalf of the citizen, and by an almost total absence of critical political interest, liberal or otherwise. The absence of accountable executive action does not bode well for Europe's future and recalls Europe's past:

> 'the violence is *authorised* (by official orders coming from legally entitled quarters), actions are *routinised* (by rule-governed practices and exact specification of roles) and the victims are *dehumanised* (by ideological definitions and indoctrinations)'.[75]

References

1. This shift was preceded by the signing of the Schengen Agreement in 1985 and the Single European Act in 1987. In this context it is worth noting that a House of Lords Select Committee Report on the 'Easing of Frontier Formalities'(HL paper 24, 1983-4) in 1983 was primarily concerned with immigration control and the possibility of identity cards being introduced if border controls were removed.

2. *Interpol*, Fenton Bresler, 1992, p161. Italics in original. It is important to note that when police want to make an arrest in another country they still have to go through Interpol and get a red notice issued. Similarly if they want to investigate an act of terrorism outside the EC they will also work through Interpol.

3. The name 'Trevi' has been open to many interpretations. It has been variously attributed to: the presence at the 1971 meeting of the Dutch Minister Mr Fonteyn (which means fountain); the name of a famous fountain in Rome; the Trevi district in Rome; and as an acronym for either 'Terrorisme radicalisme et violence' or terrorism, radicalism, extremism and international violence.

4. *Interpol*, Fenton Bresler, 1992, p160.

5. Since the beginning of 1992 the Council and Commission have been attending their meetings as observers.

6. Trevi meetings have been attended by US Attorney Generals (Dick Thornburgh and General Edwin Meese) and the Chief of the US Drug Enforcement Administration. Reports from the US have also supplemented Trevi 'security assessments'. *Associated Press*, 3.6.88 & 12.5.89.

7. Home Affairs Select Committee, 363-i, p43.

8. Home Office Circular no 153/77 issued to Chief Constables on 2 September 1977. The UK was represented by the Home Office, Security Service, HM Chief Inspector of Constabulary, the Commandant of the Police College and the Chief Constable of Derbyshire.

9. Briefing note on Trevi prepared by MS18 (the European Unit in the Metropolitan Police) dated 26.2.90; Home Affairs Select Committee, 363-I, p.xxi.

10. *Practical Police Cooperation in the European Community*, Home Affairs Select Committee, HC 363-i, 18.4.90, p6.

11. On 11 September 1986 the European Parliament passed a resolution, backed by all the main political groups, calling for more effective cooperation between the services in the EC and for the stricter application of the rules on extradition. *Report on problems relating to combatting terrorism*, European Parliament, 2.5.89, rapporteur Mr M Zagari, document A 2-0155/88, p14.

12. *Report on problems relating to combating terrorism*, European Parliament, 2.5.89, rapporteur M Zagari, document A 2-0155/88, p17. The next month, on 20 October 1986, at a follow-up meeting in London Trevi/Interior Ministers set up the Ad Hoc Group on Immigration. It was given the job of improving checks at the EC's external borders, coordinating visa policies and combating passport fraud. It met for the first time on 26 November 1986 and set up the first two sub-groups on the right of asylum and forged documents. The creation of the Ad Hoc Group on Immigration stemmed from perceived causal link between terrorism and border controls/immigration policies.

13. Trevi Senior Officials, minutes of the meeting on 16-17 November in London, Trevi Secretariat, Home Office. Confidential.

14. This assessment procedure appears to have been started in 1990. The report was also forwarded to the 'EPC Group on Terrorism', which may be a working group of the Council.

15. Trevi Senior Officials, minutes of the meeting on 16-17 November 1992 in London, Trevi Secretariat, Home Office. Confidential.

16. Home Affairs Select Committee, HC 363-i,p6.

17. Home Affairs Select Committee, HC 363-i, p6. The UK permanent correspondent is the head of the National Football Intelligence Unit.

18. It was agreed that work on the interception of communications should be drawn to the attention of national Ministers responsible for telecommunications and that the 'Friends of Trevi' grouping should also be briefed in general terms.

19. Home Affairs Select Committee, 363-i,p6. The meetings are attended by Home Office officials and a senior police officer. Pre-meetings are held with customs officers (HM Customs & Excise from the UK) and national Interpol officers.

20. Trevi Senior Officials, minutes of the meeting on 16-17 November 1992, Trevi Secretariat, Home Office. Confidential.

21. *Background report*, Commission, 26.3.92.

22. *Interpol*, Fenton Bresler, 1992, p162.

23. Home Affairs Select Committee, 363-i, p42.

24. Home Affairs Select Committee, 363-i, p44.

25. The Special Branch [or equivalent] member agencies of the Police Working Group on Terrorism (PWGOT) are: *Belgium:* Groupe Interforces Anti-Terroriste (GIA); *Denmark:* Politiets Efterentningstjeneste (PET) (Police Intelligence Service); *France:* Unite De Coordination Pour La Lutte Anti-Terroriste (UCLAT); *Germany:* Bundeskriminalamt (BKA) Abteilung Terrorismus; *Greece:* Ministry of Public Order; *Holland:* Centrale Recherche Informatiedienst (CRI) (Bijzondere Zaken Centrale); *Ireland:* An Garda Siochana (Crime and Security Branch - International Liaison Office); *Italy:* Direzione Centrale Della Polizia Di Prevenzione (DCPP); *Luxembourg:* Gendarmerie (Surete Publique); *Portugal:* Direccao Central De Combate Ao Banditisimo (DCCB); *Spain:* Comisaria General De Informacion-Servicio De Informacion Exterior (CGI-SIE); *United Kingdom:* Metropolitan Police Special Branch (MPSB) plus the following non-EC states: *Finland:* Suojelpoliisi (SUPO); *Norway:* Politiets; Overvakingstjeneste (POT); *Sweden:* Rikspolisstyreisen (RPS). See Chapter 4.

26. *The Development of Europol*, report from Trevi Ministers to the European Council, Maastricht, December 1991.

27. Programme of Action relating to the *Reinforcement of police cooperation and of the endeavours to combat terrorism or other forms of organised crime*, June 1990.

28. *Progress made in implementing the Palma Report,* the Council, CIRC 3658/4/92, 5.11.92. Confidential.

29. Home Affairs Select Committee, 363-i, p5.

30. The National Criminal Intelligence Service [NCIS] was set up in April 1992.

31. Home Affairs Select Committee, 363-i, p43.

32. In 1990 the UK representatives were: Trevi 1: Mr R B Johnson, Chief Constable of Lancashire and Mr J Sharples, Chief Constable of Merseyside and from the Home Office Mr Warne from F4 Division and Mr Potts also from F4; Trevi 2: Mr E S Bunyard, Commandant of the Police Staff College and Mr Cane from F7 Division of the Home Office and Mr Goddard from F8 Division; Trevi 3: Mr I H Kane, Chief Constable of Cambridgeshire and Mr A A Mullett, Chief Constable of West Mercia with Mr Hudson from F3 Division; Trevi 1992: Mr J S Evans, Chief Constable of Devon and Cornwall with Mr Potts from F4 Division.

33. Home Affairs Select Committee, 363-i,p42

34. Home Affairs Select Committee, 363-i, p42. One of the qualifications for becoming a member of the Special Branch has always been the ability to speak one or more languages. This historically derives from the need to keep 'foreign emigre' groups based in the UK under surveillance.

35. In early 1977 a Home Office circular 153\77 was sent to all Chief Constables. The circular is still classified.

36. Home Affairs Select Committee, 363-i,p 43. The evidence from the Special Branch observes that there is a reluctance to use Interpol for this purpose as 'the politics and motives of some of its member agencies are to say the least questionable in this context'.

37. A joint ACPO/Metropolitan Police European Unit, staffed by two Met officers (Chief Inspector and an Inspector) and two provincial officers (both Inspectors) is based at Scotland Yard. Its main function is to gather and disseminate information and examine the implications for the police, and it has established liaison with officers in other EC countries. (The changes which had occurred in the police service by 1990 were noted in evidence to the Home Affairs Select Committee. These were: 1) Establishment of ACPO International Affairs Advisory Committee; 2) Establishment of Joint ACPO/Metropolitan Police European Unit; 3) the appointment of European Liaison Officers in the majority of UK forces; 4) The inclusion of Chief Constables on Trevi Senior Officials meetings and working groups; 5) the European Liaison Section of the Metropolitan Police; 6) Appointment of a number of liaison officers abroad; 7) a number of bilateral arrangements between UK police forces and 'colleagues broad on matters of mutual interest'. Additionally, Channel Tunnel passengers will be security checked by the Special Branch which has an office at Waterloo station.

38. Home Affairs Select Committee, 363-I, p.xxi. The Commission is represented at the six-monthly meeting of Interior Ministers on immigration.

39. Home Affairs Select Committee, p5

40. *Practical Police Cooperation in the European Community,* Home Affairs Select Committee, HC 363-II, p90.

41. The first recorded parliamentary written answer on Trevi was given in 1981. This was a brief outline in the most general terms. *House of Commons,* written answer, 10.3.81.

42. See Chapter on 'Secret Europe' for a listing of the Trevi meetings in 1991 and 1992 and a sample of the information given to the UK parliament.

43. *Practical Police Cooperation in the European Community,* Home Affairs Select Committee, 1989-90, HC 363-II, pp162-3.

44. *Practical Police Cooperation in the European Community,* Home Affairs Select Committee, HC 363-II, p167.

45. see, *Interpol Today,* Raymond Kendall (Secretary General of the International Criminal Police Organisation, ICPO), Policing, Winter 1992, pp279-285.

46. Presidency conclusions, European Council, 28 and 29 June 1991, SN 151/3/91. This was one of a number of proposals under the heading of 'Future Common Action on Home Affairs and Judicial Policy', which also covered asylum, immigration and aliens.

47. *The development of Europol,* report from the Trevi Ministers to the European Council in Maastricht, December 1991.

48. *Trevi,* press release, December 1991.

49. Maastricht Treaty, p132. Article K.1 sets out the other areas of common interest as: asylum policy; external borders; immigration policy regarding third country nationals; combating 'unauthorised immigration'; drugs; fraud; judicial cooperation on civil and criminal matters; and customs.

50. Maastricht Treaty, p248.

51. European Council, 9-10 December 1991, Maastricht, *European Parliament,* 17/S-91, p5.

52. *House of Commons,* 20.11.91.

53. This has been developed through the Trevi Working Group III.

54. *House of Commons,* written answer, 18.2.92.

55. *House of Commons,* written answer, 18.2.92.

56. Report on Europol from the Civil Liberties and Internal Affairs Committee to the European Parliament, rapporteur Lode van Outrive MEP, adopted in November 1992.

57. It is sometimes also referred to as the 'Rhodes Group'. The key dates are:

1988	Coordinators' Group appointed (Rhodes)
1989	Palma Document (Madrid, June)
1989	Declaration of Trevi Ministers (Paris, December)
1990	Programme of Action (Dublin, June)
1991	Proposal for the establishment of Europol (Luxembourg, June)
1991	Report on Europol and Article K on Justice and Home Affairs in the Maastricht Treaty (Maastricht, December)

58. The new UK Police National Computer (PNC2) was set up using the same software system as the Schengen Information System.

59. This committee will report to the Council of Ministers to be known as the Council of Justice and Interior Ministers (Article K.3).

60. *European Parliament*, written answer, 5.11.92.

61. *A guide to the Treaty on European Union*, European Commission, 24.2.92, p30.

62. op.cit, p31.

63. *Migration Control at External Borders of the European Community*, Home Affairs Select Committee, 1991-2, HC 215-i,ii and iii, p64

64. Programme of work of the Coordinators group during the UK Presidency, 2.7.92, CIRC 3653/92, Confidential.

65. The Coordinators are particularly concerned to ensure 'the integration of existing areas of work in the security and enforcement sector', op.cit.

66. *Europeanisation of the police: a possibility*, Thilo Weichert, conference paper, 12-13 July, 1990, Strasbourg, refers to the similarity in objectives of the Schengen Information System and the proposed European Information System.

67. Home Affairs Select Committee, 363-i, p11.

68. Coordinators Group report on free movement of persons, 2.7.92, CIRC 3653/92, Confidential.

69. *The government reply to the seventh report from the Home Affairs Committee session 1989-90, HC 363-I*, on Practical police cooperation in the European Community, June 1991, Cm 1367, p7.

70. Note by the Presidency on the form of agreement on the European Information System, CIRC 3650/92, 29.6.92, Confidential.

71. See Chapter 9 on the provisions of the External Borders Convention.

72. The EIS will be complemented by the European 'nervous system' [ENS], developed by EC Commissioner Mr Pandolfi. A commercial group - BOS - of Bull, Olivetti and Siemens - has been formed to bid for this have opened an office in Brussels.

73. Thilo Weichert, *Freie fahrt für alle daten*, Im fadenkreuz Europas, Green Party, Germany, 1993, pp38-42.

74. See Chapter 4.

75 *Modernity and the Holocaust*, Zygmunt Bauman, p21.

Secret Europe

Tony Bunyan

The issue of secrecy permeates the work of inter-state EC bodies and working parties that are deciding the shape of the European state. Most of this work is undertaken through *inter-governmental* cooperation, working groups and agreements from which the European Commission (except in the case of immigration and asylum) and the European Parliament are excluded. Moreover, the provisions of the Maastricht Treaty ensure that much will continue to be decided in secret.

EC secrecy law proposed

In the wake of the signing of the Maastricht Agreement in December 1991 the European Commission proposed that a secrecy and vetting regulation be adopted.[1] Member governments wanted to maintain the secrecy of the new structures (eg, the K4 Committee) as the EC moved into more contentious areas like foreign affairs, immigration and asylum policies, policing and legal policies. The proposal was to introduce a UK-style official secrets regulation binding on all member states. At the Edinburgh EC Summit in December 1992, the Commission's secrecy regulation was one of the proposals withdrawn under the 'subsidiarity' clause.

The 'Explanatory Memorandum' introducing the regulation said that on 21 March 1988 the German delegation to the Council called for Community rules on security measures applicable to classified information exchanged between Member States. Nearly four years later, the Commission, 'after consultation with national experts and contacts with the administrative departments of other institutions' (presumably Interior Ministries and internal security agencies), drew up what it called 'a technical regulation' which 'should not compromise the principle of public access to information'.

The proposal was prepared by the Security Office of the EC, the Legal Service, the Joint Research Centre and the Personnel Office (DG9), and cleared with the General Secretariat of the Council of the European Communities (the Council Secretariat services the 12 EC governments). Under the Regulation officials of the Commission in Brussels and their counterparts in the 12 member states would have been able to classify documents on Community proposals and policies. The proposal was a blanket provision applicable to *any* area of EC policy.[2]

The regulation sought to establish 'security gradings' for sensitive information connected with EEC or Euratom activities and the security measures to be applied to such information inside both Member States and EC institutions. 'Classified information' was taken to mean 'all forms of information whose unauthorised disclosure could be detrimental to the essential interests of the European Communities and of the Member States'. 'Detrimental' and 'Essential interests' are not defined. The Regulation applied to information emanating both from the Commission or Council and from any of the 12 Member States, with officials determining the subjects to be classified on undefined grounds of 'essential interests'.

The Regulation ended with a section on 'infringement', ie, if there were leaks and the information came into the 'knowledge of an unauthorised person' (eg, a journalist or politician). The security department was to be informed immediately of the 'breach' of the Regulation and: 'shall take appropriate steps with the responsible officials concerned in order to limit the damage caused to a minimum and to prevent any recurrence'. The 'Penalties' imposed by the institutions and member states would be to: 'take appropriate action to penalise failure to comply with the requirements of this Regulation'.

It was drawn so widely that it could have been used to ensure that matters which may simply be politically embarrassing to the Commission and member governments were kept out of the public domain thereby bypassing democratic discussion and accountability.

The proposal came under attack from several quarters. The International Federation of Journalists, the European Federation of Trade Unions and Article 19 opposed the measure. Alex Falconer MEP, the rapporteur on the Legal Affairs Committee of the European Parliament on the EC proposals to introduce secrecy laws, said that the way the proposal had been sent to the Parliament was unusual: 1) it should have been referred to all Committees it would affect, that is several committees, not just the Legal Affairs Committee; 2) it had been sent under the 'consultation' procedure which only allows the Parliament one chance to comment, whereas proposals are usually sent under the 'cooperation' procedure which gives two chances to comment (eg, initial comments are sent back to the European Commission for revision and a proposal then goes back to the Parliament again). The Civil Liberties and Internal Affairs Committee of the European Parliament joined the call for the proposal to be withdrawn.

In the UK the proposal was considered by the Office of the Minister for the Civil Service (OMCS) in the Cabinet Office and an explanatory memorandum was circulated to MPs by the Foreign Office saying that the UK was not in favour of the proposal as drafted. The government wanted procedures to ensure an 'agreed standard of protection' to sensitive EC documents which would ensure the 'free flow of information between EC institutions and other member states', with specific areas protected (along the lines of the UK Official Secrets Act).

The spirit of the Regulation ran directly contrary to moves in the European Parliament to bring in a freedom of information law. In the summer of 1992 the parliament passed a resolution, from the Committee on Culture, Youth, Education and Media, which: 'Calls on the Commission, in particular, to draw up a proposal for a directive which, along the lines of the US Freedom of Information Act, guarantees all journalists access to information from Community and national authorities (ruling out exclusive access to such information)'.

The UK: secrecy and accountability

At national level the UK parliament is among the least informed in the EC about the work of the plethora of intern-governmental bodies. It has become the practice since 1989 for a back-bench MP to put in a 'planted' written question for the Home Secretary to provide a very brief general account from the six-monthly meetings of Interior Ministers which he attends. The UK parliament therefore has little knowledge of developments and there has been never been parliamentary debate on for example, the Trevi group in which the UK has played a leading role, during the period 1979-1993.[3]

The only opportunity parliament has to discuss substantive issues is when the UK has to ratify Conventions agreed by the Interior Ministers (and subsequently endorsed by the EC Prime Ministers at EC Council meetings). These Conventions are prepared in secret by working parties, pass through the Trevi Senior Officials or the Coordinators Group, and then a ministerial agreement is signed by the 12 Interior Ministers. Only then are the contents made officially public.

Under UK parliamentary procedure the Dublin Convention, the first EC Convention requiring ratification, was 'laid' before parliament in September 1991, when the House of Commons was not sitting, under what is known as 'the Ponsonby rules'. As no MP objected, it was formally ratified by the UK state without debate. Unlike most other national legislatures - where written constitutions give parliaments the formal power of ratifying treaties and agreements - the power rests with the government in the UK (exercising the royal prerogative on behalf of the monarch). Parliament has a say only if a very keen-eyed MP spots a proposed agreement on the packed daily order paper of the House of Commons and manages to organise opposition to it.[4] The failure to get a debate on the Dublin Convention was due partly to archaic parliamentary procedure, but the lack of debate on Trevi, the Ad Hoc Group on Immigration and Europol in the House of Commons owes more to a lack of interest in civil liberties issues.

Conclusion

The mechanism for decision-making between the EC states leaves power in the hands of officials (from Interior ministries, police, immigration, customs and security services) through a myriad of working groups. Senior officials (through the Trevi Senior Official Groups and the Coordinators' Group) play a critical role in ensuring agreement between the different state officials. The EC Summit meetings, comprising the 12 Prime Ministers, simply rubber-stamp the conclusions agreed by the Interior and Justice Ministers. It is only then, in this intergovernmental process, that parliaments and people are informed (and then often only with the barest details).

The work of inter-governmental bodies such as Trevi and the Ad Hoc Group on Immigration, and the new K4 Committee and sub-committees, are not subject to parliamentary agreement. During the two years, 1991-1992, there were 227 recorded meetings of these bodies and working parties.[5] These secret meetings are deciding issues which directly effect the rights of the citizen. For example, what about the rights of an asylum-seeker who is returned to a so-called 'safe' third country? The meeting of Interior Ministers in December 1992 decided that it would be too lengthy a process and would undermine their policies to require the receiving country to guarantee the rights of the person deported. What data protection procedures should be built into the new centres of information-gathering? If it is to be based on the Council of Europe Convention, what about countries, like the UK, who have derogated on key areas of police intelligence gathering?

The secrecy of intergovernmental decision-making through ad hoc groups has been challenged by some MEPs in the European Parliament but to little effect and national parliaments are ill-informed. The media, in the main, dutifully report press releases and official statements, critical analysis of the policies and ideology rarely appears. Uninformed parliaments and a complacent media leaves the people unaware of what is being undertaken and with no say in shaping the 'new' Europe. Faced with having to withdraw the UK-style 'Official Secrets' law the new post-Maastricht European state institutions are set to maintain the veil of secrecy used by the ad hoc groups which preceded them. Such a policy not only undermines democracy but, as important, places peoples' rights in grave jeopardy.

References

1. *Proposal for a Council Regulation (EEC) on the security measures applicable to classified information produced or transmitted in connection with the EEC or Euratom activities*, COM (92) 56 Final, 24.2.92. The full text of the provisions are available in a Statewatch briefing. There was already a limited provision in Article 215 of the EEC Treaty and the 2nd paragraph of Article 47 of the European Coal and Steel Community (ECSC) Treaty placing on officials of the Community not to disclose information 'covered by the obligation of professional secrecy'. *Draft opinion for the Committee of Legal Affairs and Citizens' Rights*, from the rapporteur, Mr Jarzemmbowksi, of the Civil Liberties and Internal Affairs Committee of the European Parliament, PE 202.537, 28.10.92.

2. Even the UK Official Secrets Act 1989 is limited to the areas of defence, security and intelligence, international agreements and policing. The UK and Ireland are the only two countries to have Official Secrets Acts in the EC.

3. The first recorded parliamentary question on Trevi was on 10.3.81.

4. *Independent*, 12 & 13.8.92; *Dublin Convention*, Cm 1623, HMSO, 1991; *Treaties and the House of Commons*, Factsheet no 57, Public Information Office. Formally, Conventions are 'laid' before parliament for 21 days.

5. See Appendix 3 for a breakdown of these meetings.

Police forces
in the EC and EFTA countries[1]

Peter Klerks

EC COUNTRIES

BELGIUM

Total no. of police officers (1991 figures collected by the European Network for Policewomen survey): total 32,691, Municipal 15,704, Gendarmerie 15,647, Judicial 1,340. No. of police officers per 100,000. Women in the police (in percentage): Municipal 4.2; Gendarmerie 0.2; Judicial 0.42 No of police officers per 100,000 inhabitants: 330 (EC av. 338).

The Belgian police has been among the most expensive forces per capita in Europe Since the second World War. After a long record of substandard performance, archaic working methods and corruption, it is currently undergoing sweeping reforms and rapid modernisation and computerisation.

Gemeentepolitie   Communal Police
Every community with at least 10,000 inhabitants can have its own police force; consequently, Belgium has 589 formally independent police forces, 334 municipal (towns and cities) and 256 rural, headed by a mayor. The Communal Police normally initiates the criminal investigation of a reported crime by informing the public prosecutor. The latter decides, in consultation with the investigating magistrate, whether further investigations are to be carried out by the Communal or the Judicial police.

A 1992 ministerial paper discussed a greater role for the Communal Police, decreasing its reliance on the *Rijkswacht* (*Gendarmerie*) assistance. Efforts to increase trans-local cooperation with the *Gendarmerie* still run up against traditional local interests which obstruct modernisation and coordination. Central government counters this by using the 'power of the purse' to ensure common standards are met.

Gerechtelijke Politie   Police Judiciaire
This plainclothes judicial police service is being reorganised from 22 independent brigades into one centralised organisation. The 23rd *Police Judiciaire Brigade* in

---

1. This Chapter has been extracted from a longer report which is available from the Domestic Security Research Foundation, PO Box 11178, 1001 GD, Amsterdam, the Netherlands.

Brussels was set up in 1986 to combat terrorism, narcotics, and organised crime. The general directorate of the Brussels *Police Judiciaire* operates the *Interpol* NCB and the *Schengen Information System* national bureau.

Rijkswacht Gendarmerie

The *Gendarmerie*, traditionally a military police force, was demilitarised in July 1991 and on 1 January 1992 became the joint responsibility of the Ministry of Justice and the Ministry of the Interior. It has 427 stationary Brigades as well as Mobile Groups, Territorial Groups and Traffic Units. Besides doing criminal investigations, its detective units, the *Bijzondere Opsporings Brigade* (BOB Special Investigations Brigade) also carry out surveillance and monitoring of political and trade union activities. Since about 1984, every Mobile Group (about 800 strong) has had its own plainclothes *POAS* (Protection, Observation, Support and Arrest) platoon.

The *Gendarmerie* supplies policing services when the Communal Police are short staffed. Apart from day-to-day assistance, the *Gendarmerie's* tasks are: guarding duties of embassies and other vulnerable targets; support of local forces at soccer matches, demonstrations etc; temporary support in case of local shortages of personnel; preventive patrols and identity checks; anti-terrorist protection of vulnerable targets (e.g. school buses with Jewish children); escorting money transports; escorting prisoner transports; traffic policing; territorial defence in case of war.

The *Gendarmerie* is characterised by a strong esprit-de-corps and little accountability to the outside world. Though a civilian organisation since January 1992, it retains some military functions (military police, tracking down deserters, etc) and military administrative and logistic staff. Observers both inside and outside the force are sceptical about the real impact of new regulations on day-to-day operations and the traditional modus operandi.

Socialist Minister of the Interior *Louis Tobback* said recently that the *Gendarmerie* should be kept as an autonomous force with its function as a standing reserve to counter domestic unrest.

Other policing services

In the countryside (i.e. in the smallest communities) there are also relatively unimportant forces of about 850 strong called the *Landelijke Politie* (rural police). In 1989, Member of Parliament *Hugo Coveliers* counted some 60 other services with police powers in the various ministries, as well as 25 institutions and commissions for the supervision, coordination or study of the police.

Special units

After the Olympic massacre in Munich in 1972, the anti-terrorist *Diane* group was established in the *Gendarmerie*. In 1977, this was reformed into the Special Intervention Squadron (SIE, or *ESI* in French), currently believed to be about 150 strong, which is constantly available at an hour's notice. Its members are recruited from the *Gendarmerie* personnel.

The *Groupe Interforces Antiterroriste* (GIA) is an intelligence unit on terrorism, created in 1984 and established formally on 17 October 1991, with the purpose of overcoming inter-agency rivalry and lack of cooperation. Belgian intelligence (*Sûreté*) is also involved. According to insiders, GIA's performance has been rather poor.

Weaponry and special equipment: *Communal police*: baton; teargas; 9 mm pistol or .38 revolver; UZI submachine gun; riot 12 mm shotgun; *Judicial Police*: 9 mm pistol or .38 revolver; riot gun; *Gendarmerie*: water cannon, tear gas; 9 mm pistol; riot gun; UZI; .50 machine guns, mortars, light artillery; armoured vehicles; 8 helicopters. In 1990 there were 106 registered cases of firearms use by the *Gendarmerie*, mostly involving the Special Intervention Squadron operations. 68% of the incidents involved firing on a fleeing vehicle.

Arrests and the treatment of detainees
People arrested on suspicion of an offence can normally be detained for up to 24 hours. After that they have a right to an attorney. A magistrate can order further detention for up to five days. Then the suspects must be presented to a magistrate who can order further detention for up to one month, pending the investigation. This procedure can be repeated indefinitely.

Accountability
The law on the control of police and intelligence services, enacted on 18 July 1991, gives the Belgian parliament considerable power to scrutinise policing activities. It is too early to evaluate the operation of this legislation.

DENMARK

Total no. of police officers: 10,269 plus 2,227 administrative, including the police forces in the Färoe Islands (pop. 47,317) and Greenland (pop. 55,385). Denmark also has a 7,000-strong 'Home Guard' that functions as a reserve force for special occasions. The 1991 national police force was estimated at 10,300 (Hazenberg and Mulschlegel 1992). Women in the police: approx. 5%. No. of police officers per 100,000 inhabitants: 183 (EC av. 338)

The Danish police form a single national force, administered through the police department of the Ministry of Justice. Policy-making responsibilities are divided between the *Rigspolitichefen* (national commissioner), the *Politimestre* (53 district chiefs of police) and the *Politidirektor* (Copenhagen's commissioner). Although the police chiefs enjoy a high degree of autonomy, final responsibility lies with the Minister of Justice. All senior ranks (above chief superintendent) are career jurists who have served in the prosecutors offices.

The national police force has over 7,733 uniformed officers for the regular police tasks, and some 2,107 detectives for serious crimes. The office of the *Rigspolitichefen* operates the Interpol NCB.

Denmark is covered by a network of district police HQs and, in some districts, a number of divisional stations. All 54 police districts are organised in seven police regions. The Danish police are currently implementing a radio-based data communication network for retrieval of relevant information from Copenhagen HQ by hand-held and mobile terminals throughout the country.

Special units
The principal anti-terrorist capability is a police unit of the Police Intelligence Service called *Politiets Efterretningstjenestre* (PET)(Thompson, 1986: 118-119). Dispersed around the country, operatives are called together periodically for training or actual missions. Best suited for dangerous operations, such as hostage rescue operations, is the 40-50 strong special unit in the *Frømandskorpset* (Navy combat swimmers) whose main responsibility is anti-terrorist operations in ports, oil rigs and ships. The Danish army is also believed to have sniper and anti-terrorist capabilities.

Weaponry and special equipment: Firearms (in 1989 a 7.65 mm pistol) are generally carried on patrols, but every use or threatened use must be officially reported, as must the use of batons. Special units are equipped with submachine guns and other weapons. Recently there has been a big increase in the use of guns, in 1990 there were 225 recorded incidents and in 1992 over 300.

FRANCE

Total no. of police officers (1991 estimate): 277,920. No. of police officers per 100,000 inhabitants: 394 (EC av. 338). The *Police Nationale* was 125,320 strong (114,900 executive, 10,420 administrative) in January 1989. The *Gendarmerie Nationale* numbered 91,800 personnel in 1991. The *Police Judiciaire* was estimated at 5,800 in 1989. Women in the police: in the *Police Nationale* in 1991 women were 10% of the total strength; the *Gendarmerie*, 1.5%. France also has a number of semi-police forces, in particular the *Police Municipale* (about 25,000) and the *Gardes Champêtres* (nearly 30,000). Including these the number of police officers per 100,000 inhabitants is 491.

France's 96 *departements* are further subdivided into 324 *arrondissements* (districts), which are made up of *communes*. A department is managed by a *Commissaire de la République* (formerly called the *Préfet*).

Gendarmerie Nationale
This strictly military organisation, which is part of the Ministry of Defence, performs police duties in all towns with fewer than 10,000 inhabitants. It is responsible for policing over 90% of the land area of France, and absorbs about 40% of the entire policing budget (i.e. of the Ministries of the Interior and Defence combined). It consists of two sections. The *Gendarmerie Départementale* forms a network of about 3,500 *brigades* with units of between five and 55 officers covering the whole of provincial France as well as its overseas territories. The officers, living in barracks with their families, are responsible for 24-hour police services.

The *Gendarmerie Mobile* (GM) is a specially trained public order force which, together with the *Compagnies Républicaines de Sécurité* (CRS, see below) forms a permanent riot control apparatus, a standing 'third force'. Some 18,000 GM are distributed over France in 24 *groupements*, made up of units of about 130 squadrons of 134 officers. The GM is solely intended to guard vital civilian installations and defend the Republic in times of war or to intervene in serious public order situations. Logistically it is almost entirely self-sufficient and has extensive weaponry including machine guns, armoured combat vehicles, helicopters, light tanks and parachute forces.

Police Nationale

CRS riot squads, the prime public order forces, are also distributed all over France and stationed around urban and industrial areas in 10 territorial group commands (*baraques*). Apart from maintaining public order, they are mostly deployed in highway patrols and on assistance duties in the mountains and on the beaches. In total, the CRS number about 16,000 men comprising 61 companies. Although organised and trained on military lines, CRS personnel are part of the civilian *Police Nationale*. Its chief operating and administrative officer is a civilian, the director general at the Ministry of the Interior, who is accountable to the secretary of state in charge of public security. Ultimate responsibility lies with the Minister of the Interior. All cities and villages with more than 10,000 inhabitants are policed by the PN's *Police Urbaine*. Another responsibility of the *Police Nationale* is to guard frontiers and airports, a task carried out by the *Police de l'Air et des Frontières* (PAF), which has about 5,000 personnel, both plain clothes and uniformed.

About 70% of the *Police Nationale* were unionised in the mid-1980s, but they do not have the right to strike.

Police Judiciaire

This locally based national detective force investigates all breaches of the law, gathers evidence and brings perpetrators before the tribunals empowered to try them.

Officiers de Police Judiciaire (OPJs) can order initial detention for four hours for an ID check. This can be extended for a further 20 hours, and a further 24 hours detention must be applied for to the juge d'instruction. For terrorist and drug arrests the periods of detention are 48 plus 48 hours. Normal *agents de Police judiciaire* have no power to impose the *garde à vue* (summary arrest).

General command over the Police Judiciaire lies with the *Direction Centrale de la Police Judiciaire* (a sub-department of the Interior Ministry) which is divided into the *Sous-Direction des Affaires Criminelles* (central executive units working on anti-terrorism, organised and serious crime etc.), the *Sous-Direction des Affaires Economiques et Financières* (fraud, counterfeiting, etc), and the *Sous-Direction de la Police Technique et Scientifique* (criminal statistics and databanks). Throughout the country the PJ has *Services Regionaux*, which in turn have their smaller branches in the *antennes* (units of 15 or more detectives). Paris has its own *Direction Régionale de la Police Judiciaire de Paris*, a very large service with over 3,000 functionaries.

The *Police Nationale* also has its own investigative branches in the larger cities, the *Sûretés Urbaines*, and every compagnie of the *Gendarmerie Nationale* has its *Brigade de Recherche* (there are some 17,000 *officiers de police judiciaire de la Gendarmerie*), coordinated by the GN's central *Service Technique de Recherches Judiciaires et de Documentation*. Investigators of all branches are formally accountable to the *juge d'instruction* (examining magistrate) when carrying out investigations.

The 25,000-strong *Police Municipale*, operate under the authority of the city mayors and have limited powers. The growth of PM, which started in 1983, reflects dissatisfaction with the services provided by the national forces. The 30,000 strong *Gardes Champêtres*, a cross between a forest ranger and a local constable, operate in rural areas.

Special units

The *Police Nationale* has the elite group (believed to number about 100) called *Recherche, Assistance, Intervention, Dissuasion (RAID)* nicknamed the 'Black Panthers'. Apart from the odd counter-terrorist mission, its main functions are shadowing and surveillance operations and VIP protection. The *Gendarmerie* has the *Groupe d'Intervention de la Gendarmerie Nationale, GIGN* (pronounced 'gigène'). Formed in 1973, by 1984 the GIGN had expanded into four 12-men teams of close combat specialists, with at least one on a permanent alert status. They perform hostage rescue operations, transporting dangerous criminals, protect high-risk VIP, deal with prison sieges, etc.

French anti-terrorist operatives were exposed in 1988 when they maltreated and killed a number of New Caledonian rebels. After revelations in 1986 that they had planted evidence on arrested IRA suspects in Vincennes in 1982, an entire unit was disbanded. The scandal continued in early 1993 when *Liberation* published evidence that the unit had illegally tapped the phones of investigative journalists and others.

In 1984 the *Unité de Coordination de la Lutte Anti-Terroriste (UCLAT)* was set up under the head of the PN for coordinating purposes. In the *Renseignements Généraux (RG)*, the French police has a dedicated police intelligence service of some 3,600 strong. The *Direction de la Surveillance du Territoire* (DST, about 1,200 personnel), the security service, is another part of the *Police Nationale* and also receives ample attention in the security services report.

Weaponry and special equipment: The *Gendarmerie Nationale*, the CRS and the PAF are equipped with a 9 mm pistol. Since 1985 the PN *gardiens de la paix* have had .357 magnum revolvers, heavy calibre for normal police duties. French police monitoring groups have listed dozens of cases over the last 20 years in which civilians, often already constrained by the police, died under police bullets. Many were ruled to be 'involuntary discharges' resulting in *homicide involontaire*, for which officers are usually not prosecuted.

Arrests and the treatment of detainees: The right to silence is not effectively guaranteed in French law - in "on the scene of crime" investigations, police officers' questions must be answered - nor is the principle of *habeas corpus*. It is not unknown for witnesses as well as suspects to be arrested. The system of public complaints against the police (either through the Public Prosecutor's office or directly to the Inspectorates General), it has low credibility.

GERMANY

Total no. of police officers (1993, our estimate): 272,000. No. of police officers per 100,000 inhabitants: 340 (EC av. 338). 1989 figures for FRG police forces (i.e. of the 11 'old' Bundesländer): state police forces total 169,000 (24,000 Kripo) plus 21,000 Bepo; Bundesgrenzschutz 21,000; Bundeskriminalamt 3,100. 1993 figures (our estimate for all 16 länder of the 'new' FRG): state police forces total ± 210,000 plus ± 25,000 Bepo; Bundesgrenzschutz ± 33,000; Bundeskriminalamt ± 4,000. Women in the police: The percentage of women in the German police forces varies greatly between the different states with women occupying between 7 to 20% of forces.

The differences between the police forces of the 16 *Bundesländer* (states) can be almost as great as those between different European countries. Although the main organisational features are roughly similar, each state has its own police law and the approach to public order problems can differ, depending upon geographical factors, local tradition and political doctrine. The police are accountable to their state Minister for the Interior for that state, through the local *Polizeipräsident* in cities or the *Oberkreisdirektor* in rural areas. Inter-state policy coordination is primarily reached through the *Innenministerkonferenz*, the Standing Conference of the 16 Ministers of the Interior. The criminal police are accountable to the state prosecutor for investigative matters.

General organisation

In general, the *Vollzugspolizei* (executive police) can be divided into the *Schutzpolizei* (known as *Schupo*: the uniformed constabulary responsible for patrolling, traffic policing etc.), the *Kriminalpolizei* (aka *Kripo:* CID) and the *Bereitschaftspolizei*, *Bepo*: paramilitary 'stand-by' force, coordinated at the federal level to provide support when large numbers of police are needed and which consists mainly of the 2nd and 3rd year recruits who live in barracks (they number more than 25,000). Apart from the *Bepo* the division between the different branches is far less strict in some states than in others. Police strength per capita can range from 1:130 in Berlin to 1:400 in some of the more rural states. The state police forces are funded by the states except for the equipment of the federally coordinated *Bereitschaftspolizei*. Most of the police officers (over 85%) are unionised, the largest union is the *Gewerkschaft der Polizei*.

Criminal Police

The general administration of the *Kriminalpolizei* is the responsibility of the federal states. The *Landeskriminalämter* (LKAs), the central criminal intelligence agencies in each of the states, have evolved since the 1960s into fully-fledged operational agencies with, in some cases, more than 1,000 personnel. *LKAs*, which operate mainly in the areas of organised crime and narcotics, can initiate and execute criminal investigations, supported by their own observation and arrest squads, infiltration teams. They have become increasingly powerful through their coordinating role in the Kriminalpolizei branches in their state.

The *Bundeskriminalamt* (BKA, Federal Criminal Police Office in Wiesbaden and Meckenheim near Bonn) also gained tremendous importance and prestige through the massive expansion of its information networks and support facilities and by increasingly initiating its own investigations into terrorism, narcotics, counterfeiting, international arms trafficking and organised crime. It has about 4,000 personnel and its annual budget is well over DM 400 million. It has a VIP protection branch and a 600-strong State Security branch. It can also engage in its own executive policing in terms of investigation, search and arrest. The German Interpol NCB at the BKA processes over 160,000 requests for information each year, one-third of all Interpol traffic worldwide.

Under the BKA's *Vorverlagerungsstrategie* (increase range strategy) close cooperation with law enforcement authorities in drug-producing countries and transit states has resulted in a German police presence outside the EC. In 1991, 33 German police liaison officers were stationed in 22 countries. A DM 4 million police development aid programme and a training programme of foreign police officers in Germany are other components of this strategy.

The German police is perhaps the world's most advanced in its use of sophisticated computer, telecommunications and forensic equipment. Its data information system allows local, regional or state police forces to communicate or cooperate through more than 6,500 computer terminals.

Federal Border Police

The *Bundesgrenzschutz* (*BGS*, federal border police), a paramilitary force organised on military lines, became a civilian organisation legally in 1991. *BGS* officers have a nation-wide jurisdiction in relation to serious crime and can be called upon to support the state forces. Other tasks include guarding FRG's borders; protecting federal state institutions and embassies abroad; patrolling the North and Baltic Seas, including environmental protection; guarding airport facilities; maintaining railroad security.

The BGS was set up in the early 1950s to enable the government to resist East German subversion and to suppress demonstrations. Since then it has been deployed in all major demonstrations. Recently a substantial part of *BGS* support for state police forces, especially in what was the East, has been riot support. It is equipped with water cannon, tear gas, assorted firearms, light artillery, grenade launchers, and armoured personnel carriers with mounted machine guns. Total spending for the BGS in 1991 amounted to DM 1.6 billion. Total personnel strength in 1991 was about 30,300 (about 10% less than its authorised strength). Bavaria has its own independent border police, the *Bayerische Grenzpolizei*. The *BGS* has separate branches for the Baltic Sea and North Sea police (*BGS See*) and for aviation services (mainly troop transport and surveillance helicopters). Policing of waterways is the responsibility of state police forces, the *Wasserschutzpolizei*.

Voluntary Police

Some larger cities have voluntary police forces. In 1992 these functioned mainly to guard asylum seekers' homes and Jewish monuments. A survey of the 2,500-strong Berlin Voluntary Police in January 1993 showed that 89 of a sample 200 Volunteers had ties with neo-Nazi groups and/or had been involved with arms smuggling, child abuse or other serious crimes. It is claimed that those with Nazi sympathies will be banned from the force.

Special units

GrenzSchutzGruppe 9 (GSG 9), the 200-strong crack anti-terrorist unit, was set up after the Munich Olympic massacre in 1972. International consultation resulted in similar initiatives being taken in most other West European countries in 1972/73.

GSG 9 reportedly consists of central HQ, intelligence, training, equipment and other support facilities and four strike units of about 42 men each, identified as GSG 9 by their green berets. Each unit has a command section and five *SpecialEinsatzTruppen* (SETs). *SETs*, can be deployed as assault squads, sniper groups, VIP protection units etc, operate on a 24-hour stand-by scheme, with helicopters available to take them anywhere in the FRG. The reputation of GSG 9 is such that it is involved in the training of many foreign anti-terrorist teams. In recent years, GSG 9 has also been used against drug dealers, a motor gang and other 'ordinary criminals'. GSG 9 is said now to be mostly deployed on covert observation missions against 'organised crime'.

Local *SpezialEinsatzKommandos* (SEK, similar to a US SWAT team) deal with terrorists where the case remains under State or city government jurisdiction. 40-60 strong and equipped like the GSG 9, the SEKs with their attached countersniper groups (PSK) are the mainstay of tactical police operations. They also deal with 'ordinary' criminals and are sometimes deployed as a shock force in riot situations. The *MobilEinsatzKommandos* (MEK) are the CID's covert surveillance units that operate in every region.

Weaponry and special equipment: All police officers normally carry a 9 mm pistol. Additional weaponry is available.

Arrests and the treatment of detainees: Arrested suspects can be detained initially for 24 hours, during which period they can consult a solicitor. A judge can order further detention for periods of four weeks indefinitely.

GREECE

Total no. of police officers (1989 estimate): 40,000. Women in the police: according to the 1992 survey of the European Network of Policewomen, women have been working in the Greek police for more than 25 years and account for 6% of the total posts per rank. No. of police officers per 100,000 inhabitants: 400 (EC av. 338).

The national police has been a unified force since 1985, when its predecessors, the City Police and the Gendarmerie, were merged. The Ministry of Public Order is responsible for the police and is its highest coordinating department.

The organisation of the police is based on Greece's 51 administrative prefectures, which constitute a police district, plus those of Attica (the Athens area) and Thessalonika making a total of 53 police districts. Each district has a Police Department which, within its jurisdiction, exercises all police powers provided by state laws; it is answerable to the Ministry of Public Order and headed by a Police Director (in Attica and Thessalonika there is a General Police Department, directed by a Major General or a Brigadier General). The Police Departments are directly responsible to the Chief of Police, the supreme police commander in the Ministry of Public Order.

Each prefecture has a Police Committee consisting of a *Nomarch* (the governmental representative in the prefecture) as its President, a representative from the local union of communities and municipalities, the Police Director (a Colonel) of the precinct in question (who acts as rapporteur) and a judge of the regional court of the precinct. The function of this Committee is to decide what action should be taken if there is a risk of public disorder through riots, fires, disasters, etc. It also acts as an advisory body on regional affairs to the Ministry of Public Order.

In recent years considerable efforts have been made to professionalise and modernise the police force, including its logistics, communications and equipment, and an Automatic Fingerprint Investigation System is currently being implemented.

Special Units
The counter-terrorist Special Security Group, formed in 1976, protects vulnerable objects and persons and has SWAT and sniper capabilities. In 1988, after the terrorist attack on the cruise ship *City of Poros*, a special 200-strong seaborne anti-terrorist unit was established. The Athens Police maintains a semi-permanent riot squad.

Other units: Tourist police (drawn from the national police) patrol airports and serve as guides. There are also Customs Guards, the Ports Police, the Forest Police, and the Agrarian Police.

Weaponry and special equipment: All police officers except women carry sidearms and clubs while on regular duty. In emergencies, heavier weapons are issued and armoured personnel carriers can be deployed.

IRELAND

An Garda Siochana (Guardians of the Peace)
The Republic of Ireland has a single unitary police force centrally controlled from Dublin. Its strength as of 31 December 1992 was 10,996 and it also employed 675 civilian workers. The Garda Siochana is headed by a Commissioner appointed by the Government and comes under the authority of the Minister for Justice who is answerable for its operations to the Oireachtas (Parliament). There are only 526 women in the Garda Siochana (4.8%). There is only one woman Superintendent and no woman is above that rank. The first women were not recruited until 1959.

Organisational structure
The state is divided into 23 policing Divisions, each headed by a Chief Superintendent, but five of those Divisions comprise the Dublin Metropolitan Area (DMA), which forms a single command unit headed by an Assistant Commissioner. A total of 3,984 gardai (36%) are stationed in the DNA, which comprises Dublin and its immediate surroundings and has a population of 1.1 million - out of 3.5 million in the state.

Uniformed/non-uniformed - unarmed/armed
The Garda Siochana has traditionally been a largely unarmed force. Uniformed gardai do not carry firearms and are armed only with batons, though all gardai now receive firearms training. There are approximately 1,700 detectives, who do not wear uniforms. They have access to firearms and depending on their duties, many will carry them. The standard weapon is a .38 revolver, but they also have access to Uzi sub-machine guns.

Each Garda Division outside the DNA has its own detective unit which deals with criminal investigation, drugs and subversive/political crime. The DMA, as well as having some 300 ordinary detectives, is also the base for the Central Detective Unit (150 members) and the Special Detective Unit (500 members).

The Central Detective Unit deals with serious crime, eg murder, in the DMA and will assist the Divisional detective units with serious crimes in their area. The Special Detective Unit deals with surveillance, and subversive/political crime mainly the IRA - as well as providing protection for Government Ministers, judges, diplomats etc. Again it will assist local Divisional detective units, which will usually have some members dealing with surveillance and subversive/political crime in their area.

Emergency Response Unit

There have been a number of special units targeted at the IRA and violent crime. In the early 1980s there was a series of Divisional Task Forces but these acquired a reputation for being aggressive, trigger happy and undisciplined. They were replaced about three years ago by a centrally controlled Emergency Response Unit. This unit -- about 75 strong - specialises in arms raids and searches, arresting suspected IRA members and dealing with bank robberies etc. It is also trained to deal with sieges, kidnaps and hijackings. One of its first actions in 1990 involved a 'shoot-out' which left a bank robber dead and two of his companions and several civilians injured. It transpired that all the shots were fired by ERU members.

The Army

The Irish Army - about 13,000 strong - is used extensively to provide back-up security for uniformed gardai at road checkpoints near the Border with Northern Ireland. It is also used to provide armed escorts for large cash shipments and to escort paramilitary prisoners to and from court and to guard the perimeter of the Republic's maximum security prison at Portlaoise, where IRA and other paramilitary prisoners are held. The Army was also used occasionally as a riot control back-up in the 1970s but this has been discontinued. On escort duties troops are armed with Steyr rifles. The Army also uses armoured vehicles to mount its own patrols in Border areas but it has no powers of arrest and must be accompanied by gardai to search vehicles, make arrests etc.

Counter-intelligence

The Republic does not have any counter-intelligence agency. The surveillance section of the Special Detective Unit presumably monitors foreign contacts by the IRA etc and the Army also has its own intelligence unit, G3. The Republic is not a member of any military alliance but has become increasing involved in the Trevi group and moves towards a common EC security policy.

Powers of arrest:

Under Section 4 of the Criminal Justice Act 1984, the gardai can detain suspects for questioning for a maximum of 12 hours - extended to 20 hours if the suspect is held overnight, but then they must be allowed eight hours rest. Under Section 30 of the Offences Against the State Act 1939, suspects can be detained for a maximum of 48 hours. Though this power was originally designed for use in connection with subversive or political offences, it is now frequently used for serious non-political offences as well. Under the pretext of questioning about suspected membership of an unlawful organisation, Section 30 is often used simply for information gathering.

The gardai have no other power to detain for questioning. And even in the case of arrests under these Acts, they must inform a relative or friend of the arrested person and allow prompt access to a lawyer. There are no provisions for audio or video-taping of interviews, however. After the expiry of the time limits, the gardai must charge or release the detained person.

ITALY

Total no. of police officers (1989 estimate, Semerak): 257,000 (*Polizia di Stato* 80,000, *Carabinieri* 85,000 (Hazenberg, 1992, gives a total of 111,400 personnel for the *Carabinieri*), *Guardia di Finanza* 42,000, *Polizia Municipale* 50,000). Women in the police: approx. 5%. No. of police officers per 100,000 inhabitants: 445 (EC av. 338)

Responsibility for keeping the peace and enforcing the law comes under the Public Security Authority in the Ministry for Internal Affairs. The *Prefetto* in each of the 92 provinces is empowered to direct all the police forces within the province, and is directly answerable to the Interior Minister. In daily practice the *Direttore General di Polizia di Stato* (Chief of Police in the Interior Ministry) instructs the senior police official in each province, the *Questore*, and the latter has an apparatus of senior civil servants to execute government policy and a *commissario* to supervise each major city in the province. The *Questore* is head of the State Police *Questura* (HQ), located in each provincial capital. The *Polizia di Stato* (State Police) also has riot control capacities in the Mobile Units, which can be deployed anywhere in the country.

Parallel to this structure are the largely autonomous **Carabinieri** who, although formally answerable to the Interior Ministry line of command during peacetime, are in fact directed by their central command in Rome. There has always been institutional rivalry between the two forces. The *Carabinieri* commander is a three-star general on temporary assignment from the army, and all personnel are recruited from the regular army. The *Carabinieri* are responsible for riot control, for which a complete miniature army is kept at the ready. Helicopters and fixed-wing aircraft as well as a small fleet of coastal patrol vessels assist in other tasks, including anti-smuggling operations, standard police work and crime detection, narcotics investigations, protection of VIPs and state institutions, supplying the secret services with trained personnel. Small villages will normally only have Carabinieri. They are also the Military Police, and have specific duties of keeping order and maintaining public security, being fundamentally a military bureaucracy with a corresponding ideology.

The Ministry of Finance has its own 40,000 strong police force, the *Guardia di Finanza*, a military force which assists in enforcing tax, excise, customs and tariff legislation. The mayors of most towns and villages also have some form of local police, the *Polizia Municipale*, covering the road network and local administration (licences, markets, public health, etc.). Numbering around 60,000, they do not play a great role in law enforcement. Several other bodies, such as the *Agenti di Custodia*

(Corps of Prison Wardens, ± 14,000), the *Forestale dello Stato* (Corps of Foresters, ± 3,000) and the *Capitanieri di Porto* (Harbour Police, ± 1,000) have their own specific responsibilities.

The latest agency set up in the ongoing battle against organised crime is the *Direzione Investigativa Antimafia* (DIA) which is equipped with state-of-the-art technology for data-processing and communications. Some feel its recent, and unprecedented, successes with *Operation Clean Hands*, has dealt a definite blow to organised crime in Italy. The 3,000 strong DIA has been described in the Italian press as the *Italian FBI*. The Justice Department is also being reorganised and there are plans to set up a dedicated anti-Mafia department parallel to the regular Public Prosecutors Office.

Special units

Italy reportedly has two anti-terrorist units. The *Carabinieri* have their *Groupe Interventional Speciale* (GIS), with 46 men, trained and armed to international standards. The other unit is the 100 strong *Nucleo Operative Central di Sicurezza* (NOCS), which became famous when it freed *General Dozier* from the Red Brigades in November 1982 (its reputation was tarnished when NOCS members allegedly tortured Red Brigade suspects). In 1990 it was disclosed that, since 1978, NOCS had mounted about 1,300 operations, 600 involving armed assault.

Weaponry and special equipment: All police personnel carry a *Beretta* pistol (7.65 mm in 1989). *Carabinieri* often carry an MP or a rifle. Special units and the Mobile Units have a range of military and specialist gear.

Arrests and the treatment of detainees

Detained suspects must be charged within 48 hours. In normal criminal cases, the maximum permissible pre-trial detention time varies according to the gravity of the crime. The government has recently moved to extend it to six years for defendants accused of serious crimes. As a safeguard against abuse, *liberty tribunals* are empowered to review evidence and decide whether continued detention is warranted. In the first six months of 1991, 2,795 men and 134 women, out of a prison population of 31,053, were released because the length of time during which they could be held had expired.

LUXEMBOURG

Total no. of police officers (1992 estimate, Hazenberg en Mulschlegel 1992): 1,100. Women in the police: The percentage of women in the *Gendarmerie* is about 3% in the NCO ranks, and in the police 5.6% in 1992. No. of police officers per 100,000 inhabitants: 282 (EC av. 338)

Luxembourg has two forces, the *Corps de Police* of around 500 personnel and the 600-strong *Gendarmerie*. Both are responsible to the Ministries of Defence, Justice and the Interior. The policing tradition is mainly based on the French system. *Corps de Police* is deployed in villages of more than 5,000. All major crimes are transferred to the *Sûreté de Gendarmerie* to investigate. Police officers are normally equipped with sidearms; additional weaponry is available. The paramilitary *Gendarmerie*, deployed throughout Luxembourg, covers all types of policing functions. A Mobile Group is responsible for riot control and observation and intervention operations. The *Gendarmerie* has its own training facilities. A pistol or .357 revolver is carried as standard sidearm; FAL rifles and UZI or Heckler & Koch sub machine guns are available.

The NETHERLANDS

Total no. of police officers (1992 estimate): 40,000. Women in the police: less than 13% of the force consists of women, most of them serving in the lower ranks. No. of police officers per 100,000 inhabitants: 267 (EC av. 338)

The police are presently going through the most far-reaching reorganisation process since World War 2. The present government is in the process of replacing the 148 *Gemeentepolitie* (municipal police) forces (totalling 32,600 personnel), the *Rijkspolitie* (state police for the rural areas, some 13,400 strong) and a handful of national specialised services by 25 regional forces (varying in strength from 450 to 4,500) and an integrated National Police Service Agency. The formal structure is broadly as follows: if the police act in a community to maintain public order or lend assistance, they come under the authority of the mayor (appointed by the Crown for six years); if involved in the maintenance of legal order or acting in a judicial capacity, they come under the jurisdiction of the public prosecutor, unless the law determines otherwise.

The regulation of authority in the new structure is the same, except for the new regional police forces. For them, general responsibility at a national level lies with the Minister of the Interior; at a regional level, with the mayor of a provincial capital or of the largest municipality in the police region who, as regional director, will be supported the local police chief. Administration will be the responsibility of the 'regional authority', chaired by the regional director. While the latter can make important decisions, in consultation with the Chief Public Prosecutor, the regional authority has the final say.

Critics believe that the 'democratic base' of the police under the new system is inadequate. Most mayors, though accountable for policing in their territory, will have little influence. They will only meet twice a year; the chair of the 'regional authority', together with the regional police chief and the Chief public prosecutor, will make all daily decisions.

The new National Police Service Agency (also referred to as 'the 26th corps') will include the present *Centrale Recherche Informatiedienst* (CRI, Central Criminal Intelligence Service), a 600-strong police support service for information management and retrieval with expertise in criminal investigations, which also runs the Interpol NCB. Other elements of the new National Agency will be the Water Police, the national Traffic Police, the VIP protection service, the police aviation service, the central police logistics and telecommunications service etc.

The *Landelijk Coördinatie Centrum* (LCC) at the Ministry of the Interior in The Hague is the crisis centre used to coordinate large-scale emergencies and events (eg: during the Pope's visit and during the Gulf War it ran anti-terrorist security operations).

The police system also includes a gendarmerie force, the *Koninklijke marechaussee* (Kmar, about 4,000 strong), a paramilitary force under the Ministry of Defence which is responsible for border controls (ie: only airports after the *Schengen Agreement* is fully operational) and identity controls on aliens in the larger cities, as well as policing duties on military establishments. Kmar personnel also provided support to the Hague and Amsterdam municipal police forces to compensate for shortages of personnel, and functions as a back-up Third Force for riot control and other large-scale operations.

The *Rijksrecherche* (State Detectives), some 70 police functionaries under the direct supervision of a *Procureur-Generaal,* investigate serious complaints against police officers and administrative and judicial authorities as well as fraud and corruption charges against public functionaries, members of parliament etc. The *Coördinerend Politie Beraad* (CPB, coordinating police council) consisting of the 25 regional police chiefs plus the chief of the national service, plays a dominant role in policy debates.

Voluntary police

In recent years, shortages of police personnel caused by financial restrictions and recruitment problems have led to a variety of 'pseudo police' groups. 'City Watches', 'police surveillants' and others comprised of low-paid and ill-trained public order assistants now number almost 1,000 operating in many cities. In Amsterdam, the 'eyes on the street', the *Stadswachten*, have gained considerable public respect in patrolling market places and neighbourhoods. They have no formal links with the police apart from radio contact and regular briefings.

Apart from the above, there are dozens of government bureaux and departments with *bijzondere opsporingsambtenaren* (special investigation officials). These are civil servants and detectives with limited police powers, whose task it is to control and enforce specific legislation pertaining to social security, railways, working-place safety, taxes, health and food matters, environmental regulations (the regular police are charged with investigating all punishable acts as well as overseeing the observance of nearly all 'special legislation'). They generally operate in close contact with the regular police, especially the criminal intelligence services, and their role in so-called 'pro-active policing' is of growing importance.

There are an estimated 10,000 *onbezoldigde opsporingsambtenaren* (unpaid investigation officials), ie: individuals with general or limited police powers due to their appointment as 'unpaid police officer'. Many are *bijzondere opsporingsambtenaren*, but at least 1,000 are employees of company security services or comparable functionaries, who may use their police powers in the performance of their duties.

Special units

In hostage rescue operations, the first option is to use trained psychologists and negotiators, an approach which has proved quite successful. Where forceful intervention is necessary, several assault units are available. Most regional police forces have 'arrest teams' deployed when suspects are considered armed and dangerous, whose record of avoiding unnecessary use of force is quite high. The

Koninklijke marechaussee has a *Brigade Speciale Beveiligingsopdrachten* (BSB, special protection brigade) for operations considered highly dangerous. This platoon-sized crack unit operates on high-risk VIP protection assignments and similar missions, but has also been deployed in evictions of unarmed squatters and raids against political clandestine radio stations.

There are also the *Bijzondere Bijstandseenheden* (BBEs, special assistance units), units seldom actually deployed, consisting of police and military marksmen and snipers and a Marines close combat unit. The *Mobiele Eenheden* (ME, Mobile Units) can be deployed throughout the country to quell riots, assist in major search operations, etc. In practice, every police officer has to serve a tour of duty with the *Mobiele Eenheid* and can always be called upon to be part of the riot police. Nowadays the ME is mostly deployed in football disturbances.

Weaponry and special equipment: All police officers are normally armed with a *Walther* P5 9 mm pistol. For special deployments, *Heckler & Koch* MP5 sub machine guns are available; these are issued to special anti terrorist teams and may be used for rapid fire only with the permission of the Minister of Justice. All other MP5s issued for guard duties and to the Mobile Units cannot be switched to automatic fire. Sniper rifles, stun grenades, tear gas and other weapons can be issued for special purposes.

Arrests and the treatment of detainees: A suspect can be detained up to six hours (midnight - 9 am do not count) before the investigation is reviewed by an 'assistant public prosecutor' (ie: a chief superintendent), who can authorise further detention for a period of four days. Suspects appearing before an examining magistrate can be detained for a further 12 days. After this period, a court can prolong detention for 30 days, and this procedure can be repeated twice, after which a suspect must be either charged and tried or released.

PORTUGAL

Total no. of police officers (1990 estimate): 47,000. Women in the police: PSP unknown, PJ 6.5%, many of whom work in the higher ranks. The GNR have no women personnel, nor does the *Guarda Fiscal*. No. of police officers per 100,000 inhabitants: 452 (EC av. 338)

The following three services are departments of the Interior Administration Ministry: *Polícia Segurança Pública* (PSP, Public Safety Police), about 20,000 strong, is responsible for maintaining public order and traffic duties in urban areas. It has a *Divisão de Segurança* for VIP protection duties and riot control capabilities in the *Corpo de Intervenção*. *Guarda Nacional Republicana* (GNR), a 18,800 strong paramilitary force, now under the authority of the Ministry of the Interior, performs the same tasks in rural areas. It has mobile units for riot control. The Aliens' Bureau is responsible for police duties connected with foreigners in Portugal. The *Guarda Fiscal* is attached to the Finance Ministry; about 8,000 officers combat smuggling and perform frontier checks.

The *Polícia Judiciária* (PJ, about 1,000 strong) deals with the prevention and investigation of crime and is an auxiliary department of the Ministry of Justice under the ultimate responsibility of the Attorney General (Portuguese NCB, 1990). It has a central headquarters (the Directorate General) and regional headquarters and local offices. The Directorate General comprises: the Central Violent Crime Squad, the Central Drug Squad and the Central Economic and Financial Crime Squad. The latter also has a Anti-Corruption Branch. The General Directorate also includes: the Higher Police Council (a consultative body which assists the Director General); the Central Information Register and Crime Prevention Department which carries out special surveillance duties and assists the Interpol NCB; the Interpol NCB; a forensic lab; and a telecommunications department.

Special units

The *Polícia de Segurança Pública* has had an anti-terrorist capability since 1979 in the *Grupo de Operacoes Especiais*, initially trained by the British SAS. Many members are former Commandos.

Weaponry and special equipment: PSP: Pistols are the standard sidearm, rifles and sub machine guns (SMGs) are optional for special deployments and at roadblocks. PJ: Pistols as well as revolvers are standard sidearms for the plain clothes PJ officers. 12 mm riot guns and SMGs are available for special occasions.
GNR: pistols and rifles; light infantry weapons.

Arrests and the treatment of detainees: No one may be held for more than 48 hours without appearing before an investigating judge. Investigative detention is normally limited to six months, but in exceptional cases it may be extended by a judge for two-three years .

SPAIN

Total no. of police officers (1992 estimate): 149,000 (70,000 *Policía Nacional*, 64,000 *Guardia Civil*. *Policía Municipal* and Autonomous Police unknown but estimated to be around 15,000. Women in the police: In 1989, about 150 women inspectors and 350 regular police officers were employed in the National Police; together they made up circa 0.7% of the total force. No. of police officers per 100,000 inhabitants: 378 (EC av. 338)

Under the 1986 Constitutional Law, there are two police forces with a nation-wide jurisdiction, the *Guardia Civil* and the *Cuerpo Nacional de Policía* (*CNP*): the former covers rural areas and small towns; the latter the provincial capitals and urban areas. Besides the normal police duties it has riot control units. While a civilian organisation, its style and structure bear many similarities to the military.
  The *Guardia Civiles* live in barracks with their families. Their main operational unit (the provincial HQ) is the *Comandancia*, totalling 56, and the *Puesto* (a detachment), commanded by an NCO. There are about 3,000 *Puestos* covering all the rural areas. The *Guardia's* tasks include preventing smuggling, guarding state buildings and institutions, enforcing laws on arms and explosives, transporting prisoners and patrolling main roads. It has separate crowd control and intelligence

units as well as a Judiciary Police Service for criminal investigations.

While at the service of the Interior Ministry (for policing), the Ministry of Justice (for criminal investigations) and the Ministry of Defence (for military purposes) the *Guardia* can be considered a military corps. The Ministry of the Interior is its main funder, but its internal regulations have to be agreed with the Ministry of Defence, giving it considerable autonomy in practice. Although no trade union activities are allowed formally in the Guardia, a quasi-clandestine grassroots United Syndicat of the Civil Guard (SUGC) reportedly has a growing influence on democratising and demilitarising the corps.

The 17 'Autonomous' police forces have jurisdiction in the 'Autonomous Communities' to which they belong. Under the direction of the Autonomous Authorities they are responsible for guarding and preserving public order. Coordination and cooperation with the national police forces is laid down by Councils of Security under the direction of the Minister of the Interior. Provincial capitals and larger towns usually have a *Policía Municipal* (PM) responsible to and recruited by the local government. Its main functions are enforcing municipal laws and traffic control, and it is normally unarmed.

On-the-spot identity checks can be carried out by police, data on the mandatory identity card give access to elaborate databases which still hold information from *Franco*'s secret services (Busch 1991: 28). Under the 1991 civil security law those found without an identity card can be arrested.

Special Units
The *Grupo Especial de Operaciones* (GEO) the *CNP's*'s anti-terrorist force, consists of about 120 men, divided into 24 five-man teams, and can be identified through their dark brown berets. The *Guardia Civil* also has an anti-terrorist capability the *Unidad Especial de Intervencion* (UEI) and the *Grupos Antiterroristas Rurales* (GAR). The UEI has a country-wide responsibility for hostage rescue operations, hijackings, prison riots and VIP protection under high-risk conditions. Said to consist of eight assault teams, backed up by technical and logistics support units and a command structure. The UEI has been deployed intensively against (suspected) ETA targets.

Weaponry and special equipment: The standard *Policía Nacional* sidearm is the 9 mm pistol, but sub-machine guns are carried regularly on the streets and on protection assignments. Rifles and rubber bullet guns can be used in special circumstances, as well as water cannon, tear-gas and electric batons. *Guardia Civil* personnel are armed with 9 mm pistols, and on guard duties and road checks, a submachine gun is usually carried. Other light infantry weapons and equipment are also available.

Arrests and the treatment of detainees: Normally, a suspect may not be held for more than 72 hours without a hearing but, under the special legal procedures applicable to detainees suspected of belonging to armed groups, extended incommunicado detention of up to five days may be imposed by judicial order and the detainee's lawyer may be appointed by the court.

UNITED KINGDOM

There are 52 separate police forces in the UK - 43 in England and Wales (128,000 officers), 8 in Scotland (14,000 officers) and 1 in Northern Ireland (8,400 officers plus a reserve force of 4,600). Each force is under the command of a Chief Constable (the head of the Metropolitan Police in London is called the Commissioner). Each force also has a police authority currently comprising two thirds locally elected councillors and one third local magistrates. The local police authorities have limited powers relating to finance, the efficiency of the force and the appointment of the Chief Constable (but the Home Secretary has to agree). Her Majesty's Inspectorate of Constabulary reports to the Home Secretary on the running of the local forces. Day to day control of the police lies with the Chief Constables who have total operational powers.

In 1993 the Home Secretary put forward a proposal to change the composition of local police authorities by cutting down the number of elected local councillors (from two-thirds to half) and introducing a so-called 'independent' element - local businessmen appointed by the Home Secretary. Under the proposals London, where the current police authority is the Home Secretary, would have an appointed 'liaison' committee. Legislation is expected in 1993/4.

Special units

There is no separate riot control police in the UK. This task is carried out by every police officer who is trained for public order situations. When the police act as a public order force they are organised in small para-military units of 10 called *Police Support Units* (PSUs). Most forces also have specialist para-military units known colloquially as *SPGs* (Special Patrol Groups) after the first group formed in London in 1965. These units are comprise officers seconded to this duty for periods varying between two and four years; in addition to specialist riot training a number also undertake firearms training.

There has been much criticism of the dual role of being a police officer in the community one day and a member of a para-military unit the next, with aggressive attitudes being brought back into the community. This long-standing criticism dates from the mid-1970s and includes the 1979 Southall demonstration against the National Front (a fascist group) when one demonstrator Blair Peach was killed by a member of the SPG; the year-long miners strike of 1984-5; the policing of the printer workers strike at Wapping; and the policing of the black community. In 1981 and 1985 there were uprisings in London and other major cities against police behaviour which led to prolonged street battles.

Political policing, the surveillance of political and trade union activists is carried out by the *Special Branch* which was formed in 1883 to try and counter Irish Fenianism. The Special Branch maintained the lead role relating to the IRA (Irish Republican Army) until 1992. MI5, the internal security agency. have now been given the lead role supported by the Special Branch.

The *Police National Computer(PNC)* was set up in 1974, and in 1991, *PNC2* came on line. *PNC2* is using compatible software with the Schengen Information System.

European developments: The *National Criminal Intelligence Service (NCIS)* was set up in April 1992 and is the UK contact point for policing matters for other EC police forces (the contact point for internal security is MI5). The *NCIS* is an intelligence gathering unit covering all policing matters - excluding the Special Branch. The European Liaison Section (ELS) of the Metropolitan Police Special Branch was formed in 1977.

Weapons: the police are not normally armed. Specialist units in each force are permanently available. They use revolvers, rifles and machine-guns.

Arrest and treatment of detainees: The powers of the police are defined in the Police and Criminal Evidence Act 1984. People can normally be detained for up to 24 hours after which a magistrate can authorise further detention up to a total of 96 hours. In the case of the Prevention of Terrorism Act people can be held incommunicado for up to 72 hours, and for a total of 7 days.

EFTA countries

AUSTRIA

Total no. of police officers (1992 estimate, Hazenberg en Mulschlegel 1992): 27,000. Women in the police: criminal service 2.94%; uniformed service 2.41%; *Gendarmerie* 0.55% Women have been deployed in the criminal service since 1951, in operational work with the uniformed police since 1985 and with the *Gendarmerie* since 1984. No. of police officers per 100,000 inhabitants: 351 (EC av. 338)

Austria is a federal state in which the maintenance of public order and security is exclusively a matter of the Federation (*Bund*) (Vetschera 1992 and Vienna NCB 1989). The provinces (Länder) have no police authority. The Ministry of the Interior is responsible for the maintenance of public order and security. The police forces in Austria have two separate branches: the *Bundespolizei* (Federal Police, about 15,000 personnel, both uniformed and detectives) in the 14 main cities; and the *Bundesgendarmerie*, 10,000 strong, operating mainly in the countryside. The *Bundespolizei* is a civilian force, yet has a paramilitary mode of organisation and supervision.
The *Bundesgendarmerie* is a paramilitary national police force under the Ministry of the Interior, with regional commands in each province except Vienna (which is exclusively covered by the Federal Police), district commands and detached stations. The *Gendarmerie* also carries out criminal investigations where the *Bundespolizei* has no presence.
For riot control and at other special occasions the gendarmerie can call on the *federal army* for assistance.

Special units
A special *Gendarmeriebegleitkommando* unit was established in 1974 to provide protection for people at risk. In 1978 it was transformed into a quick reaction team (*Gendarmerie Einsatzkommando* or GEK, aka *Cobra Unit*). The standing GEK force

is deployed in emergency situations for hostage rescue and other forms of extreme violent crime, and GEK members also fly regularly on *Austrian Airlines* flights for security purposes. Its current strength is about 200, and its training and capabilities are similar to those of most other West European countries. Standard sidearm is the *ManuRhin* .357 magnum revolver also in use with the French GIGN units. Assault and sniper rifles are also available.

In 1984 special action units (*Sondereinsatzgruppen* or SEG) of the *Gendarmerie* were established in each of Austria'ś provinces except Vienna. The SEG consists of former members of the GEK. Their task is to intervene in the first instance against terrorist or similar incidents and to contain the situation until the GEK arrives, and to support local police or *Gendarmerie* formations in dangerous incidents. Since 1985, action units (*Einsatzeinheiten* or EE) have been established within each *Gendarmerie* provincial command to assist in normal police duties connected with terrorism or similar incidents. Between 1983 and 1985, mobile action groups (*Mobile Einsatzkommanden* or MEK) were established, which perform normal patrol duties but are trained and equipped to counter emerging terrorist threats or similar violence.

A special detective group was established within the police directorate of Vienna in 1978, replaced in 1987 by a plain clothes special department for suppressing terrorism (*Einsatzgruppe zur Bekämpfung des Terrorismus* or EBT) under the Ministry of the Interior. It covers the whole of Austria and is intended to prevent violent and subversive acts. Its main task is to anticipate terrorism. A state security force (*Staatspolizei*), 2,000 strong (some sources speak of only 700) is responsible for collecting and analysing political and criminal information.

Weaponry and special equipment: The *Bundespolizei* are armed with *Glock* 9 mm pistols and, if necessary, rifles and submachine guns. The *Gendarmerie* use pistols and light infantry weapons.

Arrests and the treatment of detainees: In May 1993, a new police law came into effect setting out police conduct during investigations and limiting to seven days the time a person may be held on charges of *aggressive behaviour* without being brought before a magistrate (the normal maximum investigative detention is 48 hours). If the investigative judge agrees, the accused may be held pending completion of an investigation for a maximum of two years. The new law also requires the Ministry of the Interior to publish statistics on complaints against the police.

FINLAND

Total no. of police officers: 10,157 (excluding the Border Guard). Women in the police: ± 5% (6.6% in the Criminal Police, 3.6% in the Uniformed Police). No. of police officers per 100,000 inhabitants: 203 (EC av. 338).

The *Suomen Poliisi* (Finnish Police) are organised on three levels: the Police Department of the Ministry of the Interior, regional administration is within the Provincial Administrative Boards, and the provinces are divided into police districts for local administration (Helsinki NCB 1989). The head of the Police Department, the Chief Director of the Police, is both the administrative and operational head of all Finnish police forces. There are three operational police units under the Ministry: the *Keskusrikospoliisi* (KRP, Central Criminal Police who maintain criminal data banks, the Interpol NCB and central forensic services and handles major cases), the *Mobile Police* (LP, 750 strong, assistance in riot situations, land traffic control and national police reserve) and the *SUPO* (state security police, 160 strong).

On a regional level the Superintendent of the County Police in each of the 12 provinces is in charge of day-to-day police operations, and the local police district (usually about 12 police officers) is the administrative unit. In 1989 there were 27 City Police Departments and 226 Rural Police Districts. In the urban police departments officers only undertake police tasks, but in rural areas the police chiefs also act as public prosecutors in the lower courts.

The Ministry of the Interior also controls the Border Guard, a 3,700-strong paramilitary force which maintains public order and safety along the borders and coastal areas. The Border Guard also acts as a police auxiliary unit.

Special Units
The *Osasto Karhu* ('Bear Unit') of the Helsinki Mobile Police Department, created in 1977, is Finland's anti-terrorist unit. It is controlled directly by the Interior Ministry and has nation-wide responsibilities.

Weaponry and special equipment: All police officers in the field carry a service pistol. Rifles and sub machine guns are available for special occasions.

Arrests and the treatment of detainees: Police may hold a suspect for up to seven days without charge. The suspect has access to a lawyer during that time.
Accountability: There is a Parliamentary Ombudsman who has wide authority to enter prisons and police facilities.

NORWAY

Total no. of police officers (Hazenberg en Mulschlegel 1992 estimate): 6,000 plus about 2,000 administrative personnel and para-police functionaries. Women in the police (in percentage): ± 7. No. of police officers per 100,000 inhabitants: 139 (EC av. 338).

The *Norske Politiet* (Norwegian police) is a national force, responsible to the Minister of Justice. Central services include the *Police Security Service* (the political intelligence branch, about 150 strong plus personnel in the district offices; they have executive powers and are also responsible for anti-terrorism intelligence and VIP protection), the *Central Criminal Police Bureau* (CFC, incorporating the Norwegian Interpol NCB), the national *Mobile Traffic Police*, the anti-terrorist unit, the central police EDP service and a Narcotics Branch.

Norway is divided into 54 police districts, with a *Politimester* (Chief Constable) heading each district directly responsible to the Minister. Each district has a police area HQ (*Politikammer*) as well as a number of *Politistasjoner*. A police reserve is available for national emergencies such as disasters or wars. For coordination purposes the country is divided into five regions, each with a regional police chief.

Special units

The *Beredskapstrop* (readiness troop) is the hostage rescue unit of the Norwegian National Police (Thompson, 1986: 116-7), about 50 strong and consists of police officers who combine regular police work with additional training of about three days a week. For back-up purposes, the military has an anti-terrorist platoon which is trained and equipped to international standards.

Riot control is the responsibility of the *Utrykningspolitiet*, a 150-strong Mobile Police organised into six divisions throughout Norway (Andrade 1985). Mobile Police personnel are allocated to ordinary police units to be recalled only in an emergency.

Weaponry and special equipment: Uniformed police are usually unarmed except for a baton. In Oslo all patrol cars have firearms on board in locked safes. .38 revolvers, carbines and sub machine guns are available for specific occasions.

Arrests and the treatment of detainees: Persons may be detained without being charged for up to four hours. A person charged with a crime has the right to appear before a judge within 24 hours.

SWEDEN

Total no. of police officers (Semerak 1989 estimate) 18,400 + some 6,000 administrative personnel. Women in the police: at present, 11.1% of the Swedish police force are women, with very few women in the higher ranks. No. of police officers per 100,000 inhabitants: 214 (EC av. 338).

In Sweden the Ministry of Justice has formal responsibility for the *Rikspolis* (Swedish police), but in fact the national police are administered by the *Rikspolisstyrelsen* (RPS), the National Police Board (Archer 1985; Swedish NCB 1990). This body consists of a National Police Commissioner, his deputy and eight other members, six of whom are members of parliament and two who represent police personnel. The Commissioner is appointed for a renewable six-year period by the government and during their term of office are not subject to control by the Minister of Justice. The operational tasks of the RPS are limited to investigations into political security investigations and those crimes which because of their severity have to dealt with on a national level (terrorism, nation-wide and international crime), as well as supervision of the nation's traffic and air and sea patrols. The RPS does however give directives and operate in connection with: crimes against national security; safety and protection measures in connection with state visits and similar events; investigations of drug trafficking, economic crimes and other major crimes of a nation-wide character or with international connections; the systematic collection of information regarding persons sentenced to more than four years' imprisonment, and the search for and arrest of escaped criminals; intelligence work designed to assist police investigations.

The regional level of police organisation in undertaken by 24 county administrations. The County Police Commissioners coordinate and supervise police activities. At the local level Sweden is divided into 118 police districts, mostly with

20-50 personnel. The local Police Board is made up of the local Police Commissioner and six to eight other members appointed by the county council. It has no influence on the budget, so its powers are limited.

Special units
According to Thompson (1986:115-6) the Stockholm police has a national hostage rescue unit about 200 strong. This *Omradespolis* (Intervention police) also serves as riot police.

Weaponry and special equipment: All uniformed police personnel carry sidearms. Special weaponry is available for specific occasions.

Arrests and the treatment of detainees: Persons disturbing the public order or considered dangerous may be held for six hours without charge. Criminal suspects may be held for 12 hours maximum without formal charges. In particularly serious cases, the time between arrest and the first court hearing may be extended to four days.

SWITZERLAND

Total no. of police officers (1989 estimate, Hazenberg en Mulschlegel 1992): 10,000. Women in the police: According to information from the *Association of Swiss Women Police Officers* obtained by the *European Network of Policewomen* in 1989, Swiss women police officers mainly carry out CID work and have a special responsibility for the 'human' elements which arise in the context of police work. No. of police officers per 100,000 inhabitants: 147 (EC av. 338)

The Swiss police is said to exemplify the *fragmented system of policing* (Hunter 1990: 118. The following draws largely on Swiss NCB 1990 and Kurian 1989). The country is a Confederation of 26 sovereign cantons which are invested with their own judicial authority and police powers and which have their own police corps. A few cities also have a municipal police corps (Bern, Zürich), and there is a relatively small state police, the *Bundespolizei*. In total there are about 70 police forces. The National Gendarmerie has fewer than 1,000 personnel, the individual cantonal police forces (*Kantonale Polizei, Police Cantonale, Polizia Cantonale*) together employ about 6,000 personnel, and the Municipal Police (*Stadtische Polizei, Police Municipale, Polizia Communale*) of the major cities together are about 3,000 strong.
    At a central level, the Ministry of Justice controls: 1) The *Federal Police Division*, formed in 1935, which coordinates national police activities, including border patrol and traffic control. These Gendarmerie are a paramilitary force which also carry out normal policing roles; 2) The *Aliens Police* operates in plain clothes and enforces laws governing entry, exit and residence of foreigners; 3) The *Bundesanwaltschaft* (Attorney General's Office) is an office of the Federal Justice and Police Department which cooperates closely with the examining magistrates and police forces of the cantons. It is divided into six sections, of which the following are relevant here:
a) Bundespolizei, in charge of state security and detection and expulsion of

undesirable aliens, thought to number about 30 police officers and an equal number of administrative personnel. This *Bundespolizei* cooperates intensively with the 28 regional and local police intelligence services;
b) The Central Police Bureau, with the following sub-offices and services: *Zentralstellendienste*: working on trafficking in women and children (prostitution, vice), narcotics, illegal arms trafficking and currency offences; *Erkennungsdienst*, the Central Police Records Office, which operates an automated fingerprints database and a high-speed computerised data network enabling country-wide search and tracking operations; the Swiss *Interpol* Secretariat; Register of convictions; c) Security Service of the federal Administration (responsible for protecting buildings, persons and information).

At a cantonal level, the parliament formally decides on the size and budget of the police. A member of the cantonal government, called a *Regierungsrat*, is in charge of the Polizeidepartement or Polizeidirektion, and bears political responsibility for its functioning. A *Polizeikommandant* is responsible to the *Regierungsrat* for daily operations and management. Efforts to get a further centralised national police have failed due to on objections by sovereign cantons.

Special units

The federal police are in charge of coordinating anti-terrorist measures at the federal level. However, the cantons and their own police forces are responsible for putting these into effect. Anti-Terrorist (AT) groups within the police have been formed in Zürich, Bern and other cantons. The estimated 200 men in those AT groups perform normal police duties when not on anti-terrorist missions. There is no anti-terrorist unit at the central government level.

Weaponry and special equipment: All police personnel carry a sidearm, usually a pistol. Anti-riot equipment, sub machine guns and rifles are also available.

Arrests and the treatment of detainees: A detained person may not be held for more than 24 hours without a warrant of arrest issued by the magistrate conducting the preliminary investigation.

Acknowledgements: This report was prepared by *Stichting voor Onderzoek naar Binnenlandse Veiligheid* (Domestic Security Research Foundation) in Amsterdam. The section on the United Kingdom was written by Tony Bunyan (London), and Mike Farrell (Dublin) wrote the section on the Irish Republic. All other sections were written by Peter Klerks (Amsterdam). Peter Klerks wants to thank the following people and institutions for their help in collecting the documentation: *Activist Press Service* Amsterdam; *Amnesty International* Amsterdam; Ms Annelies Borsboom; *Bureau Jansen & Janssen*; Mrs Anita Hazenberg of the *European Network for Policewomen*; Mr Herman Jansens of the State Police Documentation Service in Brussels; Drs Berto Jongman; the library of the Amsterdam Municipal Police; the libraries of the Institute for Criminology and the Institute for International Relations at the University of Amsterdam; the libraries of the Ministry of the Interior and the Ministry of Justice in The Hague; the library of the *Nederlandse Politie Academie*; Prof Dr Alex P Schmid of *Leiden University*.

Security services in the EC and EFTA countries[1]

Peter Klerks

Introduction

This Chapter covers the intelligence and security agencies of EC and EFTA countries, with the emphasis on 'internal security'. It is incomplete for obvious reasons, as the extent and quality of information available varies from country to country. These agencies meet and cooperate through a number of groups: the Berne and Vienna groups, the Trevi group, the Kilowatt group, NATO and the Western European Union (WEU). See Appendix for descriptions of the Berne, Vienna and Kilowatt groups; the Trevi group is covered at length in Chapter 1.

The ending of the Cold War and its associated internal communist 'threat' has led to a sometimes frantic search for a new raison d'être for these agencies. European security services are shifting from a perspective dominated by counter-espionage and counter-subversion to a new 'threats' agenda.

AUSTRIA

The political police in Austria have always been part of the regular police within the Federal Ministry of the Interior. The state security police, the *Staatspolizei* (*Stapo*), is one of the five 'groups' (*Gruppe II/C*) in the Directorate-General for Public Security in the Ministry. There are also security directorates (*Sicherheits-direktionen*) for the provinces, and district offices (in the countryside) or separate police directorates (in major cities). The *Stapo* has always been responsible for protecting constitutional order and administrative roles such as the issuing of passports, the registration of foreigners and the monitoring of associations and gatherings. In 1990 the *Staatspolizei* numbered about 775. According to the Ministry of the Interior it held some 59,000 files.

In 1991 new legislation on the security police introduced a limited judicial and parliamentary control over the *Stapo* (Busch 1992). A complaint procedure was set up and information on individuals may not be collected and recorded for purely preventive purposes. But the law is so widely drawn that most monitoring can be justified, and civil servants have to cooperate with the Stapo in any investigations. Trade unions and privacy jurists have protested against the *Sicherheitspolizeigesetz* calling it an '*Emmental* in privacy protection'.

Austria takes part in several international intelligence exchange networks and

---

1. This Chapter has been extracted from a longer report which is available from the Domestic Security Research Foundation, PO Box 11178, 1001 GD, Amsterdam, Netherlands.

regular meetings (eg: the *Wiener Club*), and it has observer status in the *Trevi* Group.

Commentary

In the mid-1960s there was a scandal in Austria over the political police activities of the *Stapo*, who had assembled 1,156,000 dossiers (many dating back to the Nazi government of the Second World War). A commission was set up and in 1965 56,000 files were apparently destroyed (or archived on microfilm). But in 1990 information from some of these 'destroyed' files surfaced again and the political police also came in for renewed criticism for supplying firms with information on employees and applicants. Nearly 20,000 Austrians applied to see their security files and most were told that no files were kept on them. However, some dossiers were released showing that the police had been overzealous: for instance at least until the mid-1980s participating in a *Volksbegehren* (referendum) would be entered in one's file, even though it is part of the democratic process in Austria. Government officials told the privacy council that foreign corporations considering investments in Austria had been assured that they would get '*stapogeprüfte Arbeitnehmerware*'. This was later denied by the Minister of the Interior. The Austrian Ministry of Defence's *Heeresnachrichtenamt* (HNA, army intelligence bureau) and *Heeresabwehramt* (HAA, army security bureau) claimed they had been 'forced to supply the Americans' with information routinely collected on Austrian citizens under the threat of an all-out intelligence embargo.

In the 1980s the German doctrine of '*Befassung mit anschlagrelevanten Themen*' (involvement with attempt-relevant themes) was introduced to justify monitoring individuals and infiltrating groups who engaged in protests against gene technology, computer technology, environmental pollution, the military, EC politics, and so on. This doctrine means that people do not have to be involved in any way to be the subject of surveillance, the simple act of campaigning on an issue on which others have used violence is enough to be targeted.

People coming to the Stapo's attention for being a member, or associated with, a perceived 'extremist' organization, have all further activities, however innocent, recorded on their files. Membership of Amnesty International, writing a letter to a newspaper, going on a holiday, attending progressive academic or other study groups, signing petitions, contacting journalists, etc, all of these warrant an entry on the file.

BELGIUM

In the late 1980s evidence appeared in the Belgian press on the extent of political surveillance by *Gendarmerie* intelligence and the *Sûreté de l'État* (state security, the domestic security service in the Ministry of Justice). Investigations by progressive researchers and journalists documented the *Gendarmerie*'s wide political interest: free radio stations, Oxfam Third World shops, radical and left political parties, the peace movement, demonstrating students, trade unions, foreigners, homosexuals were registered in over 100,000 files on the *Gendarmerie*'s central computer. Trade union militants reported repeated visits and harassment by *Gendarmerie* BOB (*Bewakings en Opsporingsbrigade*) political detectives. Meetings of the radical left *Partij van de Arbeid* (Labour Party) were found to be bugged in 1987. The *Sûreté de l'État*, with 300 staff, also maintained files on scores of individuals, including politicians of all parties, especially those who had left-wing contacts in their youth. The *Sûreté* had begun computerizing their files in 1989 and the *Gendarmerie* from 1973.

In the 1980s Belgium experienced political (CCC) and criminal (*Brabant Killers*) violence which led to *Operation Mammouth* in 1984. Hundreds of offices and houses belonging to members of progressive organizations were raided by the political police in an unprecedented campaign to update its files. On 24 April 1989 the offices of the *Sûreté* were searched by *Gendarmerie* and Judicial Police detectives during the *Brabant Killers* investigations. Shortly before the searches investigating magistrate Francine Lyna had declared that the *Sûreté* had sabotaged a 1983 murder investigation of the neo-Nazi *Westland New Post* militia. The *Sûreté* had infiltrated the WNP but, according to reports, had overplayed its hand in supporting and training the WNP militia. WNP leader Paul Latinus was provided with NATO security clearance in the early 1980s by the SGR.

The *Service de Documentation, de Recherche, et d'Action* (SDRA, military security service, a section of the *Service Général de Renseignement* SGR) was particularly interested in registering those affiliated with the peace movement. In February 1987 this led to a row when a meeting of the Rainbow Group of the European Parliament was bugged and participating members of peace groups were filmed by Belgian military security. Since its premises enjoy diplomatic immunity, the EP lodged an official protest, after which Prime Minister Martens was forced to offer formal excuses.

Commentary

These incidents led to a series of reforms. Although the *Sûreté de l'État* remains under the Ministry of Justice, the Social Democrat Minister of the Interior Louis Tobback recently introduced a new form of administrative oversight by his department. The Minister of Justice now needs Tobback's co-signature for every major decision regarding competence and for new top appointments. In the summer of 1990 the head of the *Sûreté de l'État* was replaced after revelations of collusion between the *Sûreté* and the extreme right. In a rare interview in 1992, Director General Schwewebach said that new areas for his service included illegal immigration networks and Islamic fundamentalism.

Other reforms are still to be introduced. In March 1993 a Permanent Intelligence Oversight Committee, with proper support staff, became operative. A bill embodying new regulations, introduced in September 1991, is still under discussion. The 'Charter for the Intelligence and Security Services' announced three years ago is also still being considered. Vice Prime Minister and Minister of Economic Affairs and Justice Melchior Wathelet admitted on 20 January 20 1993 that the drafting of the Charter was being delayed by 'the necessity to bring the new legal operational modalities into agreement with the demands of discretion and the practices of certain foreign services'. As in Germany and Switzerland the CIA is believed to have intervened in the reform process by demanding guarantees of confidentiality of their operations and information.

DENMARK

The Danish *Politiets Efterretningstjeneste* (PET, internal security police) is

Department G of the Office of the National Commissioner's Office and is an integral part of the police. It is responsible to the National Police Commissioner in the Department of Justice. The security police have powers of arrest, search and seizure, and interrogation.

The main task of the *Forsvarets Efterretningstjeneste* (FET, Defence Intelligence Service) during the Cold War was the monitoring of ship movements in the Baltic Sea and communications intelligence on Poland and East Germany. It is now believed to have redirected its efforts to gathering political intelligence in the Baltic area and Poland and cooperating with German and US foreign intelligence. Its security branch has also been active in the surveillance of activists on the radical left.

The ruling Danish Social Democratic Party is reported to have had its own intelligence staff since at least the mid-1930s. This unofficial intelligence organization is believed to have been involved in close cooperation with the PET in monitoring communist influence in the trade unions and keeping radicals out of influential posts. Certain conservative organizations have also been reportedly active in gathering political intelligence on the Left during the Cold War.

The Danish parliament has a five-member intelligence oversight commission, following legislation in July 1988.

Commentary

In 1990 Victor Ostrovsky, who claims to be a former Mossad operative, published his controversial book *By way of deception*. This included a 1985 Mossad computer printout describing Danish intelligence and that the PET's obligations to Israel include maintaining a constant observation of the Palestinian community in Denmark numbering about 500 people. Examples are given of successful operations in which Danish intelligence helped Mossad, including giving them access to Palestinians for recruitment purposes and close cooperation in the monitoring of communications.

Danish intelligence sources say that the Popular Front for the Liberation of Palestine (PFLP) support network had been under surveillance since 1984 when PFLP members arrested at Paris Orly airport were found to carry Danish bank notes stolen during a series of armed robberies. In May 1989 Danish police officers raided a flat belonging to Carsten Nielsen and discovered an arms arsenal of anti-tank missiles and launchers, mines, hand grenades, machine guns and 100 kilos of explosives. The material had been stolen from a Swedish army depot in 1986. Police said the arms belonged to the PFLP. In the process, many of Denmark's radical political parties and solidarity groups also became the subject of intelligence operations. The case is known as the 'Blekingegade case'. After a post office robbery when a police officer was shot dead seven of the Blekinge people were arrested and sentenced to long term of imprisonment.

FRANCE

The French have traditionally excelled in keeping their secret services secret until the early 1980s. Then the Socialists came to power and began their uneasy relationship with the security world. Since 1981 successive ministers under President Mitterrand have tried to reorganise the French intelligence community so as to reduce its potential for causing embarrassment while preserving its capacity for providing quick solutions and useful sensitive information. In 1982, for the first time, the services (apart from the political intelligence police, the RG) were formally recognized under presidential decrees.

Intelligence policy coordination is effected by the number three person in the French Cabinet - the security advisor in charge of coordinating the foreign intelligence DGSE, the counter-espionage DST and the *Secrétariat Général de la Défense Nationale* (SGDN), the Prime Minister's own intelligence service responsible for overall coordination. In April 1989 the *Comité Interministériel du Renseignement* (CIR) was reactivated, meeting twice a year to prepare a National Intelligence Plan on the activities of all French services. At the same time the *Comité Permanent du Renseignement* (CPR) and a *Comité d'Experts*, a group of outsiders were charged with keeping a critical eye on the performance of the services. Overall coordination lies with the

The shift in French intelligence thinking reflects that in other Western services since the end of the Cold War: they think no longer in terms of allies or foes but of national (or sometimes European or Western) interests that need protection.

Secrétariat Général de la Défense Nationale (SGDN)

The SGDN is composed of three operational sections, the *Evaluation et Documentation Stratégique* (EDS), *Scientifique et Transferts Sensibles* (STS) and *Moyens Gouvernementaux, des Plans et de la Sécurité* (MPS) plus an *Administration Générale* (AG), totalling 584 people in 1989. The SGDN's functions are described as activities in international affairs, non-military defence, analysis of scientific and technological data, surveillance of armament evolution, export control of military material, and computer systems security. When the SGDN was reorganised in July 1987 the *Délégation Interministérielle à la Sécurité des Systèmes d'Information* (DISSI) was established with some 50 personnel.

Renseignements Généraux (RG, political intelligence police)

The RG, a branch of the Police Nationale was estimated at about 3,800 personnel in 1990 (some 400 in the *Direction Centrale*, 800 at the *Préfecture de Police* in Paris and the rest in the *départements*). RG officers do not have powers of arrest, detention or interrogation (in practice they do carry out interrogations in immigration matters although technically they do not have the power).

The RG gathers information on individuals and groups whose activities may constitute a danger to the state. It operates in every department, reporting to the *Préfet* and to the central RG directorate in Paris which is charged with 'collecting and centralising information on all matters relating to political, economic and social order, which are essential to the government'. RG officers collect information from open sources and from informers, by attending meetings, by infiltrating groups and organizations, and by intercepting mail and phone-tapping. Although a judge has to grant a warrant, illegal phone tapping occurs as well as intimidation and smear campaigns against political opponents of the ruling elite or against press institutions considered to be too well-informed (eg: *Le Canard Enchainé*, whose staff was harassed repeatedly in the 1970s).

Since 1991 under new legislation the RG has been allowed to register people's political or trade union activities, but not their opinions. It reportedly has files on 24,500 people in connection with terrorism and on 600,000 people involved in gambling, and clearly has a much wider role than most European internal security services.

Over the last five years a number of books have appeared on the RG that shed some light on the service's past and present modus operandi. Inspector Jean-Marc Dufourg worked at the RG for ten years in the 1980s and in his 1991 book summarized the experience by saying: *All I knew about the law was how to get around it without being noticed.* He was charged with illegal use of force in the Pastor Doucé affair, the kidnapping and murder of homosexual Pastor Joseph Doucé in July 1990 for which four Paris-based RG officers were arrested. He countered by disclosing details of operations including at least four break-ins in the offices of SOS-Racisme, and two large bags full of internal SOS-Racisme administration were recovered from RG offices.

Direction de la Surveillance du Territoire (DST, counter-espionage)
In 1992 some 1,500 police officers worked at the DST, which is part of the Ministry of the Interior. With its headquarters located at the rue Nélaton in Paris, its main tasks are counter-espionage, treason and anti-terrorism. In the mid-1980s the *DST* was believed to handle some 5,000 security clearance investigations annually. It has the powers to act upon its own information by carrying out judiciary investigations. It also carries out infiltration and covert surveillance operations on a routine basis. Since around 1990 the DST has been faced with a reduction in personnel and resources. In an effort to maintain its position and conquer new grounds, the service began approaching France's high-tech companies and tried to convince them that they needed the DST to protect their industrial secrets.

Foreign intelligence
Faligot and Krop (1989) probably uncovered the essence of French covert foreign policy when they described in some detail the determination of successive French governments to prevent the expansion of American influence in Africa. The French and British services also have traditionally fostered a 'whole-hearted discordance' but this may change with increased European cooperation. The French attitude towards Anglo-American influences, together with the preservation of an independent nuclear capacity, constitutes the core of French interests.

Direction Générale de la Sécurité Extérieure (DGSE, foreign intelligence)
The DGSE was called the *Service de Documentation Extérieure et de Contre-Espionnage* (SDECE) until 1981. Insiders estimate its current personnel strength at about 3,400. Its headquarters are located at the *Piscine* (swimming pool) at the Boulevard Mortier in Paris. Like the other Western intelligence services, the DGSE had to reorganise its networks in the former Soviet Union drastically to cover adequately the new centres of power in all of the republics. In 1991 new efforts on computerization and a new Africa programme were announced, and the service's networks in the Mediterranean have also been considerably expanded.

DGSE Operations Division

The DGSE's predecessor SDECE was formally established in 1945 (other sources say 1947) and originated from the World War II resistance. The *Service Action* branch expanded enormously in the early 1950s during the operations against the Viet Minh in Indochina. During the Algerian war of liberation, under the cover of the *Main Rouge* death squads, it committed many murders, sabotage and psychological operations in an eight-year long struggle against the FLN, including about a dozen assassinations of FLN supporters and cadre throughout Europe. The DGSE gained notoriety through the Rainbow Warrior affair.

Military intelligence: Direction du Renseignement Militaire (DRM, Directorate of Military Intelligence)
The DRM was created in May 1992 and works closely with the military attaches at French embassies in largely overt collection of military information.

Direction de la Protection et de la Sécurité de la Défense (DPSD)
Until 1981 this service was called the *Sécurité Militaire*, and the French military still refers to it as 'SM'. The DPSD is believed to have about 1,600 staff and is concerned with military security. Some 50 DPSD officers conduct several thousand routine security clearance investigations annually and monitor pacifist and anti-militarist groupings.

Accountability
Parliamentary oversight of the DGSE and military intelligence lies with the Defence Committee. The French privacy protection body, the *Commission Nationale Informatique et Liberté* (CNIL) has the power to systematically monitor all intelligence files except those of military security. It can look into specific files on the request of a concerned citizen and advise correction or destruction if necessary. The individual is only told that their case has been dealt with: no further information is provided. Guisnel and Violet (1988), both respected journalists, argue that parliamentary and judicial control over the French intelligence services is ineffective.

FINLAND

The Security Police (SUPO) investigates offences against the state and is one of three operational police units in the Department for Police Affairs within the Ministry of the Interior. It has 12 district offices. The Finnish Security Police have no powers of arrest or detention nor can they make house searches, which are carried out by the CID. For several years, it has received Trevi briefings from Denmark.

GERMANY

Since 1990 the federal intelligence and security services (BfV, BND and MAD) are based on formal and detailed legislation. Intrusive measures such as telephone tapping are limited under article 10 of the *Grundgesetz*. These so-called *G-10 Maßnahmen* (measures) are defined in detail in each of the separate *Länder*'s own legislations, as are the *Landesämter für Verfassungsschutz*, the lands' own domestic security services.

Bundesamt für Verfassungsschutz (Federal Office for the Protection of the Constitution, i.e. domestic security service)

The central BfV, located in Köln functions as a coordination centre for the *Landesämter für Verfassungsschutz* (LfV), the domestic security services of every land (region). As a rule all espionage investigations are the BfV's responsibility. The final criminal investigations are dealt with by the *Bundeskriminalamt* BKA and the state police services. The BfV planned a reduction in personnel from 2,432 (1991) to about 2,000 personnel, due to German reunification and the loss of its main opponent. However in November 1992 Minister of the Interior Seiters announced that the reduction would not be carried out in the light of increasing extreme-right violence. The number of BfV employees working on the extreme right had been doubled, and the police *Staatsschutz* (state protection) branches in several *Länder* had also increased their activities on the extreme right.

In September 1992 data on 1,442,291 individuals was stored in the *Verfassungsschutz* NADIS computer system (which comprises both a database and a network). 41.4% of these were registered because they held a security-sensitive position and are thus subject to periodic vetting procedures. The rest were classified as *undogmatic leftist extremists, rightist extremists, foreign extremists and counter-espionage*. In a recent interview the BfV director explained that the *Verfassungsschutz* obtains about 60% of its information from open sources, 20% is derived from the deployment of covert intelligence means and another 20% comes from other services (both German, eg: police, and foreign).

Landesämter für Verfassungsschutz

Personnel strength of LfVs in 1990 was: Bundesamt f.Verfassungsschutz 2,361, Bund and Länder together: 5,100. The exact arrangements for the *Landesämter für Verfassungsschutz* in each of the states varies considerably. In some, such as Niedersachsen, the LfV is a part of the Ministry of the Interior. In Bayern the LfV is an independent service. In the *Länder* with a red/green coalition government the Green Party wants to eliminate all secret intelligence services, but under para 2 of the *Bundesverfassungsschutzgesetz* all *Bundesländer* have to maintain a LfV. Due to experiences with the Stasi the new east German *Länder* are critical of the newly introduced *Verfassungsschutz*, but a VfS 'goodwill' campaign in 1990-1991 and the upsurge in neo-Nazi violence have muffled criticism.

The Niedersachsen Verfassungsschutz law introduced in 1992 is claimed to be the most progressive in the FRG except for Berlin. All permissible intelligence methods are listed in an exhaustive 'catalogue', thus outlawing 'new' and 'creative' initiatives. Mere 'intentions' or opinions are no longer sufficient grounds for targeted LfV activities: individuals or organizations must be clearly engaged in the use of violent means. The Niedersachsen LfV was seriously compromised in 1986 when it transpired that, in the late 1970s, a prison was bombed in a fake escape attempt to establish an agent's credentials among radical leftists. Such scandals are not uncommon: the Verfassungsschutz makes wide use of infiltrators and regularly monitors peaceful demonstrators, progressive students, refugees etc. In Berlin the LfV tried to undermine the Red-Green coalition government in the late 1980s and early 1990s, which eventually led to the transfer of several senior intelligence officers and a reorganisation of the service.

Staatsschutzabteilungen (state protection branches in the police)

When the allied occupational powers made arrangements for new police and domestic security services after the Second World War they imposed a strict separation of police and intelligence agencies, the so-called *Trennungsgebot* (separation order). To prevent another *Gestapo,* secret services were never to have executive powers in order. In practice this separation has been violated, for instance when a state security service wanted to avoid having to confirm it had an informer in a specific group, the informer was simply passed on to the police. The contacts between the *Verfassungsschutz* and the police *Staatsschutz* are extensive, while the *Staatsschutz* in many *Länder* isolates itself from other police branches. The *Staatsschutz* also, more than other police branches, employs covert methods and techniques of investigation such as informers (*V-Männer*), undercover agents (UCAs) and electronic surveillance. *Staatsschutz*-related 'crimes' affect peace activities, anti-nuclear protests, anti-Nazi violence, etc. Seemingly harmless activities, such as handing out leaflets, participating in demonstrations, publishing or providing humanitarian support for political prisoners can become defined as crimes depending on the political intentions behind them.

Each year the *Staatsschutz* investigates over 10,000 recorded crimes. *Staatsschutz* cases are extensively investigated and more often than 'ordinary' criminal cases, thus collating huge amounts of information, but the number of resulting convictions is relatively low (approx. 10%). This seems to support the thesis that the *Staatsschutz* in fact functions as a political police intelligence service. Such suspicions are heightened by recent revelations (March 1992) about the Hamburg *Staatsschutz*'s monitoring of Amnesty International and Greenpeace. Since the early 1970s intelligence reports on these and similar organisations were transferred to foreign intelligence services.

The *Bundeskriminalamt* (BKA, central federal crime service) had 238 employees in its *Staatsschutz* branch as well as 409 workers in the anti-terrorism department in 1991. The *Staatsschutz* has its own computerized registration system, APIS, with some 30,000 individuals registered in 1990.

A recent example of a *Landeskriminalamt-Staatsschutz* affair was an undercover operation by two police officers who infiltrated a left group in the Tübingen area (Baden-Württemberg) for about 18 months. One of them revealed his role in the summer of 1992 after forming a personal relationship with one of the group. The milieu in which the two had operated consisted mainly of people active in the Central America solidarity movement, Roma support groups and evangelical circles. The official grounds for the operation was an anti-terrorist investigation in the *Umfeld* (≈milieu, surrounding people and groups) of the Revolutionäre Zellen and the Rote Armee Fraktion, but there was much criticism in the press. The Umfeld argument which had been used successfully for almost two decades to legitimize the infiltration of leftist groups lost its rationale once surveillance was directed against clearly non-violent groups and (political) subcultures.

Bundesnachrichtendienst (BND, Federal Intelligence Service)

The BND is the German espionage service, responsible to the Chancellor's Office; it has no executive powers. It gathers and analyses intelligence relevant to the foreign and security interests of the FRG. The BND also monitors narcotics trafficking and illegal financial transactions. (The Directorship of the BND is a politically sensitive post and, along with the directorship of the BfV and the Federal Prosecutor, is divided between the main political parties - conservative CDU/CSU, social democrat SPD and liberal FDP).

With the demise of the GDR, it was announced in 1991 that the BND would be reduced from 7,000 to 6,300 personnel. A large number of staff had to be replaced due to the unexpectedly successful penetration of all the German services by the former East German *Ministerium für Staatssicherheit*. Since its formation in 1956 the BND, more than any other German intelligence service has featured in many scandals.

In the past the BND was known to have cooperated closely with dictatorships and extreme right insurgents, such as the Portuguese pre-1974 regime, UNITA in Angola, the Nicaraguan Contra, Iraq and the South African apartheid regime. According to Gert Hugo, chief of the Ciskei security service until 1991, the BND trained South African intelligence operators, until at least 1984, when several officers received a three-month course in Munich on electronic surveillance. The most advanced military equipment, partly in defiance of US restrictions, was shipped to Israel. BND relations with Israel had always been impeccable: in 1979, for instance, Mossad specialists disguised as BND interpreters were allowed access to four suspected PLO terrorists.

Militarische Abschirmdienst (MAD, Military Security Service)
In 1991 the MAD employed a staff of 1,834 on an annual budget of 147 million DM. In the past the military security service has repeatedly been criticized for its incompetence in tracing Soviet and East German spies. In the 1970s it repeatedly made the headlines when it bugged the apartments of Defence staff without a permit and accused senior military officers without sufficient evidence.

When the official German privacy protection agency investigated the MAD files in 1982 it ruled that 500,000 cards had to be destroyed. A considerable number of registrations proved to be ridiculous: 12,000 people were over 80 years old, others were below the age of ten. Many prominent Germans who at one time or another had signed a petition against fascism were registered, as well as motorists who had parked their car close to the departure point of a demonstration against military service.

Bundesamt für Sicherheit in der Informationstechnik (BSI, federal office for security in information technology)
This is the former *Zentralstelle für Chiffrierwesen* (ZC), a BND subsidiary in the business of coding and decoding. Since 1990 it has been headed by Dr Otto Leiberich and is known mainly for its activities in protecting against and investigating computer espionage and 'hacking'. It has about 300 personnel.

Zolkriminalamt (ZKI, customs investigators)
In 1991 this service acquired intelligence-gathering powers, including the monitoring of communications and mail, and its staff was raised to 300. The ZKI became the fourth federal intelligence service in the wake of disclosures over illegal arms and technology transfers by German firms. The *Bundeskriminalamt* also employs about two dozen officers to monitor Germany's foreign trade.

Accountability

Oversight on the German intelligence services is effected through the *Parlamentarische Kontrollkommission* (PKK) which exists both in the federal *Bundestag* and the *Länder* parliaments, and the *G-10 Kommission* which oversees telecommunications and mail surveillance. The PKK in the *Bundestag* has eight members, most of whom are senior MPs with little time to spend on their controlling duties. Most PKKs, including the *Bundestag* commission, have no power to investigate or access to files, nor do they have budgetary powers. The government has resisted demands from PKK members for powers to access to files, to interrogate intelligence personnel under oath, and conduct independent investigations. Apart from the PKKs there is also some control through the *Bundesdatenschutzbeauftragte* (Federal Data Protection Commissioner) and their equivalents in the Länder.

GREECE

The Greek national intelligence service, the *EYP* (formerly KYP), has six directorates covering national and military security, political and economic intelligence, counter-espionage, analysis and distribution, and administration. Besides the EYP there is *A2*, the military intelligence service, and a constitutional protection service (a branch of General Security).

Army General Pantelis Kalamaki took over as head of the EYP from Mr Angelopoulos, only to be replaced again by air force General Panayotis Bales on 11 December 1990. General Sklavos now heads the EYP.

Commentary

Greece has vital importance for all major Western intelligence services because of its position and relationship to the Middle East. However, its allies have been faced with some contradictions. Since the return to democracy in 1974 the socialist PASOK party, which was in power until 1989, maintained good contacts with the Palestinians (established during its years in exile under the 'colonels').

Greek intelligence officials have reportedly maintained contacts with PLO intelligence since the late 1970s to obtain information on logistics and operations of dissident Palestinian groups. In December 1990 for example, shortly before he was assassinated in Tunis on 14 January 1991, Abu Iyad had visited Athens to supply information on an 19 April 1990 bombing in Patras and on Abu Nidal networks in Greece.

In the first half of the 1980s the then-head of the KYP, Filippos Makedhos, placed PASOK militants into most key positions in the EYP. PASOK lost the June 1989 elections and the new coalition government of New Democracy and the Left Coalition opened inquiries into several PASOK scandals and ordered the destruction of about a third of all existing intelligence files. An estimated 17 million documents on suspected left-wing radicals were burned, but government critics said the operation was a tactical move by the conservative New Democracy party to eradicate all evidence of its former complicity in supplying information on its opponents to the secret police. Most of the information contained in the files had reportedly been transferred to computer files in the preceding years, an assertion the government neither confirmed nor denied.

In the spring of 1990, the EYP was suspected of interference in the election campaign. On 30 March two EYP officials were caught jamming the broadcasts of a pro-PASOK television station in Athens, after which EYP Director Dimitris Angelopoulos was forced to resign. In the same period, evidence surfaced that PASOK opponents had their phones tapped in 1988.

Cooperation between Greece and the US has improved considerably; in April 1992, for instance, high level US anti-terrorist officials visited Greece to exchange intelligence and coordinate activities. An outfit of special anti-terrorist units known under the acronym EKAM (together some 800 police officers detached for anti-terrorist duties) was substantially funded, receiving $641,000 from the US Anti-Terrorism Assistance programme. However, press reports suggest half of EKAM personnel were posted elsewhere after two bungled operations in March and May 1992. Interior Minister Theodoros Anagnostopoulos commented that EKAM units were afflicted by amateurism and intelligence leaks.

ITALY

The Italian military intelligence service has gone through a series of name changes as a result of internal scandals. This process was intended to signal a new regime but, for example, the entire staff of the SID was taken over by its successor in 1977. These were: 1949-1965: *Servizio Informazioni Forze Armate* (SIFAR); 1965-1977: *Servizio Informazioni Difesa* (SID)

1977- : *Servizio per le Informazioni e la Sicurezza Militare* (SISMI). In 1977 a new domestic intelligence service was also started, the *Servizio per le Informazioni e la Sicurezza Democratica* (SISDE).

SISMI reports to the Minister of Defence, SISDE to the Minister of the Interior. Both are also accountable to a committee, presided over by the Prime Minister, which also coordinates intelligence service and maintains international contacts. A permanent parliamentary commission has limited access to confidential material and the option of making policy recommendations.

SISMI is both a military intelligence and security service and has economic and political intelligence gathering and counter-intelligence in its mandate. The service coordinates the intelligence and SIGINT activities of the three military branches' own Deuxième Bureaux.

SISDE was estimated to be about 2,000 strong in the mid-1980s. Under its 1977 mandate it is responsible for non-military counter-espionage, counter-subversion and countering violent extremism and terrorism.

Commentary

The parliamentary commission investigating the influence of the Masonic Lodge P2 found that the heads of both the SISDE and the SISMI were affiliated to it in 1981. Some researchers have drawn links between American intelligence, Italian intelligence, Italian organized crime and terrorist organizations such as the Brigate Rosse.

Several leading (former) SISMI officials such as Francesco Pazienza, former deputy head of SISMI, General Pietro Musumeci and his assistant Colonel Giuseppe Belmonte, and Colonel Guido Pallotta, former head of industrial security at SISMI from 1975 - 1981 have all been imprisoned for crimes such as illegal arms trafficking, associating with organized crime, embezzlement, subversive association, corruption and (Musumeci and Belmonte) simulating a crime - placing a suitcase filled with explosives aboard a Taranto-Milan train in January 1981 to throw off course the investigators probing the 1980 bombing of the Bologna railway station. Many believe, however, that most of the key players and those politically responsible have so far managed to cover up their involvement in terrorism and organized crime.

THE NETHERLANDS

Introduction
After the Second World War the *Plaatselijke Inlichtingen Diensten* (PIDs, local police intelligence services) were reintroduced for domestic security purposes and in 1948 the *Binnenlandse Veiligheidsdienst* (BVD) was established to coordinate and standardize security investigations, and to improve international contacts.

The security and intelligence services stayed out of the limelight for most of the post-war period until the 1980s when a number of revelations led to reforms. In February 1992, following a series of leaks on financial mismanagement and other problems in the *Inlichtingendienst Buitenland* (IDB, foreign intelligence service), the Cabinet decided to dismantle the service altogether. Its tasks and some of the staff were taken over by the *National Criminal Intelligence Service* (CRI) and by the *Binnenlandse Veiligheidsdienst* (BVD, domestic security service). Other reforms affecting the BVD and the PID are set out below.

Reforms are also likely in the long-standing practice of monitoring and recording information on a wide range of political activists. Recent rulings by the European Court of Human Rights could lead to a review of Dutch intelligence legislation. A group of ten individuals sued the Dutch state for unlawfully registering them in intelligence files (which were uncovered after a burglary by activists in the military counter-intelligence offices in Utrecht). They have each been granted 1,000 guilders in compensation. Moreover, the Court found Dutch law and safeguards inadequate.

Commentary
In the 1980s intelligence documents were leaked and a massive amount of papers became available through a series a burglaries of military and intelligence offices. They were reproduced and analyzed in a number of activist publications and showed the secret services' outdated world view: social democrat reformers, some of them leading politicians, administrators and mayors, had until recently been registered and surveilled by the military and civilian services. Soldiers' trade unions, peace groups, anti-nuclear and other progressive organizations were closely monitored and infiltrated and, to some extent, manipulated.

This lead to reforms by Social Democratic governments. The military intelligence branches were formally merged and 'modernized'. The BVD underwent a drastic reorganization and was trimmed down from about 700 to some 570 employees. At the same time a public relations exercise started with its head, Doctor van Leeuwen on television and the organization repeatedly intervened in public debates.

In February 1992 the BVD published its first unclassified 'threat analysis' which showed how the security service's interests had expanded. The report said that corruption of civil servants, terrorism, arms proliferation, sabotage of vital infrastructural systems, theft of high grade technology, and organized crime presented dangers that Holland has to prepare for. They also emphasized the danger of political, ethnic or religious conflicts originating in the Middle East or Africa spreading to the Netherlands. The report argued that subversion of the democratic order 'from the extreme left side of the political spectrum' no longer posed a serious threat and right wing extremism was also not considered 'an especially big factor of threat'. Terrorism was seen as a real threat, centring on the 'Rara' group, which has carried out a series of bomb attacks against apartheid-related and government targets since 1985. Its targets included the Ministry of the Interior and the house of State Secretary Kosto (responsible for refugees and immigration policy) in November 1991. Special teams have failed to track down the group.

The threat report painstakingly avoids any reference to the 1991 wave of bomb attacks by extreme right activists against immigrant projects, left activists campaigning against the stricter immigration policy, and anti-militarist activists opposing the new Dutch Air Mobile Brigade (a 3,000-strong rapid intervention force currently being formed).

The BVD published its first annual report in October 1992 showing that, in 1991, it made 55,142 administrative investigations and 10,865 more intensive security investigations for government and sensitive corporate functions (excluding defence which comes under the MID). 862 full security investigations were carried out for foreign security services. The report says that 20% of the time of BVD personnel was spent in preventing unauthorized disclosures of state secrets; 15% on preventing and fighting political violence; 12% on safeguarding government integrity; 10% on the protection of democratic rights and liberties; another 10% for basic security care and vetting; the rest is distributed over nine other categories.

Accountability

A permanent closed commission on the intelligence and security services, consisting of the group leaders of the main parties in parliament, has been responsible for oversight since 1952. From 1967 the commission has produced brief activity reports and since the 1988 law on the intelligence and security services came into effect, it has been meeting more frequently. Apart from the oversight commission the services are also controlled by departmental staff, the minister, parliament as a whole, the National ombudsman (who in principle has access to all information on request) and by the magistrature. In spite of all this, the accountability of the services remains rather poor. However, it became clear during a parliamentary debate in January 1993 that a majority wanted increased control over the security services.

PID, the police's Special Branch

In June 1991 a working group report on 'Co-operation structure Police/BVD' put forward proposals to solve the continuing problem of local political intelligence mishaps by the *Plaatselijke Inlichtingendiensten* (PID's) which resulted from outdated concepts and amateurish methods of spying on pacifists and communists.

The report stressed the importance of a professional approach to local political intelligence gathering in line with police reorganization, which is to transform the Dutch police into one national body with 25 regional departments. One important element in the reforms will be the central administration of all political intelligence in a region, including the detailed registration of all 'work contacts' with agents and informers 'for the protection of the employees themselves'. This is a reaction to instances where PID case officers started deploying their contacts for their own private undertakings, including cases of fraud, extortion and arson.

BVD infiltrators

There have been at least a dozen documented incidents of BVD infiltrators inciting activists to violence or breaking the law themselves by initiating or taking part in violent activities. Usually the people concerned were not BVD officers but paid and trained agent-provocateurs.

In a recent case Lex Hester, living in Wormer, a small town 10 miles north of Amsterdam, had been working for the security service and the police central anti-terrorist branch (*Bijzondere Zaken Centrale*) for 12 years. Mr Hester, who has dozens of convictions for violence and drugs-related offences, began as an informer on local squatters. Later he worked for several activist book stores gathering information on European radical movements which he passed on. In 1989 he was the driving force behind a new periodical called 'Het Info', which published manifestos and press releases from organizations such as ETA, RAF, Action Directe and PIRA. Repeated attempts by Hester to provide Semtex explosives to astonished activists led to his unmasking in January 1991.

BVD and political refugees

In 1991 the activist research group Buro Jansen & Janssen in Amsterdam, together with a refugee support group (LSV), published a report on the activities of the security services against political refugees. The report lists 70 cases in which the BVD or a local PID branch sought to get asylum seekers to provide information or to work as informers. In a number of cases the security services reportedly used some form of pressure to attain cooperation.

A well documented case of recruitment under pressure was that of Nathan Quimpo from the Philippines who was granted asylum status early in 1993. On 26 October 1991, Dutch VARA television filmed a meeting in an Amsterdam hotel between Mr. Quimpo, BVD officer 'Kees Overveen' and CIA officer 'Charles Taylor'. Mr Quimpo, a member of the New People's Army (NPA), was in a Philippine prison for two years and tortured, he fled to Holland in 1990 with a price on his head.

At the meeting Mr Quimpo was offered $1,000 a month, a passport and world-wide protection to infiltrate NPA structures. The first payment was handed over on the spot. When the TV programme exposed the meeting the BVD stated that it worked on the Philippines because there had been indications that the NPA was preparing assaults on US assets in Europe, and this would endanger Dutch state security. This also explained the presence of the CIA officer.

In parliament the Minister of the Interior, Ien Dales, said that the BVD investigated the activities of solidarity movements because the threat of harmful activities on Dutch soil against other governments, even non-allies, constituted a violation of the international legal order and were therefore, by definition, a matter of concern for the BVD.

NORWAY

The Police Security Service is responsible for domestic intelligence gathering, anti-terrorism intelligence, VIP protection and counter-espionage. The Police Security Service has executive police powers and employs 150 officials at its headquarters in Oslo. Norway has a parliamentary Intelligence Control Commission. The security service is a separate branch of the police and is responsible to the Minister of Justice.

Commentary

Unlike most other European countries, Norway has traditionally had a strong alliance between the long-governing social democrats, the intelligence services and the trade unions.

Norway has a common border with the former Soviet Union and since the Second World War the United States has collaborated closely with the Norwegian government, operating a network of listening posts and submarine detection equipment. This has ensured that Norwegian radical and communist influences were closely watched. The unions reportedly exchanged information freely with the security services throughout the Cold War to keep communists out of sensitive public and private posts.

In 1991 the head of the security service, Svein Urdal, resigned after it was revealed that Mossad agents had been allowed access to ten Palestinian refugees who had defected from the PLO because of its position on the Gulf War. The Mossad officials were given Norwegian passports to hide their identity.

In 1992 the Norwegian parliament decided that the security service would be more strictly controlled and the head of the security service has to give explicit approval for all operations involving foreign intelligence services, and the Minister of Justice also has to be kept informed. An internal oversight committee will monitor sensitive operations and develop guidelines for international cooperation.

PORTUGAL

Portugal's civil security service is the *Serviços de Informaçâo e Segurança* (SIS) which was created in 1984. The military intelligence service, the *Serviços de Informacâo Militar* (SIM) is still better known under its old name DINFO, which stood for *Direcçâo de Informaçâo*. SIM's activities cover both military affairs and foreign intelligence.

Commentary

Lisbon became a legendary 'city of spies' during the Second World War. Under the Salazar and Caetano dictatorships the CIA, BND, SDECE and other western intelligence services had good relations with the PIDE (later DGS) secret police. After a group of junior military officers ousted the Caetano regime in April 1974, the CIA channelled funds into the country through West European Social Democrat parties.

Portugal played a key role during the Iran-Iraq war, acting as a transit point. An indication that Portuguese intelligence is taken seriously by other countries is the reported promotion of Vice Admiral Fausto Morais de Brito e Abreu, former director of Portuguese Naval intelligence, who became director of NATO intelligence in February 1989.

The services have been active in Portugal's former African colonies. The SIM supported the Mozambique RENAMO insurgents and until late 1992 when the rebel movement's HQ in Lisbon expressed the desire to distance itself from its covert Portuguese sponsors. SIM is similarly suspected of supporting the Unita movement in Angola. The civilian SIS is strongly opposed to this and has attempted to sabotage support for RENAMO on several occasions. It is known to maintain good contacts with the security services of Portugal's former colonies. Both Unita and RENAMO have in the past accused the SIS of allowing the Mozambique and Angolan intelligence services to operate freely on Portuguese soil. In April 1988 RENAMO leader Evo Fernandes was assassinated in Lisbon by killers with proven Mozambican intelligence contacts.

Both the military and the civilian intelligence services have also been implicated in providing support to the GAL death squads that assassinated at least 29 suspected ETA members in Southern France between 1983 and 1987.

SPAIN

In 1977 the counter-espionage *Centro Superior de Información de la Defensa* (CESID) was established to replace the Francoist intelligence services. At the outset many of its staff came from the 'Documentation Service', Carrero Blanco's notorious SDPG, responsible for counter-subversion under the Franco regime. In 1982 a government decree expanded its role to include domestic and foreign counter-espionage, anti-constitutional movements and the coordination of the intelligence departments of the three military services. The head of the CESID is responsible to the Minister of Defence. CESID's strength in the mid-1980s was estimated at 2,000 plus two operational sections, 400 Civil Guards and 100 members of the *Cuerpo Superior*.

The *Policía Nacional's Comisaría General de Información* (the Intelligence Division) is concerned with gathering intelligence on public order and security. Its major role has been the central direction of anti-terrorist work through its *Brigada Central de Información* (a *brigada* is a squad). The *Comisaría General de Información* is responsible directly to the secretary of state for security in the Ministry of the Interior.

The *Guardia Civil* has its own intelligence branch, the *Servicio de información de la Guardia Civil* (SIGC). Every *Guardia* officer supplies information to the SIGC which is concerned with combating terrorism, "subversion" and crime.

Commentary

A senior CESID employee was prosecuted and convicted to several years imprisonment for leaking information to *Interviu* magazine in February 1988. The information showed that the CESID had an Operational Group with an interior and an exterior section, a technological and economic division active in the acquisition of *Tecnologia Punta*, and an arms trafficking and an industrial security branch. The foreign intelligence division was divided into the Maghreb, Latin America, Arabic, Western and Eastern areas, a structure reflected in the counter-intelligence division.

The interior intelligence division had sections on revolution, terrorism, subversion and liaised with the rural *milicias*. Liaison offices were maintained in over a dozen countries. CESID has repeatedly attracted unwanted publicity by spying on senior government officials, such as the Spanish Foreign Affairs Ministry delegation at the Trevi meeting in 1987.

To deal with domestic terrorism, Spain has resorted to specific anti-terror legislation, a special court to handle all terrorism-related cases and a crown witness system to encourage former members of terrorist groups to come forward. Throughout the 1980s all the Spanish intelligence services have been accused of unnecessary violence, torture and extrajudicial killings in the battle against ETA and other terrorist groups.

SWEDEN

The *Säkerhetsavdelningen* is colloquially known as Säpo - short for *Säkerhetspolisen* (security police in Swedish), and is formally accountable to the Ministry of Justice. It reports directly to the Commissioner of the *Rikspolisstyrelsen* and the National Police Board and is formally Department D of the *Riksspolis* (Swedish police). Säpo has three offices. Office O is concerned with counter-espionage, mail interception, tapping radio traffic and with defence security. Office P deals with bombs, terrorists, political extremists, the control of foreigners living in Sweden, and foreign powers' activities. Office L deals with the administration of the security service and the data on those observed by the service.

The Säpo has local and regional branch offices and numbers 950 personnel, half in the Stockholm HQ. The Secretariat processes and analyzes all incoming data (including about 80% from open sources). It employs a range of academics, computer specialists, military experts, and police officers.

Accountability is exercised through the Standing Committee on the Administration of Justice and the Standing Committee on the Constitution. The four largest political parties also have had members appointed to the board of the National Police Board, but they are not allowed to pass information to their parliamentary groups. The Parliamentary Ombudsman and the Attorney-General also have a role in the control and oversight system. There is, however, a reluctance to control the agencies actively; the Ombudsman reportedly has remarked that it is probably 'just as well if we don't know so much'.

Commentary

After disclosures in the late 1960s that Säpo was carrying out surveillance and making records on left wing dissidents, this function was transferred to an even more secretive branch of the *Informations Byrå* (IB, military intelligence service). The existence and functioning of the IB was disclosed by journalist Jan Guillou in 1973. Reportedly the IB currently works under the acronym SSI (section for special gathering. Töllborg 1991: 68). Over the past decade Säpo has been criticised again for concentrating on monitoring left wing groups.

The assassination of Prime Minister Olaf Palme in 1986 initiated a period of severe tension for Swedish society as a whole and for the security service in particular. Internal conflicts over the direction of the investigation (the PKK trail), the methods and the secrecy-vs-openness debate led to several scandals, the resignation of a Säpo chief, a Minister of Justice, and to few results and much discontent.

In 1989 a *Terroristlagen* (Terrorist Act) was passed making it easier to conduct surveillance on foreign citizens in Sweden (this formalised powers already available since the mid-1970s under the law on foreigners). Telephone tapping is allowed in certain cases and happens relatively frequently, but the use of hidden microphones (bugging) is not allowed. When Säpo officers tried to smuggle such equipment into the country in 1988, this led to arrests and later the resignation and conviction of several senior officials in the so-called Ebbe Carlsson affair (Töllborg 1991: 48-56). Since the Conservative government came to power in October 1991 the intelligence service has increased its strength significantly and initiatives taken by the former social democrat government for reform and greater accountability have been dropped.

Sweden is a neutral country with a substantial military industrial complex. It has always maintained a relatively large military intelligence service responsible for foreign intelligence gathering and communications intelligence. Collaboration with other Western intelligence services (notably the CIA, SIS and Mossad) is intensive.

SWITZERLAND

The *Bundespolizei* (federal police) and the *Bundesanwaltschaft* (federal prosecutor's office) are responsible for both criminal and political investigations and report to the Ministry of Justice and Police. In addition to *Bundespolizei* (Bupo) the *Kantons* (federal states) and some of the larger cities have their own intelligence services. The Bupo employs nearly 100 functionaries, in the kantons about 200 people (some part-time) work on *Staatsschutz*.

Commentary

The Swiss public became aware of the extensive political police surveillance of leftists, liberals and pacifists and the vetting of 'sensitive' jobs in the wake of a scandal in 1988 when the Minister of Justice and Police, Elisabeth Kopp, warned her husband of a pending criminal investigation against a bank where he was vice-president. In March 1990 there were mass demonstrations against the political police and a campaign for open government which led to the creation of the Komitee Schluss mit dem Schnüffelstaat (stop the snooping state). It forced the government to make available the political police files and 350,000 people applied to see their files.

In September 1992 the Nationalrat decided to give access to those who had asked to see their files before April 1990, provided they put in another request. So far only Fichen (index cards) have been released but now the Akten (dossiers) are being made available. Of the 350,000 individuals who requested their files some 40,000 were indeed registered. According to the authorities 80.5% of the total of 728,000 registered individuals were foreigners. Half of the 142,000 registered Swiss civilians had been entered in the files since 1980. On the basis of several hundred index cards released so far the impression is that, up to the 1970s, a communist party (Partei der Arbeit) was the main subject of Bupo's attention but from the mid-1970s it shifted to new social movements such as the anti-nuclear movement, communes and the libertarian youth movement. The traditional concept of subversion was replaced by targeting protest movements against poverty, environmental pollution, inhumane technologies, militarism and exploitation of the Third World.

Reportedly about 5% of the old files will be taken over in a new file system, but 30,000 new entries have been made since 1990 (many in relation to threat alerts during the Gulf campaign). A new, computerized system, *Informationssystem Staatsschutz und Innere Sicherheit* (ISIS), was introduced through a ministerial directive in 1992. In theory access to these new files is also possible, but the usual restrictions such as 'only when not detrimental to state security' and 'no violation of a third person's rights' will make this right difficult to exercise. Information will be held on people and organizations involved in violent extremism, acts of terrorism, intelligence activities and organized crime, and will include 'those who advocate or condone' such activities.

The interim directives are to be replaced by a new law in 1993 which will allow the police to draw up a list of special issues that are not covered by the four named areas, and the security service will also operate a data bank on organizations 'susceptible to threaten Swiss security'.

There was a close cooperation between the Bupo and the *Untergruppe Nachrichtendienst und Abwehr* (UNA, section intelligence and security) in the *Eidgenössische Militär Department* (EMD, Ministry of Defence) through the office of the *Bundesanwaltschaft*. The UNA also monitored 'subversives' and other domestic threats and in November 1990 a parliamentary investigation commission (PUK-EMD) reported on the many improprieties in the military intelligence and security services. Subsequently the P-27 military intelligence 'stay-behind' was reorganised and the P-26 covert army disbanded. Later it was decided to disband the UNA and replace it with a new military security service and a foreign intelligence service. The new National Intelligence Service will gather intelligence abroad and employ 2-300 officers. To ensure proper cooperation between the Bupo and the military, the director of the Zürich municipal police Peter Hofacher was appointed head of the Military Security Division in January 1993.

The Swiss government is currently attempting to integrate into the European internal security structure, but it faces a problem because a referendum in 1992 came out against joining the EC. With the partial release of confidential material the US and other intelligence services said they feared too liberal legislation on the Swiss services.

UNITED KINGDOM

The intelligence and security organisations in the UK comprise: MI5 (the Security Service, founded in 1909), MI6 (the Secret Service, the external intelligence agency, founded in 1911), DIS (Defence Intelligence Staff) and GCHQ (Government Communications Headquarters at Cheltenham). MI5 is theoretically accountable to the Home Secretary (but with direct access to the Prime Minister if necessary). MI6 and GCHQ are theoretically accountable to the Foreign Secretary, and DIS to the Minister of Defence. Policy is coordinated through the Joint Intelligence Committee.

MI5 has a full-time staff of 2,000 and an annual budget of £200 million. It is divided into branches: 'A': deals with bugging, breakins and surveillance; 'B':

personnel; 'C': protective security - the vetting of civil servants, security of state offices; 'F': internal surveillance of subversives: trade unions, radical and campaigning groups, and of terrorist groups (including the IRA); 'K': counter-espionage against 'hostile' agents.

Commentary

The 1989 Security Service Act recognised the existence of MI5 for the first time. The Act defined its main role as protecting 'national security' against, 'threats from espionage, terrorism and sabotage, from activities of agents of foreign powers, and from actions intended to overthrow or undermine parliamentary democracy by political, industrial or violent means'. Its role also covers safeguarding the 'economic well-being of the UK'.

MI5 has been involved in the work of Trevi 1 (terrorism) since 1976 and takes part in a number of working groups. In 1992 it took over the lead role against the IRA from the Special Branch. In 1993 its undercover officers appeared in court for the first time in a case concerning alleged Welsh nationalist fire-bombings.

Its work is covered by the 1989 Official Secrets Act which makes it an offence to publish information about its operations and personnel. It also remains an offence under the 1920 Official Secrets Act to 'retain' (ie, to hold) information concerning MI5 and the other security agencies.

Policing the New Europe: The Northern Ireland Factor

Mike Tomlinson

Introduction

This article examines some of the key features of the Northern Ireland conflict and its management in the context of the emerging European state. It seeks to shed light on why the conflict is important for Europe and vice versa. To date, interest in 'Europeanisation' and how it is shaping Northern Ireland has for the most part been confined to questions of economic and social policy. The deployment of structural funds and the application of special initiatives such as INTERREG (targeted specifically on border areas) or the LEADER programme (rural development), provide fairly visible manifestations of the new European state at work. Far less clear, however, is what goes on within those structures, such as TREVI Group I, which lie beyond the European Parliament and the Commission and which are laying the foundations of the European secret state.[1]

One of the key themes of the article is the lack of accountability of intelligence, military and policing agencies. After more than twenty years of mainly low-level warfare, the Northern Ireland conflict has become so institutionalised and interests so entrenched that only the most curious and persistent ask questions on what the state agencies in the frontline are up to. The deployment of thousands of troops in the cities and countryside of Northern Ireland is now so taken for granted that no-one even bothers to calculate what it costs. Intelligence agencies and covert military units have acquired enough power and autonomy for few questions to be raised when they kill. Misleading the media and the courts have become part of routine statecraft. The decision-makers are unidentifiable or else bluff their way through, using the crude rhetoric of counter-terrorism which substitutes for proper political consideration. Critics, if they dare to pop their heads up, are demonised. Some are threatened: some eliminated.

The importance of Northern Ireland for the European secret state is that it is, at present, the foremost source of armed conflict in the EC, within Britain and, of course, in Ireland itself. Equally important, the conflict has produced the most developed counter-terrorist policies of anywhere in Europe, even if these do rest on shaky intellectual and political foundations.[2] It is the management of the conflict itself which gives Northern Ireland its significance in Europe.

The main body of the article is in seven sections. The first examines the build up of armed forces, gathering together the available information on the security agencies, their size, cost, and changes over the last two decades. It considers how the Army is being deployed and the difficulties arising from defence cuts. The second section is on the role of intelligence agencies and undercover units, in particular, the rise of MI5. Counter-terrorist policy has been at the centre of the restructuring of intelligence and police work. The closer the date for the removal of all border controls in Europe, the more fortified the border has become, and the more pressing has been the issue of North/South collaboration on security policy. This is the subject of the third section. The long-standing issue of extradition is covered next and then the fifth section looks at the movement of sentenced prisoners between Britain and Ireland. The sixth section looks at the rhetoric surrounding killings and the issue of collusion. Finally, the efficacy of the European Convention on Human Rights is considered.

Armed forces

In his evidence to the British House of Commons Defence Committee in November 1992, General Sir Martin Farndale drew a distinction between the Army's primary function - the ability to engage in the 'high intensity operations' of general warfare - and the secondary function of what he described as 'short term low intensity tasks'.[3] Included in the latter is the British Army's role in Northern Ireland where it has had an active presence on the streets for twenty-four years.

When the first deployment of 2,690 troops was sent to Derry and Belfast in the summer of 1969, there were already around 2,500 soldiers stationed in Northern Ireland. At the time, the Royal Ulster Constabulary (RUC) contained 3,044 officers. There was, however, a part-time auxiliary force known as the Ulster Special Constabulary numbering 8,581.[4] This was disbanded and replaced by the Ulster Defence Regiment (UDR) in 1970. At the start of the current conflict, then, there was an active deployment of just over 5,700 troops and police officers. By the time Direct Rule from London was instituted in 1972, the British Army had over 17,000 troops committed in Northern Ireland. From the mid-1970s these numbers began to decline as part of an official policy of 'police primacy' - to give the RUC the primary role in managing the conflict. 'Ulsterisation' is a better description of the policy at this time because the main objective was to replace or downgrade the role of the British Army with forces recruited from within Northern Ireland itself. This meant building up not only the RUC but also the UDR which, although formally a regiment of the British Army, was entirely dependent on local recruits and had no military role outside of Northern Ireland. To begin with, the UDR was largely a part-time force. The Ulsterisation process involved reducing the number of part-timers and increasing the full-timers. By 1979, the Army had reduced its numbers to just over 13,000, UDR full-time numbers stood at 2,400 and the RUC at 7,300 - a total of 22,700.

The decline of Army numbers, matched by the build up of the RUC and UDR, continued in the early 1980s. The RUC had reached 10,300 full-timers by 1984 while the Army had been reduced to 9,500. Full-time UDR numbers stood at 2,670, giving a total full-time deployment of 22,470.[5] This pattern changed in the late 1980s and early 1990s. In more recent years, there has been a continuing commitment to the expansion of the RUC and UDR, but Army numbers have been increasing as well.

In 1992, as part of the 'Options for Change' restructuring of the British Army, the UDR was merged with the Royal Irish Rangers to become the Royal Irish Regiment (RIR).[6] At the time the UDR was 6,200 strong, of whom 700 were women and about half full-timers. When the merger was announced the commander of the British Army in Northern Ireland, Lt General Sir John Wilsey admitted that the UDR had a serious image problem. The regiment, he said, 'has not sought to be sectarian, one-sided or filled its ranks with Protestants, but that's the way it turned out'. More than a dozen members/ex-members of the UDR are in prison for murder and an estimated 120 are in prison for other serious offences related to conflict. Members of the regiment are twice as likely to commit a crime than the general public, on the basis of recorded crimes.[7] The Rangers numbered 1,300 but were to lose a battalion in the merger. The Army claimed that the Rangers were 30% Catholic - the UDR was thought to be about 3% Catholic - but a few months later it appeared that the real figure was only 6%. 'It seems the figure for Ballymena barracks got into our system as the overall regimental breakdown', an Army spokesman stated.[8] The RIR has a target size of 6,750.

Two extra battalions were committed to Northern Ireland early in 1991, one of which was to reinforce border garrisons to ensure the continuation of the building programme of new checkpoints and bases (see below). As the Defence Committee's recent report confirms, the two extra battalions are still stationed in Northern Ireland and there is every reason to believe that at least one will be required for at least a further year.[9] Army and RUC numbers as of 1st March 1993 are given below.[10]

	Males	Females	TOTAL
RUC full-time	7,613	739	8,352
RUC Reserve			
Full-time	3,000	79	3,079
Part-time	1,047	420	1,467
TOTAL RUC	11,660	1,238	12,898
Army			12,173
RIR			5,627
Navy			240
RAF			1,100
TOTAL RUC and Army			32,038

These figures exclude the RUC's civilian backup workforce of 3,250. The total uniformed RUC numbers are projected to rise to 13,460 by 1994/5 or a total of 16,840 including civilian workers. By next year there will be one Army/RUC member for every 3.7 Catholic males aged 16 to 44.

In terms of military deployment and certainly as far as the infantry is concerned, Northern Ireland could neither be described as a short-term commitment nor a secondary one. As General Farndale himself sees it, 'force levels in Northern Ireland are low and could easily have to be increased at short notice'.[11] The actual number of troops involved in the Northern Ireland commitment is much higher than the above figures of those stationed in Northern Ireland suggest because of the cycle of preparation, training and re-training. The Deputy Director of the International Institute for Strategic Studies stated recently: 'the British Army in particular is overstretched. With 12,000 troops, mostly infantry, stationed in Northern Ireland and as many again caught up in the Northern Ireland cycle, that is either training for an emergency tour there or having just completed a tour in the province, there is little spare capacity to most additional commitments. Moreover, the degree of overstretch is particularly acute at present while commitments remain inflated'.[12]

Army units are deployed in one of two ways in Northern Ireland. They may be sent as resident battalions, of which there are currently six, or they be part of the 'Emergency Tour Plot' involving a further six battalions. Resident battalions spend two and a half years in Northern Ireland. The length of an Emergency Tour was recently increased from four to six months and the average interval between tours of 15 months is now considerably below the target average of 24 months. For some units, the tour interval is down as low as eight months.[13] The tour interval is used by the Army as the key indicator of 'overstretch', a recognised problem of the stress and strain on soldiers and their families which is leading to an increased drop out rate. Another indicator is 'nights out of bed', defined as the number of nights each year on average that individual soldiers are away from their normal home. One unit experienced 271 nights out of bed in 1990, 154 in 1991 and 287 in 1992.

To maintain infantry levels on the ground, the Army is having to use gunner units. In fact almost a third of the infantry in Northern Ireland is made up of non-infantry units. Gunner units are no longer able to train at full strength and some regiments have not fired their artillery guns for two years. Units are further depleted by the recent decision to keep 50 men from every unit at 'home' bases in Britain and Germany to guard barracks and families from IRA attacks.

Add to this the pressures of amalgamations and disbandments initiated by the 'Options' review and it becomes clear why the Defence Committee concluded that 'overstretch is fundamental and chronic' and is 'symptomatic of a fundamental failure to match infantry forces to foreseeable commitments'. A lobby within the Conservative Party and the military is now arguing for the cancellation of all cuts in the infantry, as well as for an expansion of the RIR to take on less specialised roles such as guarding prisons.

Costs

Given the high level of armed forces in Northern Ireland and the political attention which has been paid to scrutinising public expenditure over the past fifteen years, it is surprising to find that relatively little information is available on costs. For example, it is not possible to compare the costs of different operations or the policing of the border as compared to Belfast. Capital expenditure on border checkpoints, watchtowers and bases is not visible in the Defence Estimates, although the Northern Ireland Office has admitted that border checkpoints are 'very costly to operate'.[14] The checkpoint at Clonatty Bridge near Newtownbutler, which in 1989 only saw an average of thirty vehicles per day pass through, is thought to have cost over £1.5 million.[15] While there is virtually no information on the Army, data are available for the RUC. The RUC, for instance, spent £28 million out of its £477 million budget on building work in 1990/1, reflecting the major refurbishment, rebuilding and repairs programme that has been in progress for some years. A further £6.4 million went on computers and other communications equipment in the same year.[16] The direct financial costs of the Army in Northern Ireland cannot easily be determined from published sources.[17] According to one source, a unit of the UDR cost about £7.2 million in 1991/2, while a resident battalion cost £9.8m and a short tour unit £4.8m, but whether or not these figures refer to the additional cost of these units arising from the nature of their task in Northern Ireland is unclear.[18] Such additional cost figures used to be routinely given in public expenditure white papers but they were excluded in the early 1980s. The last of such estimates was for the year 1981/2 and was given as £149m.[19] Allowing for changed troop levels and inflation, today's additional cost is likely to be around £470m.[20] The full cost is in the region of five or six times this figure. Taking the additional cost figure, adding the 1993/4 planned spending on prisons of £147m - or what amounts to a weekly cost per prisoner of £1,600 - and the projected cost of the RUC for this year of £602m, and the identifiable 'law and order' budget comes to £1,219 million per year.[21] It is estimated that the additional cost to the Irish government of the conflict in the North totals IR£2.5 billion and is now running at IR£200 million per annum.[22] Recent compensation costs are detailed below:[23]

	£millions Criminal Damages	Criminal Injuries
1989/90	18.2	6.5
1990/91	18.8	8.0
1991/92	29.8	10.9

Such figures present only one side of the costs of the conflict. There is an ongoing debate about the impact of the conflict on the economy of Northern Ireland, particularly in relation to employment and unemployment.[24] This debate has recently acquired some significance in Britain. The direct costs of the Baltic Exchange bombing were put at £800 million but of longer term significance is the threat to London's bid to become the financial centre of Europe should commercial property become uninsurable. Regular disruptions to commuter traffic, increased security measures, both public and private, and the latest threat to bomb industrial targets, all contribute to an economic cost of the conflict within Britain itself which one estimate suggests was £5 billion for 1992. Operation Isis, the security programme drawn up to protect the Prime Minister and the Cabinet at the 1992 Conservative Party annual conference, was budgeted at £2.5 million.

The numbers of armed forces, therefore, far from reducing or even stabilising, are increasing. Likewise, the directly identifiable costs of the conflict are escalating. Those costs currently amount to over £9,200 per year for each Catholic male between 15 and 44 years of age.

Intelligence and covert operations

'Be clear on one point above all else. The intelligence world is not answerable to secretaries of state. It is accountable to nobody - not the Prime Minister, not Parliament, not the courts'.[25]

Even more invisible than Army costs is expenditure on intelligence agencies and undercover operations. This aspect of British policy on Ireland is, of course, the least accountable of all both politically and in terms of the law. Covert operations have become the central feature of British security policy and ensuring that personnel, informers, and techniques remain secret has in itself become a key objective. As Urban concludes:

'attempts to protect intelligence sources and techniques have frequently resulted in the deception of the courts in Northern Ireland. It is also apparent that deception has been used to allow soldiers or police officers who have acted mistakenly to escape criminal charges. The powers of the courts, in particular those dealing with inquests, have been modified in such a way as to make it extremely unlikely that they will ever uncover dishonesty on the part of the security forces'.[26]

A good example of this is the inquest into the deaths of three men killed by the RUC Special Branch's undercover surveillance unit E4A in November 1982, which has to date involved five different coroners and has still not been concluded. These killings formed part of the investigation into 'shoot-to-kill' allegations carried out by John Stalker.[27] Deception and censorship of the media has been another important ingredient. In his review of the period 1976 to 1987, Urban identifies the emergence of a pattern of aggressive covert operations 'with the acquiescence of politicians and senior officers'.[28] Covert units have become more autonomous and powerful so that supervision and knowledge of what they are up to has lessened even within the Army and RUC themselves. Latterly, there has been less political compulsion to justify 'shoot-to-kill' operations.

During the earliest years of the current conflict, the British government favoured the use of MI6 in Northern Ireland (and in the Republic). On the basis of countering IRA bombing campaigns in Britain, MI5 pushed for a presence in the North and from 1973 onwards began to build itself organisationally. It was this period of the mid-1970s that gave rise to intense rivalry and conflict between MI5 and MI6, as well as between the British military and the RUC.[29] Army and RUC officers alike derided MI5 efforts in the 1970s.[30]

The rivalries between RUC SB and military intelligence agencies came to the attention of senior MI6 officer, Maurice Oldfield, who was appointed as Security Co-ordinator for Northern Ireland in October 1979. Less than a year later, Oldfield was removed from this position because, as Mrs Thatcher's statement in the Commons claimed, he had 'confessed' to being homosexual. But for a brief period, Oldfield sided with the British intelligence agencies, arguing that it was dangerous to rely too heavily on the RUC.

By the late 1970s, most MI6 agents had been taken over by RUC SB or MI5 and MI6 itself had withdrawn from RUC and Army headquarters, although it retained an office at Stormont. In contrast, MI5 installed itself to the extent that its operational head, the Director and Co-ordinator of Intelligence (DCI) at Stormont, is now a key adviser to the Secretary of State. This relationship is formally recognised under the Security Service Act with the DCI reporting to the Secretary of State for Northern Ireland, not to the Home Secretary in London - though clearly MI5 in Northern Ireland retains close links with London. MI5 has offices at Army HQ in Lisburn and at RUC HQ. It floats in and out of the three intelligence co-ordinating Tasking and Co-ordination Groups (TCGs) based at Castlereagh (Belfast), Gough Barracks (Armagh) and in Derry, depending on its interests in a given operation.

The first TCG was set up in Belfast in 1978 and proved so successful in 'tasking the SAS for executive action' (ie: identifying targets for the SAS to eliminate) that two more were established soon afterwards for the RUC's other regions.[31] From the late 1970s the TCGs combined the CID, SB and the Army, allowing the linking together of informer-based intelligence and the surveillance and ambush activities of undercover units. The Army representative on TCGs 'is almost always a veteran of an SAS or 14 Intelligence Company tour'.[32] The Army also contributes intelligence gathered from its agents run by the Field Research Unit, set up by Commander of Land Forces Major General Glover in 1980. Brian Nelson, the Ulster Defence Association intelligence officer sentenced to 10 years imprisonment in February 1992, worked for FRU for 10 years.[33] The bulk of intelligence available to the TCGs comes not from MI5, FRU or 14 Intelligence Co., but from RUC SB.

From the mid-1980s, counter-terrorist work became much more important to MI5. 'High flyers' in the service were often sent to Northern Ireland: Patrick Walker, appointed director general of MI5 in 1989 and current director Stella Rimington's immediate predecessor, served in Northern Ireland in the late 1970s. Eventually, counter-terrorism became a branch of its own and the director of counter-terrorism acquired the same status as director of counter-espionage. As such, the director of counter-terrorism sits on MI5's board, as does Northern Ireland's MI5 head, the Director and Co-ordinator of Intelligence. Rimington herself worked on Northern Ireland matters prior to her move to F branch ('internal subversion'). She was director of counter-terrorism before taking over as director general.[34]

On 8 May 1992 Home Secretary, Kenneth Clarke, announced that MI5 was to be given the lead responsibility for intelligence work against the IRA in Britain. The change followed two reviews of the role of intelligence services undertaken by the former head of the Secret Intelligence Service (MI6), Sir Christopher Curwen, in 1990 and 1991. Curwen argued for a strictly limited and subordinate role for MI5 but the Home Secretary rejected this advice. MI5 already had primary responsibility for intelligence work in relation to loyalist and international terrorism, as well as IRA activity in Europe and elsewhere.

Curwen's reviews and opposition within the police itself, were not enough to dissuade the Home Secretary from the promotion of MI5's role. As he made clear in the House of Commons, the ending of the Cold War meant, 'we simply have the opportunity to switch more resource within the security services into this key area of Irish republican terrorism in this country... As a result of political changes, there is greater opportunity for the Security Service to put more of its resources into that activity'. Clarke went on to state, 'it is important that all the work on the mainland of Britain, in Ulster and in the Republic of Ireland is co-ordinated to a certain extent and that all the authorities co-operate as they properly should in action against the joint threat which they all face from the Provisional IRA. I am sure that proper contacts will be maintained and will not be affected in any way by the announcement today'.[35]

The rise of MI5, which ends police primacy in Britain in relation to anti-IRA operations after 109 years of Special Branch responsibility, raises the question of MI5's role in Ireland on both sides of the border. The response to the announcement from senior Garda officers was reported to be 'angry'. They had not been forewarned of the change and, as one officer put it:

> 'we are very worried about this latest development in Britain. We believe there are a large number of MI5 agents now working here, particularly in

Dublin and along the border, but we've not been officially notified of their presence. The (British) Special Branch would notify us of any activities it carried out in the Republic. But since the changeover, MI5 has not been in contact with us.. For obvious reasons we don't want an army of agents operating here and carrying out dirty tricks'.[36]

In the North the RUC officially retains primacy in intelligence and operational matters. The relationship between MI5 and RUC Special Branch (RUC SB) is somewhat different than the British equivalent.[37] Because of its dependence on the RUC's extensive network of informers, MI5 is more respectful of RUC SB. But MI5's influence has clearly expanded over the years even if its role is confined primarily to securing intelligence on potential IRA activity outside of Northern Ireland. MI5 has an estimated 100 full-time operatives in Northern Ireland.[38]

It is unlikely that the restructuring of relationships between MI5 and police forces in Britain and Ireland will resolve the tensions and rivalries between these agencies given recent operational experiences and proposed developments. RUC Chief Constable, Sir Hugh Annesley in his Police Foundation lecture of July 1992 questioned the need for 43 police forces in Britain and made the case for a national force operated on a regional basis. This is close to the model for reform announced by the Home Secretary in February 1993 except that regional police authorities - now to have the proportion of elected local councillors reduced from two-thirds to a half - will retain a sense of regional autonomy. Annesley also proposed two new operational units, a National Crime Squad and a National Anti-Terrorist Unit. The latter would have four divisions, one concerned with the cultivation of informants, the second with the gathering, analysis and assessment of intelligence, the third with providing an operational capacity to respond to such intelligence, and the fourth, a training, legal and support service wing. The unit, Annesley suggests, would incorporate the Security Service, the Metropolitan Police Special Branch and Anti-Terrorist Unit, with a significant input from provincial CID and Special Branches. It would also include military and customs personnel with the capacity to co-opt specific skills from other agencies or departments as appropriate. The National Anti-Terrorist Unit would provide a 'single police and intelligence focal point for liaison with the RUC, the Garda and the police forces and intelligence services of Europe and North America'.[39] The head of the unit would have a line of command to the Home Secretary 'but with direct access to the Prime Minister'. The Unit is being actively considered following a number of operational fiascoes including the escape of an IRA unit in London which was under observation by MI5 and was being tailed by a twelve-strong police firearms unit. MI5 and the police were using different radio frequencies. A National Anti-Terrorist Unit of the kind envisaged by Annesley would involve MI5 as a partner, not as the lead authority.

Within Northern Ireland, the Nelson case shows that RUC SB/Army rivalry continues to be an issue. The head of FRU from 1986 to 1990 was the Colonel 'J' who ran Nelson as an agent and who gave evidence at his trial. One RUC officer is reported to have described Colonel 'J' as 'a liar, a cheat, a manipulator with no integrity in his approach'. In a Panorama programme broadcast 8 June 1992, it was claimed that FRU knew the Ulster Defence Association had targeted Brendan Davison, an IRA member who was supplying information to RUC SB. Davison was important to the RUC because he was part of the IRA's counter-informer unit and RUC SB was reportedly outraged at the murder of their key informer.[40] Following the Nelson trial and a review of Army/RUC relations, a Provincial Executive Committee has been established which includes the Army's Commander of Land Forces, the head of RUC SB, a Deputy Chief Constable with special responsibility for police/Army liaison, and MI5's Director and Co-ordinator of Intelligence.

Covert units have been responsible for an estimated 60 killings. Urban claims that the SAS killed 25 IRA volunteers between 1976 and 1987, and another five since then.[41] The SAS was first sent to Northern Ireland in 1969, although its presence was not publicly admitted for several years. Between 20 and 25 SAS men are kept in Northern Ireland most of the time, but these numbers are reinforced for shoot-to-kill operations. Operation Judy, the Loughgall ambush which resulted in the killing of eight IRA members and one civilian, involved 39 SAS men as well as fifty of the Army and RUC's most experienced undercover operatives. Urban's figures suggest that up to 1987, the SAS had killed six innocent civilians. As he recognises, however, many of the killings of IRA volunteers have been in disputed circumstances in that they were unarmed or were not arrested when they could have been.[42] Murray lists 42 SAS killings up to 1989. Whatever the true figures, it is evident that the SAS has killed considerably more people than 14th Intelligence Company or the RUC's E4A.

Fortifying the border

Northern Ireland has not only been heavily militarised for many years, it is becoming more so. During the 1980s, a major programme of new RUC and Army base building has been in progress. To some extent, this has been accelerated by IRA attacks on police stations and army installations, especially border checkpoints. Some 35 attacks on RUC stations, for instance, were recorded for 1980 but these had risen to over 200 by 1991.[43]

Since the mid-1980s, the Army has been fortifying the border with a mixture of road closures, new permanent bases, watchtowers and checkpoints, including all the usual paraphernalia of cameras and telecommunications. The new border post at Killeen on the main Belfast to Dublin Road, for example, now consists of a steel-clad military base, an inspection shed with X-ray equipment, and a system of traffic lights, cameras and barriers, including hydraulic pistons sunk in the road which can be triggered to stop vehicles which attempt to drive through the other barriers. In 1989, 9,000 vehicles passed through this checkpoint on average each day. Following an IRA attack, it was re-built and relocated without warning next to a large primary school which was forced to close in September 1992.

In 1989, 65 out of the 291 'recognised' border crossings were closed.[44] Three years later, a total of 103 border roads were subject to closure orders under the Emergency Provisions Act although actual closures are higher than this at 160 according to the Department of Foreign Affairs in Dublin.[45] Many border communities have been disrupted by road closures particularly in the Fermanagh and Tyrone areas. At Tulleyvogey, a remote community where some houses have neither electricity nor running water, some residents, although living in Northern Ireland, have been cut off from the North by a road closure. To reach a neighbour on the Northern side of the closure - a neighbour who ironically gets her electricity supply from the South - one resident must drive 26 miles to bypass the Army blockade set up in March 1991. Other communities have similarly been annexed from Northern Ireland by the night-time closure of permanent vehicle checkpoints.

The Army closes border roads by means of trenches, craters and huge concrete blocks into which steel posts are embedded - known locally as 'dragon's teeth'. Of 59 border roads in Fermanagh, only ten remain open. The Lackey Bridge crossing, near Clones in County Monaghan, has been the focus of conflict between local people and the authorities for decades. It was first closed in 1922, reopened in 1925, spiked in the 1950s, reopened again in the 1960s until closure in the early 1970s. In the last few years, local people using heavy earth moving equipment have reopened the crossing on several occasions, including new year's day 1993, the day on which border controls between EC member states were supposed to disappear. Under the Emergency Provisions Act, it is an offence to use a crossing which the authorities have closed and an offence to build a by-pass around a closed road within 200 yards of the blockade. The Act also introduced new powers to seize equipment such as tractors and JCBs which may be used to reopen roads.

Not all border crossing closures have been instituted by the British Army. After the IRA killed a UDR man and his wife in 1972, Aghalane bridge was blown up by a loyalist group. A temporary bridge was put in place but this too was blown up. The bridge has not been re-built even though much investment has gone into dredging and landscaping the Woodford river, which it once crossed, as part of a major tourist development scheme to link the Erne waterway in the North with the Shannon.

In addition to campaigns to reopen roads, residents in the South Armagh area have been concerned for some years about the health effects of military equipment in use in border areas. They believe that the Army may have established a 'microwave fence' along parts of the border and is using electronic grids for navigational and communications purposes.[46] Although the Army claims there are no health hazards relating to its equipment and has even invited selected people to view some of the equipment in use at the Bessbrook base, the Secretary of State for Defence, Archie Hamilton, has declined to give details of the make, model and emission levels of each type of equipment in use by the military in border areas of NI which emits electromagnetic radiation.[47]

EC integration has brought the border into sharp political focus. Many unionists and nationalists, albeit from opposing political perspectives, believe that Europeanisation may weaken the significance of partition. For the latter, Europeanisation is a welcome form of 'creeping re-unification', a process which will finally render the border irrelevant. But for unionists the fear is that EC integration will weaken the relationship to Britain. So far from reducing its significance, the progress of EC integration has increased the importance of the border as a political boundary.[48]

In the early 1970s, British troops regularly crossed the border, generating much local hostility and general political embarrassment. Between 1973 and 1976, 304 border incursions were recorded by the Irish government - an average of two per week. 63 of these were on foot, 18 in armoured vehicles, 55 in other transport, 151 by helicopter and 17 in other aircraft. The most controversial of these incursions involved suspected SAS kidnapping and murder in 1976. On one occasion eight SAS men were arrested, brought to trial and convicted in Dublin for possession of weapons with intent to endanger life. They were fined £100 each.[49] These incidents were prior to the introduction of the policy of police primacy and prior to any meaningful cross-border police co-operation on the ground. As Mark Urban writes, 'the advent of police primacy in 1976 was a positive step for Dublin since it removed the Army, with whom the Gardaí would not deal, from control of operations'.[50]

High level contacts between RUC Chief Constable Flanaghan and Garda Commissioner Malone began in 1974. These meetings gave rise to a series of study groups called the 'Baldonnel panels' which were designed to facilitate intelligence exchanges as well as co-ordinated border patrolling.[51] Around the same time, European-wide co-operation was being established by London's Metropolitan Police Special Branch, specifically with a view to responding to anti-terrorist matters, and in 1976 the TREVI Working Group I on terrorism began work. TREVI-I has been cited as proving 'valuable in relation to the United Kingdom's response to the Provisional Irish Republican Army' when the latter mounted a series of operations in Europe in the late 1980s.[52] In the early 1980s, however, a rift between Chief Constable Hermon and Garda Commissioner Wrenn over the 'Dowra affair' meant that the two had no meetings for three years.[53] Relationships were further soured by Hermon's public criticisms of Gardaí inefficiency and policy with respect to border security and extradition.[54]

The Hillsborough Agreement (the Anglo-Irish agreement, 1985) established an Intergovernmental Conference as the framework for regular North/South meetings of government Ministers, officials, police and security personnel. Article 2 states that the Conference should deal with i) political matters, ii) security and related matters, iii) legal matters, including the administration of justice, and iv) the promotion of cross-border co-operation. Article 7 covers security policy. The goals mentioned under security policy include the discussion of policy issues, serious incidents and forthcoming events, as well as improving relations between the security forces and the community. This may include increasing the proportion of Catholics in the RUC, thought to be 6.0% in 1992. Under Article 8, the Conference considers the harmonisation of criminal law and 'the possibility of mixed courts in both jurisdictions for the trial of certain offences'. Extradition is also listed as a concern, as is 'extra-territorial jurisdiction as between North and South'. Article 9 states, 'the Conference shall set in hand a programme of work to be undertaken by the Chief Constable of the RUC and the Commissioner of the Gardaí Síochaná and, where appropriate, groups of officials in such areas as threat assessments, exchange of information, liaison structures, technical co-operation, training of personnel, and operational resources'.[55]

The Agreement resulted in the setting up of three joint RUC/Garda working groups on operational and technical co-operation. Groups of officials also began meeting on extradition and other legal matters. Progress on implementing recommendations on RUC/Garda operational co-operation were considered at a special meeting of the Conference held in London on 31st October 1986. By the end of 1989, the Conference had held 32 meetings, with many more meetings of officials and police personnel taking place behind the scenes. Most of the intergovernmental meetings were (and are) attended by the Garda Commissioner and the RUC Chief Constable. At the April 1990 meeting, it was agreed to set up a working party on how to deal with 'fugitive offenders'. By February 1993, the Northern Ireland Office was referring to the 'high level of security co-operation' between North and South, but very few details have emerged as to what this amounts to.[56]

Clearly, intelligence and operational information is regularly exchanged and co-ordinated operations are routinely mounted either side of the border.[57] In its 1989 memorandum to the Home Affairs Select Committee on police co-operation, the NIO describes the border as 'a major strategic resource for terrorists' although it is unable to put a figure on the actual number of 'terrorist-related crimes which have a cross-border element'.[58] Accordingly, it had developed a border policy with three elements: i) road closures, ii) Permanent and Selective Vehicle Check Points (PSVCPs), and iii) mobile patrols. The 18 PSVCPs in existence in 1989 were all permanently occupied by the military, with an RUC presence at most of them. The majority of mobile patrols in border areas are on foot, supported by top cover from helicopters and by 'satellite mobile patrols'. Patrolling is co-ordinated between the RUC and Garda by Border Superintendents and by respective Operational Planning Inspectors.[59] Major Garda and Irish Army reinforcements were deployed to assist the British Army with road closures and the building of permanent checkpoints during 1991, but it appears that these operations are organised through RUC/Garda channels: according to the Irish Army, 'there is no army-to-army communication'.[60] When questioned about the role of intelligence services in October 1992, Security Minister Michael Mates replied, 'co-operation between the intelligence services of the Republic and ourselves has never been as good as it is now'.[61] Ryder claims that arrangements now exist for bomb disposal teams to cross the border and for helicopter 'overflights'.[62]

Nevertheless, there is much debate as to how to increase further the effectiveness of cross-border security co-operation. It has been suggested at Westminster, for example, that for border security purposes Garda patrols should be armed or the Irish Army put in the front line.[63] Another idea is that joint RUC/Garda mobile units should be established along with common radio communications, and procedures for 'hot pursuit' have been proposed on a number of occasions.[64] The RUC apparently favour the latter, not so much for its practical use which seemingly would be rare, but because it would send an 'important psychological signal' to the IRA.[65]

Extradition

Over the last twenty years the issue of the extradition of political offenders or suspects has created considerable tension between the British and Irish governments. The problem lies in differences in the way the 'political exception' to extradition has been interpreted by the authorities. The political exception - the refusal to hand over political fugitives to the requesting state - has a long history dating back to the French Revolution. It is based on the idea that enemies of a state cannot expect a fair trial and also on a basic sympathy with oppressed groups. The European Convention on Extradition of 1957 places a requirement on contracting parties to hand over wanted persons for a set of defined offences in defined circumstances. Under Article 3 (1), the Convention states that 'extradition shall not be granted if the offence... is regarded by the requested party as a political offence or as an offence connected with a political offence'. The taking or attempted taking of the life of a head of state (or his/her family) cannot be regarded as a political offence, but otherwise the

Convention leaves the definition open. Article 6 allows a country to refuse to extradite its own nationals, but in so doing it may be requested to proceed against the suspect in its own courts. Another important feature of the Convention is the Rule of Speciality under Article 14. The idea of this is that a person who has been extradited shall only be tried and sentenced for the offence for which they were extradited. Unlike the British 1870 Extradition Act, the Convention did not require the requesting party to establish a prima facie case against the person sought.

The Irish government signed the Convention in 1966, having passed an Extradition Act modelled on the Convention the previous year. The British, however, did not sign and ratify the Convention until 1990. Following partition, the legal position on extradition between North and South was confused. Until the late 1920s, the authorities relied on mid-nineteenth century legislation governing the issue of warrants to transfer offenders between Ireland and Britain. This procedure was successfully challenged from the South by two political suspects in 1929 and for the next 35 years no official extradition machinery existed between North and South. As Farrell writes: 'Such a situation was highly inconvenient between two states with an open land frontier and free passage across the border. Eventually the Gardaí and the RUC began to co-operate unofficially by simply dumping fugitive offenders across the border where the local police would be waiting to pick them up. This arrangement was quite illegal but the courts on both sides turned a blind eye to it'.[66] Soon after the Dail passed the Extradition Act of 1965, the meaning of the political exception clause was being tested in the Irish courts. In the early 1970s the Supreme Court upheld the political exception in relation to the conflict in the North on several occasions. Justice Finlay concluded in one case that 'it seems to me that the safekeeping of explosives for an organisation attempting to overthrow the state by violence is... an offence of a political character' and he went on to characterise the situation in Northern Ireland and Britain as 'a political disturbance'.[67] Since that time, Britain has applied continuous pressure on the Irish government to pass legislation re-defining the political exception. The carrot on two occasions, 1973 and 1985, has been to give the Irish government some sort of consultative role on Northern affairs. In the 1970s this was resisted on grounds that the political exception was a principle of international law. Instead, the South would pass legislation allowing Northern fugitives to be tried in the South - the Criminal Law Jurisdiction Act, 1976.

Britain's attitude to extradition and the political exception hardened following the passing of the Suppression of Terrorism Act in 1978. This Act enabled the British to ratify the European Convention on the Suppression of Terrorism which came in to force the same year. The Convention was designed to redefine the political exception to extradition in such a way as to compulsorily exclude bombing, hijacking, and hostage taking from being regarded by the courts as political offences. The Convention also provides that contracting parties may ignore the political nature of an offence, such as violence against people or property, if they so wish. In its own Act, however, Britain chose to ignore the political nature of all the offences listed in the Convention. Ireland refused to sign the Convention on the grounds that it contravened asylum rights written into the constitution. Nevertheless, the British Act is so drafted that it can be applied unilaterally to Ireland.[68]

By the time of the Hillsborough Agreement, the Irish courts had hardened their judgements on the political exception. Britain still pressed for further concessions. As part of the Agreement the Irish government would be regularly consulted about the North and in exchange it would sign the European Convention on the Suppression of Terrorism, as well as amending its own legislation on extradition accordingly - the Extradition Act of 1986, which was amended a year later. The new Act 'de-politicises' the offences listed in the Convention which the Irish government signed 'with touching naiveté... without reservation, unlike most of the other signatories, 12 of whom retained the right to regard some offences as political, eight of whom will not extradite their own nationals, and seven of whom will not extradite to states which operate special courts'.[69]

The new Act, and judgments under it, have significantly narrowed the political exception. Britain's 1989 Extradition Act brought British law in line with the Convention, abolishing the prima facie criterion. The table below shows that the bulk of extradition traffic between Britain and EC countries is between Britain and the Republic of Ireland.[70] Some of the cases between the UK and other EC countries concern Irish suspects.

	UK to Ireland	UK to other countries	Ireland to to UK	Other EC countries
1985	15	12	17	4
1986	9	18	2	4
1987	13	30*	3	8
1988	17	5	6	7

*Included 25 Heysel stadium football supporters.

When he was British Home Secretary, Kenneth Clarke advocated that the already weak safeguards in the European Convention on Extradition should be demolished. At a conference on extradition in London in October 1992 he argued that extradition was often a complicated, difficult and drawn out process: 'that is good news for the criminal. Too often, it encourages continuing challenges to extradition in the hope of finding a loophole'.[71] To simplify procedures, he suggested scrapping the rule of speciality, the right of countries to refuse to extradite their own nationals and removing the political exception altogether.

The main reason for this tough stance on extradition is that the British believe that other countries cannot be relied upon to convict Irish political suspects. The Dutch acquittal in 1991 of Donna Maguire, Sean Hick, Paul Hughes and Gerard Harte, who were held on murder and IRA membership charges, caused a minor political storm amongst British MPs, some of whom suggested that there were now serious diplomatic problems between the British and Dutch governments. Ivor Stanbrook of the Conservative back-bench Northern Ireland Committee, who is a legal expert on extradition, called for Holland to be excluded from the TREVI Group because 'the Dutch have shown a totally unrealistic attitude with regard to the battle against terrorism in Western Europe'.[72] Labour called on the Foreign Office to insist that the Dutch revise their 'flawed' laws on terrorist activity.[73]

Repatriation of prisoners

Although British governments have fought hard to break down the barriers to the movement of political offenders between jurisdictions, they have taken a somewhat different line regarding the movement of sentenced political prisoners. In November 1992, the long-awaited Ferrers committee Report of the Interdepartmental Working Group's Review of the Provisions for the Transfer of Prisoners Between UK Jurisdictions was placed in the House of Commons library. The long-standing issue behind the report concerns the position of the small number of Irish prisoners being held in Britain for politically-related offences. For twenty years these prisoners have been protesting against the refusal of the Home Office to transfer them back to Northern Ireland. It has stood behind eight different reasons for refusing transfer over the years.[74]

While transfer from Northern Ireland to Britain has always been easy, moves in the other direction have generally been refused, or only conceded after considerable lobbying. Between 1973 and 1987, 57 prisoners were moved from the North to Britain while only 15 were moved in the other direction.[75] The suspicion has always been that it is easier to be transferred to Britain because such requests generally come from ex-military personnel or loyalists, whereas the transfers in the other direction mainly involve republicans. Between 1985 and 1990, 229 requests were made for permanent transfer to the North from prisons in England and Wales, resulting in 32 transfers or a 14% success rate. The success rate in the other direction, albeit based on much smaller numbers (27), is 33% over the same period. Among those successfully applying for transfer to Britain were British Army agent Brian Nelson and Private Thain, the only serving British soldier to have been convicted of murder in Northern Ireland, who was released from a life sentence after less than two-and-a-half years. In the 1970s two men died on hunger strike while seeking repatriation to the North. After a prolonged hunger strike lasting 216 days and which included 166 days of forced feeding, Marian and Dolores Price were transferred to Northern Ireland in 1975 and were released in 1980 and 1981. By 1991, there were 38 Irish Category A prisoners in British jails whose offences were 'related to paramilitary activity'. Among these were Roy Walsh, William Armstrong and Paul Holmes, jailed in 1973 along with the Price sisters and three others for causing and plotting explosions. They caused no fatalities but were nevertheless given life sentences. Gerard Kelly, one of 38 who escaped from the H Blocks in 1983, was another involved in the case. He was later captured in Holland and extradited back to the North, a condition of the Dutch court being that the British authorities drop his life sentence, which they did. The court regarded the offence for which Kelly had received life as a political one. Kelly was released in 1989. The other two in the case, Hugh Feeney and Martin Brady, were released not long afterwards. Walsh, Armstrong and Holmes remain in prison and have had their requests for transfer repeatedly rejected. In 1991 they were told that they will next be considered for release in 1994. Finally, the three were transferred to Northern Ireland in November 1992.

Another Irish prisoner in Britain, John McComb, who is serving a fixed 17 year sentence, sought a judicial review of the Home Office refusal to grant a transfer. The Home Secretary turned down the transfer application on the grounds that, if transferred, McComb would be released earlier in Northern Ireland because the rules on remission are different. McComb's case was that this is an unlawful criterion since transfer decisions are supposed to be about prisoner welfare.[76] Justice Taylor, in rejecting McComb's case, argued that it was quite reasonable for the Home Secretary to consider sentence length in his decision.

It is evident from the Ferrers Report that when the 'principle' of upholding 'the integrity of the original sentence outweighs the compassionate circumstances involved,' as it seems to do in Irish political cases, then a refusal of transfer may result. But the important point is that this practice, adopted in the case of Irish political offenders with respect to transfers within the United Kingdom, seems to be setting a precedent for the British approach to the European Convention on the Transfer of Sentenced Persons: 'the United Kingdom's approach in such cases reflects that adopted for internal transfers'.[77]

The government has now agreed to implement the Ferrers Report recommendations. Prisoners will be transferred but only on a temporary basis. The prisoners and campaign groups had sought transfer as of right. The main change in policy is that 'crimes undeserving of public sympathy' have been deleted from the criteria for refusing transfer. However, a permanent transfer can be refused on the grounds that it will result in a substantial reduction in sentence. The idea that transferred prisoners might benefit from shorter sentences because of different remission rates (up to 1989, prisoners in Northern Ireland got 50% remission) and different lifer review considerations, has meant Home Office resistance to transfer. However, under the new system, the 'temporarily' transferred prisoners will remain under the British sentencing regime. Those given life in Britain will serve around seven years longer than those sentenced in Northern Ireland, partly due to Leon Britain's 1983 decision that 'terrorist murderers' (amongst others) should serve a minimum of 20 years.

The repatriation question also concerns the Republic of Ireland. The Dublin government has failed to ratify the European Convention on the Transfer of Sentenced Persons, even though it signed it in 1986, mainly because its prisons are already overcrowded and it fears large numbers would be involved. This is challenged by groups campaigning on the issue, notably the Dublin-based Irish Commission for Prisoners Overseas which raised the Irish government's non-ratification with the Council of Europe's Committee of Experts on the Operation of Conventions in the Penal Field in May 1992. The ICPO has now convinced the government that the numbers seeking transfer, after an initial groundswell of 30-40, will be in the region of 5 to 7 applications per year. Repatriation to the South from Britain and elsewhere in Europe is likely to be offset by transfers to the North.[78]

Killings and collusion
Over 3,200 people have now been killed as part of the conflict within Northern Ireland itself and more than ten times that number have been injured. Half the killings took place during the six years 1971 to 1976. Since then, the annual death rate has varied between 113 for 1979 and 54 in 1985. In the last two years the rate has climbed back to close on 100 reflecting the increase in killings by loyalist groups which now outnumber those by the IRA and official armed forces. The resurgence of loyalist attacks has featured firstly members of Sinn Féin, including elected councillors, and secondly attacks on places where Catholics are likely to be

congregated, such as the bookmaker's shop on the Ormeau Road which saw five killed in February 1992. In a number of statements, loyalist groups have declared all shades of nationalism and associated cultural groups as legitimate targets, including the SDLP and members of GAA clubs. The IRA, in contrast, has concentrated more on economic targets and a campaign in Britain in recent years - there were 48 attacks recorded by the Home Office in 1992 and the campaign has claimed 26 lives since 1988. It continues to kill members of the official armed forces, as well as those defined as supporting security policies, such as the building workers killed at Teebane crossroads. It has also executed several of its own members found to be supplying information to RUC SB, a reflection of the increasingly intelligence/informer-based nature of the conflict.

One of the main controversies of the conflict concerns the status of victims and what this says about the relationships between official and unofficial armed forces. Between 1969 and 1990, loyalist groups killed 11 members of the official armed forces but republican groups killed between 850 and 1,000 (depending on which set of figures is used).[79] Over 80% of loyalist killings have been of randomly targeted Catholics, whereas 'deliberate sectarian killings' of Protestants amount to around 7% of republican killings.[80] Army and RUC undercover units did not kill a member of a loyalist paramilitary group between 1976 and 1987.[81] Between November 1982 and January 1992, on-duty RUC and Army personnel killed 75 people, many of these in disputed circumstances.[82]

Increasingly, different moral and political constructions are being placed on violence, depending on the perpetrators. In the midst of a spate of loyalist killings in the autumn of 1991, Official Unionist MP John Taylor, in a widely reported speech, said: 'the harsh reality is that as one walks down the street or goes into work, one out of every three Roman Catholics one meets is either a supporter of murder or worse still a murderer'.[83] There is a growing idea that the recent upsurge in loyalist violence is expressive of a new 'loyalist alienation' associated with the failure of constitutional talks and growing levels of unemployment. Certainly, the Chief Constable and British politicians have adopted the position implying that loyalists are not entirely culpable for their violence in that they are only responding to the actions of the IRA. For instance, former Secretary of State for Northern Ireland, Peter Brooke, has written, 'I think it is significant that the Provisional Irish Republican Army, which offers the main, if not the only threat in Northern Ireland, has not advanced one millimetre towards securing its declared political objectives. Obviously, it is still the determined and effective action of the security forces which bear most heavily upon the Provisionals, and our first priority is to ensure that there is no let up here'.[84] Similarly, Annesley, the RUC Chief Constable, has stated that 'the principal resources of the RUC are and will continue to be deployed against the Provisional IRA... Almost all loyalist activity is reactive to that threat'.[85] Again, there were echoes of this selectivity in Prime Minister John Major's statements during his visit to President Clinton in February 1993. When asked about human rights in Northern Ireland he retorted by saying that the only threat to human rights came from the bombers.[86]

Statements such as these not only encourage the conclusion that security policy is partisan, but also the view that there is co-operation of some sort and at some level between loyalist groups, the Army and RUC, otherwise known as 'collusion'. Critics of this view, while accepting that 'rogue' members of the security forces have assisted loyalist groups, usually deny that collusion exists by saying that they have found no evidence of an official or stated policy, or of solid links between loyalists and senior Army/RUC personnel.[87] This judgement needs to be put alongside the following. Firstly, central to current security policy is the widespread recruitment of informers. There is nothing accidental about this: it is a systematic part of counter-terrorist policy. At any one time, as events have shown on many occasions, RUC SB (and less often FRU and MI5) will have informers placed at some level within the IRA and loyalist groups. On grounds of protecting their sources, handlers will turn a blind eye to the participation of informers in operations. The Nelson case illustrates this very clearly although whether or not there are major differences between RUC SB and military intelligence in terms of what they are prepared to tolerate is less clear. In terms of collusion, the use of informers allows the authorities the choice of what to do with the information they acquire. The informer system creates relationships with proscribed organisations through which the authorities can encourage, modify, ignore, intercept or prevent operations.

Secondly, there does not need to be a conspiracy or direct order for groups to know that a particular strategy or action has been signalled in high places - even if perpetrators still risk being caught in the act. Three weeks before the murder of Belfast solicitor Patrick Finucane in February 1989, British government Minister Douglas Hogg publicly stated (and refused to retract) that in Northern Ireland 'a number of solicitors' were 'unduly sympathetic to the Irish Republican Army'. From the point of view of loyalist groups, this is tantamount to a British government Minister declaring that a few solicitors are 'legitimate targets'. Finucane was killed by a British Army weapon, sold to a loyalist paramilitary group, according to evidence revealed at the inquest. His murder has also been linked to the Nelson case.[88]

Thirdly, the social composition of the RIR and RUC is such that one in ten of all Protestant men works in the security services in some capacity.[89] This means that, 'Protestants can be said to have a vested interest in the continuing emergency . . . (and) the policy of Ulsterisation has effectively created an armed Protestant force of considerable magnitude'.[90] An estimated 45,000 people passed through the ranks of the UDR during its 21 year history.[91] There is a further implication which is that the social background of those in the security industry means that some are likely to have a degree of identification with, and local knowledge of, loyalist groups, both of which may be used at an informal level to facilitate such groups. One study of the RUC has concluded that 'the RUC is not selective or partisan' in its law enforcement and that most rank-and-file officers are able 'to divorce their opinions from their conduct': It acknowledges, however, that the conflict 'introduces features that are core characteristics of RUC occupational culture... most notably Protestantism and sectarianism', even if 'both are less prominent than might be imagined from the social composition of the force'.[92] In addition, police resources and strategies differ according to Catholic and Protestant areas - obviously the simple absence of police can assist a loyalist attack.[93]

The strongest evidence that social composition translates into practical assistance for loyalist groups, however, comes from UDR involvement in killings and other activities. Regarding the 1970s, one study suggests that, 'over the first ten years of the UDR's existence nearly 200 members were convicted in the courts'. The same study goes on to give a detailed examination of 113 killings by loyalist groups in the 1980s, concluding that in 70 of these 'collusion was a likely factor'.[94]

A fourth factor which needs to be looked at in the collusion debate is related to the last point. Information from RUC and Army intelligence files regularly finds its way to loyalist groups. The RUC frequently approach individuals to warn them that their personal details are in the hands of loyalist groups.[95] The most dramatic illustration of this process occurred in the late 1980s when the Ulster Freedom Fighters started to publicise information it had secured from the RUC and UDR. The group did this because it wanted to prove that its killings were not random or 'sectarian' but well-targeted on the basis of lists of republican suspects held by the security forces. The information leaks mainly took the form of photomontages of these 'suspects'. It was during the Stevens' Inquiry into the leaks that Brian Nelson was arrested.[96] When the Inquiry started, Nelson had over 1,000 leaked documents in his possession. Before he was arrested he returned these to his military intelligence handlers for safe keeping. For four months, FRU resisted handing these documents over to the inquiry team. The Stevens' Inquiry resulted in 51 people being convicted. Ten of these were members of the UDR, eight of whom were charged with having extra ammunition and two of whom were accused of taking photomontages from a police station. One British soldier was charged with leaking a photomontage which ended up on the front page of The Sun, but no RUC officers were charged.

A final point is that some forms of collusion need not be extensive in order to have great impact. Following the Nelson trial, it has been alleged that British intelligence had full knowledge of Nelson's trip to South Africa to organise a substantial arms shipment which included 200 AK47 rifles, a dozen rocket launchers, 90 pistols and 500 fragmentation grenades. One source has even suggested that Nelson's visit was cleared by a government Minister as well as the Ministry of Defence.[97] The RUC seized about a third of the shipment but the remainder has never come to light, other than from its usage in subsequent loyalist killings.[98] The latest allegation is that British intelligence may have had two agents involved in the South African deal. Panorama's John Ware has described the weapon's shipment as 'one of the least publicised and biggest intelligence scandals in two decades of Northern Ireland's dirty war... You've got a massive weapons shipment going into the hands of terrorists who are now exceeding the killing rate of the IRA. For the intelligence services to have failed to prevent that shipment coming in when they had such an early lead to my mind demands an answer'.[99]

In many respects, the language and concepts which surround the status of the conflict are confusing. Sometimes it is described in terms of war, or a terrorist war, or a war against terrorism, or a conflict between the state and terrorism. Sometimes it is referred to as a fight between terrorism and human rights. Nevertheless, the British government is obliged by its policies and the practices of the agencies for which it is responsible, to be somewhat ambiguous about human rights.

Human rights

Approaching the Northern Ireland conflict from a human rights perspective has gathered considerable momentum lately, both in non-governmental organisations and within state bodies such as The Standing Advisory Commission on Human Rights.

SACHR advocates that the European Convention on Human Rights be incorporated into domestic law. This would have the advantage that those with serious human rights grievances would have a swifter remedy than that available through the various European mechanisms. The problem for the government is that it would have to drop certain powers and practices if it were to do so, such as the seven day detention power under the PTA. It has little incentive to speed up the legal processes which test its powers against international human rights standards.

Britain is a signatory to the UN Covenant on Civil and Political Rights which it ratified in 1976. At the time, the government entered a derogation with respect to Northern Ireland which it withdrew in 1984. It derogated from the European Convention as long ago as 1957 with respect to Northern Ireland. This was also withdrawn in 1984 and, as a result: 'Northern Ireland is no longer officially designated under the international instruments as a territory where "a public emergency threatening the life of the nation" exists'.[100] But after the Brogan case concerning seven-day detention in 1988, a further derogation was entered which leaves the question of whether Britain is justified in doing this with reference to the circumstances pertaining in Northern Ireland at the present time.

British Ministers have shown a cavalier attitude to international human rights processes. For example, in August 1992 the International Federation of Human Rights submitted a five page report to the Economic and Social Council of the United Nations concerning 'the ongoing intimidation of lawyers in Northern Ireland by elements within the police force'. It also covered the absence of safeguards to prevent the ill-treatment of detainees held under 'emergency' legislation.

The IFHR report states that 'detainees regularly report that police officers make threats against the lives of their lawyers, question their lawyers' professionalism and suggest that their lawyers are in the pay of or are members of terrorist groupings'. It is being increasingly asserted by defenders of current interrogation powers and practices that detainees must be denied access to legal representatives in the early stages of detention to prevent lawyers assisting or warning the detainee's associates in some way. The assertion is that there is collusion between elements within the legal profession and the IRA.

Professor Claire Palley, Britain's representative on the UN Sub-Commission on the Prevention of Discrimination and Protection of Minorities (which received the report), commented that the concerns about the intimidation of lawyers 'appear to be wholly justified'. She also said that suspicions of official collusion in solicitor Pat Finucane's murder could only be put to rest by an independent inquiry.

Former Security Minister, Michael Mates, responded by accusing Palley of making unsubstantiated allegations, and by stating that 'the only people in Northern Ireland who do not respect human rights are the terrorists'. Mates, however, is aware that a dossier of 268 cases of alleged ill-treatment of detainees was submitted to the UN's Commission on Torture in November 1991. These cases involve 143 instances in which RUC officers allegedly made death threats against detainees' solicitors.

Pursuing cases under the European Convention on Human Rights, while providing an international mechanism for addressing human rights grievances, has limitations.[101] The process of taking cases to Europe is time-consuming and costly. More importantly, several important judgements have been delivered over the years in support of the British government's position. Internment, for example, was judged to be acceptable. The notorious five techniques developed by the British Army in Malaya, Kenya and Aden, which involved prolonged interrogation alongside sleep deprivation, no food, white noise, wall-standing and the use of hoods over suspects heads, and which were used in Northern Ireland in the early 1970s, did not amount to torture according to the Commission. It was also found that neither the refusal of special category status nor the treatment of prisoners on the no-wash protest in the late 1970s was in breach of the Convention.[102]

Some local groups within Northern Ireland have taken up the government rhetoric regarding the real abusers of human rights, and have sought to persuade civil liberties lobbies and human rights bodies to examine and monitor the conduct of paramilitary organisations. Civil liberties organisations explicitly condemn terrorism so are not morally at odds with such a stance. They do, however, face the practical difficulty of the problems surrounding international law when it comes to human rights abuses by paramilitary groups. International humanitarian law, such as the Hague Convention and the 1949 Geneva Convention (and subsequent Protocols which sought to define the nature of conflicts within countries as opposed to between them) has no enforcement machinery. Besides, the British government has refused to sign the protocols under which it might be possible to define Northern Ireland as an 'armed conflict'. As Campbell writes, 'before anyone rushes into applying humanitarian law to Northern Ireland, some markers must be put down: a) it must apply across the board, to all paramilitary organisations and emanations of the state; b) it must not be used to divert resources or attention from abuses by the state; and c) it must be applied by independent competent organisations, without political axes to grind - preferably established international groups who can bring sufficient clout to bear'.[103]

Conclusion

This article has tackled seven aspects of the Northern Ireland conflict which have significance for the construction of the new European state. It began with the situation of the armed forces, their expansion in the 1990s and the enormous financial costs involved. Regarding the British Army, although the Defence Committee says that the 40,000 cut in troops under Options for Change is 'Treasury-led', the government had chosen to implement the cut at a time when it judged that its NATO commitment and the changing threat to Europe was such that it could manage with a smaller army. Yet the Northern Ireland commitment is now under some strain and in itself has come to dominate the Army's function. This presents two basic options. The first is to find ways to sustain the Northern Ireland commitment and, accordingly, it has been proposed that more forces are recruited locally to free up the British infantry to do the real soldiering. The problem with this is that, in the same way in which it is not exactly clear how the PTA prevents terrorism, it is not at all self-evident as to how the growing numbers of armed forces and their form of deployment is actually defeating loyalist or republican armed groups. Even the notion that large numbers of armed forces contains the conflict is looking increasingly dubious. On the contrary, the more deeply institutionalised the military conflict becomes - the low-intensity equivalent of escalation - the more it takes on a life and momentum of its own, with all the self-perpetuating characteristics which we associate with all large institutions. At the level of political culture, Britain's defence of its role in Northern Ireland brings to Europe the idea that the militarisation of society is the appropriate response to political conflicts. The second, alternative option is to explore imaginatively how militarisation is put into reverse.

British government perceptions of the changing European threat are also important for the restructuring of the intelligence agencies. Counter-terrorism, and specifically combating the IRA, is now MI5's major priority. It is on this basis that the Security Service is seeking to rescue its tarnished reputation and to resist increasing pressure for more accountability. Countering the IRA threat is also an important factor for MI5 in forging its role in Europe. This ranges from the surveillance of Irish communities in Germany, the Netherlands, France etc. to developing mechanisms of co-operation between European intelligence agencies geared towards the British agenda in relation to the Northern Ireland conflict. TREVI Group I, for example, has agreed to intensify regular exchanges of detailed information on terrorist groups, their techniques, logistic supports, financing and the incidents they provoke. Member states must communicate without delay any information they have about groups or suspects in which another state is interested. It has also been agreed to examine the legal means required to allow police investigations into the financing of terrorist activities and, no doubt, the powers under the Prevention of Terrorism Act will be the model.[104] And during the debate on the renewal of the PTA in March 1993, the Home Secretary announced that several new offences would be incorporated into the Criminal Justice Act. Failure to report suspicion or knowledge of terrorist funds or transactions will carry a five year sentence, while those knowingly in possession of terrorist assets will face up to 14 years.[105] The TREVI Group is to achieve the co-ordination of counter-terrorist measures through a network of liaison officers who will enjoy 'diplomatic immunity'.[106]

Another example of how Britain's secret state is being pursued in Europe, is the proposed Council Regulation on security procedures - the UK-style European Official Secrets measure which was withdrawn at the Edinburgh summit in December 1992. Should this ever be introduced, article 12 allows for the political vetting of appointments in relation to the Commission's work along the lines of practices which have become all too familiar in Northern Ireland.[107] It appears that the political vetting of Irish appointees to the Commission by MI5 may already be in train with or without the proposed Regulation.[108]

Lastly, the gestures towards accountability embodied in the Security Service Act are meaningless when it comes to covert operations in Northern Ireland. The intelligence agencies appear to be immune from legal and political accountability, even if some of their contract workers are occasionally sacrificed on the altar of criminal justice. When asked in the Westminster parliament what steps he had taken to investigate the involvement of the security services in terrorism following the conviction of Brian Nelson, Michael Mates replied, 'the investigation of any allegations of criminal conduct is a matter for the RUC'.[109] This sounds plausible enough until it is remembered that MI5 is bound by the law not to reveal evidence of MI5 unlawful actions.[110] Furthermore, covert operations are protected in court cases and at inquests through the Secretary of State for Northern Ireland's power to issue a Public Interest Immunity Certificate.[111]

One of the most revealing aspects of Europeanisation is the physical fortification of the border. Since the mid-1980s the process of EC integration has presented a new challenge and framework for the politics of the Northern Ireland conflict. In response to international pressures, Britain calculated early on that formal intergovernmental co-operation with the Irish was preferable to US or EC interference, whatever the risks in terms of unionist opposition. As Coughlan writes: 'despite, or perhaps because of, Ireland's strategic importance Britain's failure to solve the northern problem in recent years has become an increasing embarrassment vis-a-vis the Americans and the continental countries. The Foreign Office hopes that the Hillsborough Agreement, which prevents Dublin from openly criticising Britain about partition and which seeks to tie Dublin into British security policy in the north, will remove the embarrassment'.[112]

The fortification of the border has become the basis around which cross-border policing and intelligence liaison has been developed. At times the relationships at the level of policing and between the British and Irish governments have been difficult, especially when proposals or actions seem to threaten Irish sovereignty, or when the British appear to ignore Irish representations on the North. Recent border security policy has been of some comfort to unionists, who welcome both the restrictions on cross-border traffic and the mobilisation of the Irish authorities in increasing levels of counter-terrorist work. They remain nervous, however, that British/Irish co-operation may further weaken the prospects of Northern Ireland remaining part of the UK. Unionists are more likely to make calls for the sealing of the border than to go along with the SDLP's idea of an all-Ireland anti-terrorist force.[113] Even self-styled 'realists' who advocate North/South co-operation on security, industrial development, tourism, transport, energy and so on, find it necessary to settle the constitutional question once and for all in favour of the union.[114]

The physical build-up of the border, however, directly contradicts Article 8a of the Single European Act which defines the single market as an area without frontiers and which allows the free movement of goods, services, capital and persons. Although the Act is qualified by the declaration permitting member states to take necessary measures against terrorism, the fortification of the North/South border is of dubious legality and certainly contradicts the spirit of EC integration. As a counter-terrorist measure, however, the fortified border suits Britain's opposition to the general relaxation of border controls. And should the Irish government depart from the British position - it recently adopted the 'Bangemann Wave' but went no further - 'London would be obliged to rethink its Irish border policy'.[115] One implication is that the border would acquire the status and controls of an 'external' border, requiring all travellers to produce passports or identity cards.[116] The Home Office is now studying new technology which will be able to check travellers when they press a thumb or hand against a screen.

A similar complex of political interests surrounds the question of extradition and the movement of sentenced prisoners. Britain has persuaded the Irish government, if not always the Irish judiciary, to get rid of the safeguards which have traditionally surrounded the consideration of extradition in cases of political suspects. A large chunk of extradition traffic between EC countries and the UK concerns Irish political offenders and this is driving Britain's policy of seeking yet further relaxations in procedures and safeguards. But this attitude does not extend to sentenced persons. There has been a long-term reluctance within the Home Office to agree to requests by Irish political prisoners to be transferred to Northern Ireland. Although the recommendations of the Ferrers Report were accepted in November 1992, there was little additional movement by mid-March 1993.[117] This is matched by the Irish government's reluctance to ratify the European Convention on the Transfer of Sentenced Persons. Whatever domestic reasons are put up for this, there may be lingering fears within the Home Office that ratification may provide a 'backdoor' route to Ireland for the prisoners it has been refusing to transfer over the past twenty years.

The penultimate section of this Chapter reviewed recent developments in the characterisation of the conflict. There is a continuing debate over the morality and politics of the killings and the status of victims. This in turn is reflected in arguments over the role of official armed forces in the conflict. The formal British government position of neutrality is that, 'the first priority of government in Northern Ireland will always be the defeat of terrorism, from whatever side of the community it comes'.[118] But this is gradually being replaced by a doctrine which describes loyalist terrorism as less culpable than IRA terrorism - loyalist groups are 'reacting', 'retaliating' and 'defending', exactly the language used by loyalist groups themselves. As such, security resources are primarily directed against the IRA and nationalist communities. The primary objective is to 'combat', though sometimes 'defeat' IRA terrorism, language which appears to have become enshrined in the workings of the TREVI Group. The sense of partisanship which comes from this, is confirmed by the social composition of the security forces and further by continuing evidence of involvement with loyalist groups - collusion.

The conventional retort to the above concerns is that, whatever the sins of the security forces with respect to human rights abuses, these are nothing like as serious as occur in South and Central America, nor as damaging as those committed by paramilitary organisations, particularly the IRA. Civil liberties organisations, the argument continues, should spend their efforts condemning and monitoring paramilitary human rights violations, because without these, there would be no abuses by the state. It was pointed out, however, that this adds little or nothing to the resolution of issues or the prevention of practices. Unless there is some way of enforcing humanitarian law, or getting all parties to a conflict to recognise the force of the Geneva Convention, then moral invective will achieve little by way of de-escalating the Northern Ireland conflict.

Wars of whatever intensity can be ended either militarily or politically. Britain's policy towards the conflict is to keep the military aspects separate from the 'constitutional' and 'political' aspects. This has contributed to the growing militarisation of Northern Ireland and has failed to produce a locally workable political relationship between the British government and the political parties it is prepared to talk to. Its European agenda with regard to Northern Ireland is to persuade other countries that the emerging structures of intelligence and policing are geared towards its stewardship of the Northern Ireland conflict. In so doing, to quote Chomsky, it has 'little use for instruments that might lapse into excessive independence'.[119]

References

1. Tony Benn criticises traditional responses to the secret state which have either been to dismiss it as a conspiratorial fantasy, or to accept it as the natural order of things. See Benn T, 'The Case for Dismantling the Secret State', New Left Review, 1991, pp127-130.

2. See Rolston B, 'Containment and its Failure: The British State and the Control of Conflict in Northern Ireland' and George A, 'The Discipline of Terrorology', chapters 7 and 4 of George A, (ed.) *Western State Terrorism*, Cambridge: Polity Press, 1991.

3. *Britain's Army for the 90s: Commitments and Resources, Defence Committee, Second Report*, HC 1992/93: 306. London: HMSO, 1993. p32.

4. Hillyard P, 'Political and Social Dimensions of Emergency Law in Northern Ireland' in Jennings A, (ed) *Justice Under Fire: The Abuse of Civil Liberties in Northern Ireland*, London: Pluto Press, 1988, pp191-212.

5. Rowthorn B and Wayne N, *Northern Ireland: The Political Economy of Conflict*, Cambridge: Polity Press, 1988, p46.

6. For the political background to this change, see 'Reforming the UDR?', Statewatch no 4, September/October 1991, pp3-4.

7. Ryder C, *The Ulster Defence Regiment: An Instrument of Peace?* London: Methuen, p184.

8. See Statewatch Vol 2, no 1, p11.

9. Op cit. p.ix-x.

10. British Army HQ and RUC HQ Press Offices.

11. Defence Committee, op cit. p34.

12. Colonel Michael Dewar, 'The Military Overdraft', The Guardian, 29.1.93.

13. Op. cit p33.

14. Northern Ireland Office Memorandum to the *Home Affairs Select Committee on Practical Police Co-operation in the European Community, HC 1989/90: 363-II*, p175.

15. 'Border craters prevent widow from visiting husband's grave', Irish News, 10.7.92.

16. Police Authority for Northern Ireland, Statement of Account, HC Papers 1991/2: 69.

17. The costs of keeping the Army in Northern Ireland are included in the Supply Estimates under Class I, Vote 1: personnel costs, support and other services; Vote 2: defence procurement; and Vote 4: works services, but they are not disaggregated. Hansard Written Answers, 1st July, 1992, col. 651.

18. *Eleventh Report of the Defence Committee, HC Papers, 1990/1:394*, p76.

19. *The Government's Expenditure Plans, 1982/3 to 1984/5, Cmnd. 8494-II.*

20. A recent Irish government publication gives a figure of £218m for 1990/1. See *Ireland in Europe: A Shared Challenge. Economic Co-operation on the Island of Ireland in an Integrated Europe.* Dublin: Stationery Office, p18.

21. Cm 1908.

22. Justice minister, Maire Geoghegan-Quinn, Dail debates, 1.4.93.

23. Hansard, 27.10.92, written answer col 602.

24. See Rolston B and Tomlinson M *Unemployment in West Belfast: The Obair Report'*, Belfast: Beyond the Pale Publications, 1988, pp45-52. Also, Rowthorn B and Wayne N, *Northern Ireland: The Political Economy of Conflict*, Cambridge: Polity Press, 1988, p93-99.

25. Irish Times 24.4.80. Cited in Burke M, *Intelligence Services in Ireland*, Washington: Irish American Unity Conference, 1989.

26. Urban M, *Big Boys Rules: The SAS and the Secret Struggle against the IRA*, London: Faber and Faber, 1992, p245.

27. See Statewatch July/August, 1992, p11.

28. Op cit p247.

29. Foot P, *Who Framed Colin Wallace*, London: Pan Books, 1990.

30. Colin Wallace, who himself was involved in the 'dirty tricks' campaigns of this period, gives a useful account of MI5 incompetence in The Oldie, 15.5.92, pp12-13. See also, Lobster, No. 11, pp. 41-45.

31. Philip C and Taylor A, *Inside the SAS*, London: Bloomsbury, 1992, p64.

32. Urban, op cit, p95. 14 Intelligence Co. is an Army undercover surveillance unit which is about 200 strong.

33. See Statewatch, March/April 1992. Also, British Intelligence, Brian Nelson and the Rearming of the Loyalist Death Squads, Belfast, 1993.

34. See The Guardian, 17.12.91 and 18.12.91.

35. Hansard, 8.5.92, col. 302.

36. Police Review, 5.6.92, p1028.

37. Urban, op cit, p97.

38. Intelligence Newsletter, 5.11.92, p5.

39. Police Journal, October 1992. The RUC already has direct access to Britain's PNC2 computer which came online in 1991. Police Review 20.12.91.

40. FRU had knowledge of at least four other targets who were later murdered, including the solicitor Pat Finucane. At least 16 people on Nelson's target list have been killed or wounded, including 8 since his arrest. FRU is implicated in this because it helped Nelson to organise and streamline his UDA intelligence files, in some instances assisting with photographs of intended targets and premises.

41. Op cit, pp248-253.

42. The most publicised of these killings were in Gibraltar in 1988. See Bolton R, *Death on the Rock and Other Stories*, London: Allen, 1990. Miller D, *Whose Truth? The Media and the Gibraltar Killings*, Glasgow University Media Group, 1989. Jack I, *Gibraltar*, Granta, 25, 1988. See also Committee on the Administration of Justice, *Inquests and Disputed Killings in Northern Ireland*, Belfast: CAJ, 1992. *Report of the Public Inquiry into the Killing of Fergal Caraher and the Wounding of MicÅal Caraher 30th Dec. 1990*, Irish National Congress/Cullyhana Justice Group, 1992.

43. RUC Chief Constable's Annual Report for 1991.

44. Northern Ireland Office Memorandum to the *Home Affairs Select Committee on Practical Police Co-operation in the European Community, HC 1989/90: 363-II*, p175.

45. Sunday Tribune, 10.1.93.

46. See Statewatch, January/February 1993. Also, Porter, S. *Unhealthy Surveillance: Investigating Public Health in South Armagh*, Critical Public Health (forthcoming).

47. See Hansard, Written Answers, 17 February, 1993. A statement by the Army discussing emissions and claiming that any radar equipment which it uses has power outputs one five-hundred-thousandth of those coming from radar at airports, was carried in the Newry Reporter, 23.7.92.

48. For an assessment of the impact of EC integration on border communities see O'Dowd L, 'Strengthening the Border on the Road to Maastricht', Irish Reporter, no 9, 1983, pp12-15. (ISSN 0791-4067)

49. Murray R, *The SAS in Ireland*, Cork: Mercier Press, 1990, pp175-182.

50. Urban M, *Big Boys' Rules: The SAS and the Secret Struggle against the IRA*, London: Faber and Faber, 1992, p29.

51. Ryder C, *The RUC: A Force Under Fire*, London: Methuen, 1989, p133.

52. *Home Affairs Select Committee, Practical Police Co-operation in the European Community, HC 1989/90: 363-i*, p6.

53. A Garda officer, the brother-in-law of the Minister for Justice, was to appear in court at Dowra (in the South) for assaulting James McGovern who lived in the North. The case was dismissed when McGovern failed to turn up, the reason being that he had been arrested and detained by the RUC, allegedly at the request of a senior officer in Dublin.

54. Brewer J et al, *The Police, Public Order and the State*, London: Macmillan, 1988, p78-9.

55. Agreement between the Government of the United Kingdom of Great Britain and Northern Ireland and the Government of the Republic of Ireland.

56. Northern Ireland Information Service press release, 3.2.93.

57. Northern Ireland Office, The Day of the Men and Women of Peace must surely Come, Belfast: NIO, 1989, p32.

58. NIO Memorandum to the *Home Affairs Select Committee on Practical Police Co-operation in the European Community, HC 1989/90: 363-II*, p176.

59. On 20 March 1989, the IRA ambushed a car carrying two senior RUC officers on their way back from a meeting with their counterparts in Dundalk, killing Border Superintendent Bob Buchanan and Chief Superintendent Harry Breen.

60. See 'Last Barrier in Europe', Sunday Tribune 10.1.93.

61. Hansard, 29.10.92 col 1118.

62. Ryder C, op cit, p370.

63. Hansard, 10.5.90, col 390.

64. Hansard, 2.5.91, col 418.

65. *Home Affairs Select Committee on Practical Police Co-operation in the European Community, HC 1989/90: 363-I*, p xv.

66. Farrell M, *Sheltering the Fugitive? The Extradition of Irish Political Offenders*, Cork: Mercier Press, 1985, p31.

67. Op cit, p61.

68. State Research Bulletin, no. 8, October/November 1978, pp6-7.

69. Farrell M, 'Extradition: The Life and Times of the Political Exception', Irish Reporter, Summer 1990, p9.

70. *Home Affairs Select Committee, Practical Police Co-operation in the European Community, HC 1989/90: 363-i*, p2.

71. Home Office, press release, 12.10.92.

72. Stanbrook I and Stanbrook C, *Extradition: The Law and Practice*, Chichester: Barry Rose Publishers, 1980.

73. Irish News 13.7.91.

74. The Committee for the Transfer of Irish Prisoners, Double Sentence, Belfast, 1991.

75. Rolston B and Tomlinson M, 'The Challenge Within: Prisons and Propaganda in Northern Ireland', in Tomlinson M et al (eds) *Whose Law and Order? Aspects of Crime and Social Control in Irish Society*, Belfast: Sociological Association of Ireland, 1988, pp167-192.

76. Irish News, 26.3.91.

77. Ferrers Report, p9.

78. Newsletter for Irish Prisoners Overseas, no 10, January/February 1993, p2.

79. For a discussion of 'Who Kills Who', see Statewatch, January/February 1992, pp9-11.

80. *In Whose Name? Britain's Denial of Peace in Ireland*, London: Troops Out Movement, 1991, p18.

81. Urban, op cit, p238.

82. This total excludes cases where there are allegations of collusion with loyalist groups, and cases involving off-duty personnel. Committee on the Administration of Justice, *Inquests and Disputed Killings in Northern Ireland*, Belfast: CAJ, 1992.

83. Statewatch, January/February 1992, p10.

84. 'Politicians, Soldiers and the Place of the Security Forces', RUSI Journal, April 1992, p2.

85. Interview on BBC Radio Ulster, Sunday 20th October 1991.

86. Although the RUC has recently warned that loyalists were planning a bombing campaign in the South, it is generally acknowledged that they lack explosives. Major could only have been referring to the IRA.

87. Bruce S, *The Red Hand: Protestant Paramilitaries in Northern Ireland*, Oxford: Oxford University Press, 1992. Dillon M, *The Dirty War*, London: Arrow Books, 1990.

88. International Federation of Human Rights and Committee on the Administration of Justice, *Report to Sub-Commission on Prevention of Discrimination and Protection of Minorities*, 4th August 1992.

89. This figure includes prison officers and other security jobs. Rowthorn B and Wayne N, *Northern Ireland: The Political Economy of Conflict*, Cambridge: Polity Press, 1988, p112.

90. Hillyard P, 'Political and Social Dimensions of Emergency Law in Northern Ireland' in Jennings A, (ed) *Justice Under Fire: The Abuse of Civil Liberties in Northern Ireland*, London: Pluto Press, 1988, p200.

91. Statewatch, September/October 1991, p3.

92. Brewer J, *Inside the RUC: Routine Policing in a Divided Society*, Oxford: Clarendon Press, p 271 & 247.

93. West Belfast Catholics often remark that the way the RUC and Army set up road blocks means that it is easy to drive into the area but not to get out. People in the Protestant Shankill area of West Belfast became quite indignant at the untypical police presence and arrests in the area at the beginning of March 1993. Irish News, 5.3.93.

94. The Ulster Defence Regiment: the Loyalist Militia, Dublin: Sinn Fëin Publicity Department, p8 & 72.

95. This, of course, does not necessarily mean that information has been passed on to loyalist groups by police officers. In Gillen v. The Chief Constable the court ruled that potential targets were not entitled to be given any of the details which had led the RUC to warn them.

96. The authorities in Belfast and London were aware of leaks to loyalist groups at least two years prior to the setting up of the Stevens' Inquiry.

97. Private Eye, cited in *British Intelligence: Brian Nelson and the Re-Arming of the Loyalist Death Squads*, Belfast, 1993, p14.

98. For example, Michael Stone used some of these weapons to kill three mourners in Belfast's Milltown cemetery who were attending the funerals of the three IRA members killed by the SAS in Gibraltar. Statewatch, March/April 1992, pp 5-6. See also Dillon M, *Stone Cold: the true story of Michael Stone and the Milltown massacre*, London: Hutchinson, 1992, pp 105 & 139.

99. BBC Northern Ireland, Spotlight, 18.2.93.

100. Hadden T Boyle K and Campbell C, 'Emergency Law in Northern Ireland: The Context', in Jennings A, (ed) *Justice Under Fire: The Abuse of Civil Liberties in Northern Ireland*, London: Pluto Press, 1988, p22.

101. See Appendix for country by country survey of applications.

102. Hadden et al op cit, p22.

103. Campbell C, 'Humanitarian Law: Not as Simple as it Seems', Just News, Vol. 6 No. 11, December 1991, p7.

104. Under Section 17 of the 1989 Act, there are powers to enable the police to obtain warrants to secure such information they need, for example from banks and building societies, for the general purpose of investigating terrorism. The Emergency Provisions Act 1991 allows for the seizure of documents and computer discs to find out if they are 'of use to terrorists'.

105. Guardian, 13.3.93.

106. Programme of Action relating to the Reinforcement of Police Co-operation and of the Endeavours to Combat Terrorism or other forms of Organized Crime. June 1990.

107. The Political Vetting of Community Work Group, *The Political Vetting of Community Work in Northern Ireland*, Belfast: Northern Ireland Council for Voluntary Action, 1990.

108. See the case of Mary Reid, discussed in Statewatch, March/April, 1993.

109. Hansard, 26.11.92, written answer col 784.

110. Should an MI5 officer disclose evidence of illegal MI5 activities, even to an MP, they are committing a criminal offence under the Security Service Act. The Guardian, 18.2.93.

111. This may be a sensitive issue for the authorities. A recent parliamentary question asking for the numbers of certificates issued since 1972 drew the terse response that there is no central record. Hansard, 30.11.92, written answer col 17. CAJ record two certificates with respect to inquests. See Committee on the Administration of Justice, *Inquests and Disputed Killings in Northern Ireland*, Belfast: CAJ, 1992.

112. Coughlan A, *Fooled Again? The Anglo-Irish Agreement and After*, Cork: Mercier Press, 1986, p42.

113. See Statewatch, January/February 1993 and Irish News, 1.3.93.

114. *Northern Limits: Boundaries of the Attainable in Northern Ireland Politics*, Belfast: Cadogan Group. 1992, p26. For a critique of this position which equates it with hardline unionism, see Anderson J and O'Dowd L, 'Limited Thinking', Fortnight, March 1993, pp30-31.

115. Sunday Telegraph, 17.5.92.

116. At present, driving licences (which in the North have machine readable photographs) and car registrations are the main forms of identification used by the RUC and Army.

117. Hansard 11.3.93.

118. Brooke, op cit, p3.

119. Chomsky is referring to Washington and mass media disdain for the World Court. Chomsky N, *Year 501: The Conquest Continues*, London: Verso, 1993, p21.

The Prevention of Terrorism Acts and the new European state

Paddy Hillyard

Introduction

The Prevention of Terrorism (Temporary Provisions) Act was introduced in 1974 in the wake of the Birmingham bombings. Within a week of the bombings, a bill was presented to Parliament, suggesting that one had already been prepared for some time, and it then passed through all its parliamentary stages without a division and was on the statute book within 24 hours. It was modelled on two different sources. First, it drew upon the Northern Ireland (Emergency Provisions) Act, 1973. This, in turn, was based on the recommendations of a Commission, which was chaired by Lord Diplock, a British High Court judge, to consider legal procedures to deal with political violence in the North of Ireland.[1] Second, it drew upon the Prevention of Violence (Temporary Provisions) Act, 1939. The PTA has now been through three major revisions - 1976, 1984 and 1989 - and was expanded on each occasion. It covers both Northern Ireland and Great Britain.

After third decade on the statute book its permanency belies its title. Although introduced by a Labour government, the Labour Party announced its opposition to it in the early 1980s. In February 1993, however, Mr Kevin McNamara, the Northern Ireland shadow secretary, set out possible pre-conditions for the Labour Party to support it. Although, this was immediately rejected by Mr Kenneth Clarke, the Home Secretary, it is unlikely to be very long before there is a broad consensus among all the political parties on the legislation, which was described, when introduced by the then Home Secretary, Roy Jenkins, as 'unprecedented in peacetime' and 'draconian'.[2]

The aim of this chapter is to describe, in broad terms, the provisions of the legislation and to draw out the implications of the existence of the legislation for the development of the European state.

Major provisions

The original Act contained five major elements. The first element radically extended the existing police powers of arrest and detention. It provided the police with the power to arrest anyone on reasonable suspicion of being involved in the preparation, instigation or commission of acts of terrorism. Terrorism is defined as using violence for political ends and includes the use of any violence for the purpose of putting a member of the public, or any section of the public, in fear. What is unique about this arrest power is that it does not require that a specific offence has been committed or that a person is reasonably suspected of having committed any offence. This arises because 'acts of terrorism' are not offences in ordinary criminal law and no specific 'acts of terrorism' are defined. Coupled with this extraordinary arrest power, is the power to detain those arrested for up to 7 days.

The second element provided the Secretary of State with powers to establish a comprehensive system of control at ports and airports. Using mainly delegated powers, a sophisticated system of surveillance coupled with an comprehensive examination process has been established to monitor the movement of people between Britain and Ireland. In effect, a border has been established between the two islands and is policed with similar intensity as the land border between the North of Ireland and the South.

The third element introduced a system of internal exile within the United Kingdom. The Act provides the Secretary of State with the powers to serve an exclusion order on anyone who he or she believes is involved in the preparation, instigation or commission of acts of terrorism and can instruct that the person be prohibited from being in or entering Great Britain or Northern Ireland. The person served with an exclusion order has no right to know the evidence against them and, more importantly, has no right to a trial. The decision to exclude is purely an executive decision.

The fourth element gave the Secretary of state a power of proscription. He or she may proscribe any organisation which appears to him or her to be concerned in, or in promoting or encouraging, terrorism occurring in the United Kingdom and connected with the affairs of Northern Ireland.

The fifth element introduced a wide range of new criminal offences. In relation to the powers at ports and airports, it is an offence to contravene knowingly any prohibition or to fail to comply with any duty or requirement. This effectively abolishes the person's rights to silence and to privacy. There are also a number of new offences relating to activities concerning proscribed organisations. For example, it is an offence to solicit, to collect, or to receive money for such an organisation or being a member of one. Further, it is an offence to break an exclusion order or to help someone to do so.

Finally, and perhaps the most important, it is an offence to withhold information concerning acts of terrorism. This offence effectively prevents journalists investigating aspects of political violence because if they come across information concerning some specific incident they must report the matter to the police and hence break their confidence with their informant.

The changes in 1976 and 1984 mainly consolidated these provisions except in 1984 the legislation was extended to cover international terrorism. The 1974 and the 1976 Acts covered only terrorism relating to Northern Ireland. The only area, therefore, which the PTA does not cover is political violence arising from activities within Great Britain.

The 1989 Act substantially expanded the powers under the PTA. It introduced a new concept of an 'investigation into terrorism' and provided further extra powers when such an activity was in process. This was modelled on the concept of a 'criminal investigation' which had been introduced under the Police and Criminal Evidence Act, 1984, which, in turn, had drawn upon the Northern Ireland Emergency Provision (Temporary Provisions) Acts. The '89 Act also drew upon other ordinary criminal law, particularly, the powers concerning the confiscation of proceeds arising from drug related activity. Over the years, therefore, a symbiotic relationship has been developed between this extraordinary legislation and the ordinary criminal law with each influencing the other and providing the police and the executive with ever increasing new powers. As Jim Marshall emphasised in one of the renewal debates on the legislation; 'This is an example of the insidious circular process in which draconian laws soften us up to similar laws which become the desired standard for further measures'.[3] Many of the powers of the Secretary of State under the PTA are subject to no Parliamentary scrutiny.

The Acts have been subject to three major reviews and a number of yearly assessments.[4] While successive governments have emphasised the independence of the reviews, this misleading. In the first place, all the inquiries were given restricted terms of reference which did not allow any consideration of why the ordinary criminal law was considered to be insufficient to deal with the problem. All major reviews were therefore based on the premise that extraordinary legislation was necessary. In addition, all the reviews were carried out by people who were close to government or the executive and all obtained most of their information from those responsible for implementing the legislation. No attempt was made to obtain systematic evidence from those examined, detained or arrested under the Acts.[5] Hence none of the reviews can be considered to be independent of government or the authorities with responsibility for implicating the legislation.

The PTA in Britain in the last eighteen years shows that the arrest and detention powers have been principally used to collect intelligence on the Irish community living in Britain and moving between Britain and Ireland. So few people are subsequently charged or even excluded that it is clear there is often no reasonable suspicion whatsoever that the person detained is involved in the preparation, instigation or commission of acts of terrorism. Second, the Irish community whether living in Britain or moving between Britain and Ireland has been seen as a suspect community and subject to increasing surveillance. This tendency is likely to increase even more rapidly with the announcement last May that MI5 were to be given the lead responsibility in gathering intelligence against the IRA.

The PTA and the European state

There are two principal issues concerning the PTA and the new Europe. In the first place, there is the question as to what will happen to the port control powers of the PTA in the context of a commitment to a borderless community within the EC. The edifice of control which has been developed between Britain and Ireland is the very antipathy of the notion of freedom of movement. Second, there is the broader issue as to what extent will the PTA be used, or perhaps already has been used, as a model for policing both the external borders and the internal territory within the EC.

Over the last few years there has been considerable acrimony between member states over the control of EC nationals at ports and airports irrespective or whether or not they are suspected of any crime or political violence. Although the aim was to abolish all internal border controls by 1 January 1993, this has not been achieved. The British government, along with Denmark and Ireland, has long opposed any relaxation of controls.

It is not clear what has been negotiated in relation to the PTA. In the last major review of the PTA, Lord Colville emphasised that it would be 'foolish to contemplate dispensing with the core controls in the foreseeable future'.[6] In addition, the building of massive fortifications along the border between the North and South of Ireland suggests, in a very concrete form, that the British government has no intention of eliminating controls for many years to come. But the retention of the PTA together with the fortification programme is totally contrary to the abolition of all internal controls for persons travelling within the territory of the EC.

In evidence to the Home Affairs Committee on *Migration Control at External Borders of the European Community*, the Home Office stated the government's current position on the PTA in the context of strengthening the external borders and abolishing internal borders:

> ...the Government does not believe that the implementation of the External Frontiers Convention would enable the United Kingdom to relax or abolish existing frontier controls under the Prevention of Terrorism Act. No strengthening of the external perimeter of the Community would in the Government's view offer sufficient protection against the movement of terrorists to enable controls that are purely internal to the Community to be lifted. Police controls are concerned primarily with the movement of small number of people who may often have acquired considerable skills, for example as terrorists or drug traffickers. It is unrealistic to think that the external frontier could ever be strengthened to the point where it was able to provide a certain barrier against such people.[7]

It should be noted that although the PTA powers apply only to terrorism, the Home Office refers to terrorists and drug traffickers in the same context.

There is a consensus among the EC governments that the external borders should be as secure as possible. A House of Lords Select Committee expressed this as the need to impose a 'cordon sanitaire to keep out drug traffickers, terrorists and other criminals, refugees together with unwanted criminals'.[8] If the British government and the British Police Service have they say, then the comprehensive system of control which has been developed at ports and airports under the PTA to control the movement of people will form the basis of a common control system at external borders.

The most likely outcome of the disagreements over abolishing internal borders is that the UK will be allowed to continue with port controls until such time that there is a general agreement on a more extensive system of internal control within the community. In other words, the internal borders will remain until all countries are agreed upon a set of what have been widely referred to as 'compensatory measures'. One commentator has suggested that they will involve 'more effective surveillance away from the frontiers as required and based on transnational information exchanges of a more intense kind among relevant enforcement agencies'.[9]

The Home Office, in its evidence to the Home Affairs Committee on *Migration Control at External Borders of the European Community*, did not think the proposed External Borders Convention sufficient to compensate for loss of the PTA port control powers:

> ...If port controls under the Prevention of Terrorism Act were abolished, the introduction of identity cards, coupled with new police powers to demand their production away from the frontier, would not compensate for the loss. Although the island geography of the United Kingdom means that there is

some prospect of controlling the movement of terrorists through selective checks at ports and airports, the present arrangements could not realistically be replaced by a system of purely internal checks.[10]

The British Police Service's position on internal controls is similar to the Home Office's position. In its evidence to the Home Affairs Committee it argued that the PTA and identity cards should form the core of any new system of internal control together with increased powers of arrest under the PTA and powers to demand proof of identity. It is not only the Home Office and the British police who consider that ID cards should form the basis of internal control. The Home Affairs Select Committee report on Practical Police Co-operation in the European Community supported the introduction of a machine-readable identity card. Although the use of the card would be entirely voluntary, it was felt that it would enhance 'our European sense of identity and make Europe an easier and safer place for its citizens'. [11]

The introduction of machine readable identity cards would be inevitably accompanied by a new power for a wide range of state and quasi state officials to stop and examine anyone, anywhere, to establish their identity. The need for this power was clearly flagged in the Home Affairs Committee Report. It pointed out that under the current legislation in England and Wales the police have no power to detain a person inland and hold them while their name and address is verified. They recommended that the police should therefore have the power to detain people for a short period until their names and addresses are established. [12] This power, it should be noted, is virtually identical to the examination power under the PTA.

Conclusion

In the long run it is unlikely that the British Government will be able to resist the pressure from the Commission to do away with all internal controls at ports and airports. The 'compensatory measures' will lead to greatly increased security at the external border and a wide range of new internal forms of control. All the indications are that PTA type powers coupled with the introduction of compulsory ID cards will probably form the core of a new system of surveillance and monitoring of the community. At the same time the comprehensive intelligence gathering system which has been developed under the PTA to police the Irish community will, in all likelihood, be combined with the intrusive new intelligence network for the whole of the internal community - the European Information System.

It is inevitable that the introduction of new extensive forms of internal control will involve a considerable reduction in the civil liberties of all EC nationals and further erode the sparse civil liberties of the 15 million non-EC nationals who live and work in the EC. But whatever its form, it is clear that the repressive apparatus of the new European state is being developed in secret and with no democratic discussion.

References

1. Diplock Commission. (1972). *Report of the Committee to Consider Legal Procedures to Deal with Terrorist Activities in Northern Ireland*, Cmnd. 5185. London: HMSO.

2. Hansard, Vol. 882, No. 24, Col. 35, 28 November, 1975.

3. Quoted in Sim, J. and Thomas, P.A. (1983) 'The Prevention of Terrorism Acts', *Journal of Law and Society*, Vol. 10, No 1, p75.

4. Shackleton Report (1978) *Review of the Operation of the Prevention of Terrorism (Temporary Provisions) Acts, 1974 and 1976*, Cmnd. 7324, London: HMSO; Jellicoe Report (1983) *Review of the Operation of the Prevention of Terrorism (Temporary Provisions) Act 1976*, Cmnd. 8803, London: HMSO; Colville Report. (1987) *Review of the Operation of the Prevention of Terrorism (Temporary Provisions) Acts 1984*, Cm. 264, London: HMSO.

5. For a detailed analysis of 115 people's experience of being arrested, examined or detained under the PTA in Britain see: Hillyard, Paddy (1993) *Suspect Community: People Experience's of the Prevention of Terrorism Acts in Britain*, London: Pluto Press.

6. Colville Report (1987) op. cit. para. 3.1.8.

7. Home Affairs Committee (1992) *Migration Control at the External Borders of the European Community*, Minutes of Evidence, Session 1991-92, HC 215-i,ii,ii, London: HMSO, p69, para 4.

8. *Border Control of People*, 22nd Report, Session, 1988-89, HL 90, London: HMSO, para 5.

9. Philip, A.B. (1991) 'European Border Controls: Who needs them?' *Public Policy and Administration*, Vol. 6, No. 2, pp. 35-54.

10. Home Affairs Committee (1992) Op. cit. p. 70, para.5.

11. Home Affairs Select Committee (1992) Vol.1, paras 137-138.

12. Ibid. para 128.

Anti-terrorism and Ireland:
the experience of the Irish Republic

Michael Farrell

Discussion about anti-terrorist legislation and strategies in connection with Ireland invariably focuses on the situation in Northern Ireland or the steady contamination of the British legal system by seepage from the Northern Ireland conflict. The Republic of Ireland rarely rates more than a passing mention.

But the Republic merits more than mention in passing for a number of reasons. In the context of a discussion in Britain, the Republic is the place of origin of the vast majority of the Irish community in Britain, so what happens there is of considerable interest to them. But it has a wider significance as well. The Northern Ireland experience can be represented - at least to a West European audience- as unique and of limited relevance to other European states. The political conflict there is so fundamental - over the very existence of the state itself - that it is unlikely to be paralleled or replicated in any other West European country, except perhaps as between the Basques and the Spanish state. And even the British experience - the development of the Prevention of Terrorism Act etc could be regarded as peculiar to Britain, where there has been a series of bombing campaigns arising out of the Northern Ireland conflict over the last 20 years.

Of course, the Republic of Ireland also has a unique relationship with Northern Ireland, where a significant minority owes allegiance to Dublin rather than London and where the two states/areas share a land frontier. But, in addition, the Republic is an apparently highly stable West European democracy, a member of the European Community, a major contributor to UN peacekeeping operations and a signatory to almost all the international conventions and covenants on human rights. The population of the Irish Republic is very homogeneous. There are no very fundamental divisions in society there and it has been a functioning parliamentary democracy for almost 70 years without interruption. Apart from a penchant for maintaining extremely conservative Catholic social legislation - such as bans on divorce and abortion and criminalising homosexuality - the Republic could, at least on a superficial view, almost be described as a paradigm of Western democracy. If human rights and civil liberties can be severely curtailed in the name of anti-terrorism in the Irish Republic, then they could be at risk in any European democracy.

In fact, the Irish Republic introduced or re-activated anti-terrorist legislation in 1972, two years before the introduction of the Prevention of Terrorism Act in Britain. The legislation had been on the statute book but it was not in use. All that was necessary, however, was for the Minister to make orders bringing it into operation. And the Republic now has special courts, special rules of evidence and a broadcasting ban beside which the British ban, which was inspired by its Irish counterpart, looks almost liberal. This has been introduced in response to the conflict in Northern Ireland, which has steadily seeped across the Irish border, bringing with it a new array of anti-terrorist measures. Obviously, the Republic is more affected than most countries by this seepage, but as the IRA spreads its activities to continental Europe, other countries may be tempted to follow the Republic's lead. And in any event, the ideas and tactics employed by the security forces in one European state have a tendency to spread to all the others.

Over the last 20 years, the Republic has also introduced new laws providing for trial within its jurisdiction of persons accused of offences committed in Britain or Northern Ireland. And the courts and the legislature have steadily amended the extradition laws in a bid to remove the political offence exception to extradition and to make it easier to hand over IRA and other Irish republican paramilitary suspects to the authorities in Britain and Northern Ireland.

In fact, as we shall see, there has been more litigation in the Republic over the question of extradition, and in particular the implementation of the European Convention on the Suppression of Terrorism, than in any other European country. Anyone anxious to know how the issue of extradition will be handled in other European countries in the future could do worse than look at the developments and definitions under the Irish legislation, which seem likely to influence the shape of the law in the rest of Europe.

The Irish Republic has also been in a permanent state of emergency for the last 54 years, with the effect that any law passed by the Oireachtas (legislature) and specifically stated to be necessitated by the existing emergency can override the provisions of the Constitution. The state of emergency was first declared in 1939 in connection with the looming second world war, though there was also a link with the Northern Ireland conflict as the IRA had just begun an earlier bombing campaign in Britain. The Dublin government was worried that the activities of the IRA might endanger its neutrality in the world war and wanted to crack down severely on that organisation. Of course, the second world war has now been over for some time, as even the last of the Japanese soldiers who hid in the jungles of Asia seem to have realised. But the Irish Republic did not rescind the state of emergency declared in 1939 until 1976 and then it promptly replaced it with a new one, this time specifically linked to the conflict in Northern Ireland.

The powers granted under the state of emergency have only been used once since then - to permit the passage in 1976 of an Emergency Powers Act allowing the Gardai (police) to detain suspects for seven days for questioning. This was an example of the Republic copying from British emergency legislation. The traffic has not all been one way however as we shall see in connection with the respective broadcasting bans. The seven-day detention power lapsed after 12 months and was not renewed, but the Emergency Powers Act is still on the statute book and seven-day detention could be revived at any time simply by Ministerial order.

The Emergency Powers Act had followed a series of actions by republican paramilitary groups that led to an almost hysterical reaction by the government of the day. A leading Dutch industrialist had been kidnapped in 1975, a mail train had been held up and robbed in March 1976 and the British ambassador to Ireland had been assassinated in July 1976. As well as introducing seven-day detention, the government allowed a group to emerge in the Gardai, popularly known as the Heavy

Gang, who specialised in the use of brutality to secure confessions. The activities of the Heavy Gang led to an Amnesty International mission to the Republic in 1977, which produced a highly critical report. The Heavy Gang was also responsible for the Republic's own version of the Birmingham Six, Guildford Four and Judy Ward miscarriage of justice cases - the Sallins mail train case. In the Sallins case, three innocent men were convicted of the robbery of the mail train on the basis of confessions which were beaten out of them, followed by a less than satisfactory trial in the non-jury Special Criminal Court. Two of the convictions were quashed on appeal *(The People (DPP) v. McNally and Breatnach, 2 Frewen)*. The third, that of Nicky Kelly, was only finally quashed by Presidential pardon last year.

The mid 1970s was the worst period for emergency legislation and police repression in the Republic but dramatic over-reaction by the authorities by no means ended then. In 1987, following the interception of a Libyan arms shipment for the IRA, the authorities launched the largest search operation in the history of the state. Proportionate to the population of the Republic, it must also rank as one of the largest such operations in Western Europe since the second world war. A total of 50,132 houses, or rather more than one house in every 20, were searched in this exercise, code-named Operation Mallard. Very little was found and much of the search appeared to be a giant intelligence-gathering exercise.

The basic anti-terrorist law in the Republic is the Offences Against the State Act. First passed in 1939 on the eve of the second world war, it neatly illustrates how coercive legislation originally supposed to deal only with a specific emergency situation can very quickly become a permanent feature of the legislative landscape.

Some of the powers granted under the Act, which was amended and strengthened in 1972, are less extensive than their British counterparts, some are more draconian, and some are quite bizarre. The powers to detain, search and question without warrant and to proscribe organisations are permanently in operation. Other sections of the Act, such as the power to establish special courts, require a ministerial order to come into effect. That section has been in operation since 1972. A further section which provides for internment without trial has not been invoked in recent times, though it was in use during the second world war and briefly during an IRA campaign in the 1950s. Once again it requires only a Ministerial order to come into operation. There have been periodic calls over the last 20 or so years for internment without trial to be introduced in connection with the Northern Ireland conflict. They have recently been renewed by former Labour Cabinet Minister Dr Conor Cruise O'Brien and Opposition party leader John Bruton in the wake of the Warrington bombing in March 1993, when an IRA bomb in a north of England town left two children dead and many others wounded. The fact that no parliamentary sanction would be required creates a danger that such a measure could be taken in a panic reaction to some particular atrocity.

Under Section 30 of the Offences Against the State Act, persons can be detained without charge for up to 48 hours for questioning about a scheduled offence - membership of a proscribed organisation, possession of firearms, malicious damage etc. The maximum period for which someone can be detained for questioning under the ordinary law is 12 hours, which can be extended to 20 hours if it is overnight, but the detained person must be allowed to sleep for eight hours of that period. Section 30 arrests were averaging around 1,800-2,000 per year in the mid 1980s;

more recent figures are not readily available. They are widely used for information gathering, often about purely political activities. And although the Section 30 powers when passed were clearly intended to deal with IRA activities, they have also been widely used over the years to question people about more serious non-political offences because of the longer time for which suspects could be detained.

A non-jury Special Criminal Court was established by ministerial order in 1972. It consists of three judges, which is some slight improvement on previous courts established under the Offences Against the State Act, which consisted of military officers. Jury trial is the norm for all but minor offences in the Republic. The Special Criminal Court was ostensibly established because of fears of intimidation of juries but no evidence of such intimidation was ever produced. There is no mechanism for periodic reviews of the necessity or otherwise for such a court, which has now become a permanent feature of the judicial system. In fact, the Criminal Law (Jurisdiction) Act, which was passed in 1976 as part of regular legislation, effectively incorporates the court into the permanent judicial structure by providing for trial there of persons charged under that Act.

Scheduled offences are tried in the special court and non-scheduled offences can also be tried there if the DPP certifies that the ordinary courts are inadequate to deal with the case in question. The DPP's decision is not reviewable and over the years a number of non-politically related cases, or cases with only the most marginal political connections, have been tried by the Special Criminal Court. This writer is aware of a case of unlawful taking of a motor car which was tried in the special court, presumably on the grounds that the accused were suspected of being members of the IRA. This trend was criticised by the current President of Ireland, Mary Robinson, in a pamphlet she wrote in 1975 when she was a practising lawyer and again in an article in 1982. It is a good example of how emergency measures begin to contaminate the entire legal system.

The rules of evidence in the Special Criminal Court were altered in 1972 so that the sworn testimony of a Garda Chief Superintendent that he believes that the accused is a member of a proscribed organisation is sufficient evidence to secure a conviction unless the accused denies it on oath. The Chief Superintendent need not know the accused personally, nor can he be required to disclose the source of his information. If the accused denies membership, then corroboration of the Chief Superintendent's word is required, but in 1987 in *(The People (Director of Public Prosecutions) -v- O'Leary,* Irish Times, 20 November 1987) possession of a number of pro-IRA posters was held to be sufficient corroboration.

In 1972 an amendment to the 1939 Act also provided that failure to deny a published report that a person was a member of a proscribed organisation could constitute evidence of membership, though that provision has not been used for a long time. Another bizarre provision of the 1972 Act gives the authorities power to close down buildings which they suspect are being used for the purposes of a proscribed organisation. This provision was used in the early 1970s to close down two buildings in Dublin used by Sinn Fein. The potential closure period was later extended to three years, though again this provision has not been used for some time. A further amendment in 1985 gave the Government power, without notice to freeze bank accounts and order the payment of the monies in question into the High Court on suspicion that the funds are intended for the use of a proscribed organisation. It is then necessary for the account holder to prove his/her title to the property. This peculiar provision was obviously a precursor to recent British legislation to curb alleged terrorist fund-raising.

The other two main areas of anti-terrorist legislation in the Irish Republic which may be of wider interest are the broadcasting ban and extradition. The Irish broadcasting ban dates back to October 1971, when the then Minister for Communications made an order under Section 31 of the Broadcasting Act 1960 prohibiting the broadcast of anything that could promote the aims or activities of an organisation that engaged in or encouraged the use of violence.

One year later, the Government dismissed the entire membership of the broadcasting authority after the national station, RTE, had broadcast an account of an interview with the alleged chief of staff of the IRA. After that RTE management banned all interviews with members of the IRA or other paramilitary organisations, but then in 1976 the Act was amended and a new ministerial order was issued. It banned interviews with spokespersons for named organisations. One of the organisations named was Sinn Fein, which was and still is a legal political party in the Republic where it has a number of members elected to local authorities. The new order also prohibited interviews with spokespersons for any organisation which was or is proscribed in Northern Ireland, a unique example of one government allowing another government to decide what may or may not be broadcast on its national broadcasting network.

The ban has been rigorously enforced since 1976. There is no relaxation during election campaigns, even when Sinn Fein, which is the real target of the ban, has nominated candidates, and Sinn Fein elected representatives cannot be interviewed even about constituency business, unlike under the British ban. As a result when Sinn Fein president Gerry Adams was elected MP for West Belfast in 1983, RTE, alone of all the media covering the election, was unable to interview Mr Adams and had to be content with speaking to the defeated candidate. More recently, when Mr Adams was defeated last year, RTE was again unable to interview him. One reporter was sacked in 1988 for including a few innocuous words from a Sinn Fein official in a report on the funeral of the three IRA members shot dead in Gibraltar in that year.

RTE management adopted an extraordinarily rigid interpretation of the ministerial ban, prohibiting not alone interviews with Sinn Fein spokespersons, but with any member of that organisation on any topic whatsoever. The results were often bizarre. Thus, when an eyewitness to a fatal fire in a hotel in a seaside town some years ago turned out to be a Sinn Fein member, an interview with him was not used. And when a Sinn Fein member rang up a phone-in gardening programme with a query about mushroom growing, his question was not broadcast.

In 1990 there was a major industrial dispute at Dublin bakery plant. RTE had broadcast one interview with the chairperson of the strike committee, Larry O'Toole, before they discovered he was a Sinn Fein member. Though other interviews with him were recorded, they were never used. Mr O'Toole challenged this blanket ban on all Sinn Fein members, no matter what the topic under discussion, in an action before the Irish courts. In a judgment given at the end of March, the Irish Supreme Court held that for RTE to impose such a blanket ban on all members of Sinn Fein was an impermissible extension of the Ministerial order. Accordingly, the blanket ban has now gone, but the court indicated that it would probably support the ban on spokespersons and it has yet to be seen exactly how RTE will deal with the new situation.

In the meantime, RTE had engaged in an even more extraordinary extension of the ban by refusing to carry an advertisement for a book of short stories written by Sinn Fein president Gerry Adams and set in the nationalist community in Northern Ireland. The advertisement was totally innocuous but RTE, in less than pellucid prose, justified its refusal to carry it on the grounds that the publication of the book could only have as its aim the 'portraying of Mr Adams as an artist, a man of culture and a man who writes stories which by their nature are intended to enable the readers to identify with both the story and by inference the writer and the message which he conveys...' The overall effect of publicising the book, said RTE, would be 'to promote or incite to crime or...tending to undermine the authority of the state.'

Mr Adams's stories may not rank with Joyce, Yeats or O'Casey, but it is an alarming development that works of fiction, whatever their quality, should be banned or excluded from access to advertising because of their authors's political views or because they portray a community where the IRA has a certain legitimacy among the population. A slight extension of that attitude could lead to a refusal to screen the Oscar-winning film 'The Crying Game'. A not dissimilar attitude led to the dropping of two scheduled films, Hidden Agenda and Angel, by British television channels in the days just after the Warrington bombing. 'Hidden Agenda' was presumably dropped because it was highly critical of the security forces in Northern Ireland and portrayed Sinn Fein members as fairly normal people. Angel seems to have been dropped because the IRA and the republican community in Northern Ireland lurked in the background, albeit in a none too favourable light.

The ban on the Adams advertisement is also being challenged in the Republic's courts, but even success in that action would still leave the overall ban in place and there is nothing to hope for by taking a case on to the European Court of Human Rights. The European Commission on Human Rights in 1991 rejected a challenge to the Section 31 ban, holding that it could 'reasonably be considered 'necessary in a democratic society'.

Finally, the Republic's law and practice in relation to extradition should be of some interest to those interested in extradition law, especially concerning political offences, in any European country. The Republic's Extradition Act 1965 is based on the European Convention on Extradition, and there has been more case law in the Republic in recent years on the political offence exception to extradition than in any other European country, as the Republic has been pressed by Britain to hand over IRA and other republican fugitives.

In the early and mid 1970s, the Irish courts held firmly to the view that there should be no extradition for political offences - first laid down in the case of Sean Bourke, an Irishman who helped Soviet spy George Blake to escape from a British prison *(Bourke v. The Attorney General 1972*, IR 36) Thereafter the courts held that offences committed by the IRA or similar groups in Britain or Northern Ireland were politically motivated and so exempt from extradition - most clearly expressed in *Burns v. The Attorney General* (unreported, 4 February 1974). Pressed ever harder by Britain, in 1976 the Republic enacted the Criminal Law (Jurisdiction) Act to allow for the trial in the Republic of persons accused of offences in Britain or Northern

Ireland. There was *still* a distinct reluctance to hand over suspected IRA fugitives to the regime which they had been opposing.

The British authorities made no secret of the fact that they preferred extradition with its subliminal message that the Republic no longer saw the conflict in Northern Ireland as a political conflict, but instead a 'terrorist' problem. By degrees the Irish courts changed their stance during the 1980s, performing some extraordinary legal somersaults along the way. In 1982 in *McGlinchey v. Wren* (1982 IR 154), the Irish Supreme Court narrowed the concept of political offence to what 'reasonable, civilised people' would regard as political, forgetting that violent political conflicts rarely break out where people have the opportunity to lead 'reasonable, civilised' lives, Then in 1985 the Supreme Court delivered an extraordinary judgment in the case of *Quinn v. Wren* (1985 IR 322). The court held that a member of a republican splinter group called the Irish National Liberation Army could not avail of the protection of Section 50 of the Extradition Act (the political offence exception) because his organisation supposedly sought to overthrow the Irish Constitution by force.

The Quinn decision smacked of reintroducing the concept of outlawry. In effect the court was saying that someone who sought to overthrow the state was not entitled to the prottection of the laws enacted by the state. Three years later in *Russell v. Fanning* (1988 IR 505), the court was confronted by an IRA member who declared that the IRA did not seek to overthrow the Constitution by force. The court came up with the bizarre argument that because the IRA was seeking to achieve one of the aims of the Irish Constitution (Irish unity) by means which were not sanctioned by the Irish government, then IRA members could not avail of the protection of the law either.

This convoluted logic proved too much for some of the judges, however, and in 1990 a differently composed court reasserted in the case of *Finucane v. McMahon* (1990 IR 165) that IRA attacks on members of the security forces in Northern Ireland could qualify as political offences, though it made clear that attacks on civilians would not qualify.

By then, however, as a result of the Anglo-Irish Agreement of 1985, the Republic had ratified the 1977 European Convention on the Suppression of Terrorism, which seeks to depoliticise a number of offences for the purpose of extradition between states parties to the Convention. Two Extradition Amendment Acts were passed in 1987 declaring that certain offences - whatever their motivation - could not be regarded as political. They included aircraft hijacking, attacks on diplomatic personnel and offences involving the use of explosives or automatic weapons, or involving cruel or inhuman methods, or endangering civilians.

The Republic entered no reservations when it ratified the anti-terrorism convention, unlike most of the other states parties which will not extradite their own nationals, or reserve the right to regard certain offences as political. There may be increasing pressure on other states parties in the future to follow Dublin's example and withdraw their reservations. Already a number of cases have been heard in Dublin under the amended Acts - *Ellis v. O'Dea* (1990 ILRM 346) and *Sloan v. Culligan* (1991 ILRM 641) - and offences that would otherwise have been regarded as political have been ruled out because they involved the use of explosives or automatic weapons. So far, the Irish courts have held that it is only *actual* use as opposed to mere possession, of explosives or automatic weapons that depoliticises the offence. However, there is now a strong lobby to have the Extradition Acts amended yet again, so as to exclude *use* as well, thereby making the Irish legislation more restrictive than the anti-terrorism convention. And if that amendment is brought in, it may not be long before there is pressure on a Europe-wide basis to amend the anti-terrorism convention to the same effect.

The sheer volume of anti-terrorist, emergency or exceptional legislation in a relatively peaceful democratic backwater like the Irish Republic may come as a surprise to those unfamiliar with the Irish state. It did not develop overnight and it may serve as a reminder that emergency-type laws rarely expire with the 'emergency' that produced then and that even in a democratic state, a whole corpus of repressive laws and threats to civil liberties can accumulate before many people realise what is happening. It may also seem surprising that such inroads on human and democratic rights could be made with so little protest in a state which is a functioning democracy with regular changes of government.

The lack of protest comes from a variety of causes. The present Irish state had its origins in a bloody and vicious civil war when the victorious party, which had opted for Dominion status within the British empire rather than independence, ruthlessly suppressed the then IRA and then maintained a formidable apparatus of repression for a decade afterwards. Their successors, once in power, were little better and the Republic never developed a strong culture of democratic rights. When the Northern Ireland conflict erupted at the beginning of the 1970s, the more conservative elements in the Republic feared that they would be drawn into it and the stability of the state undermined. That provided the impetus for the first spate of emergency measures. As time went by, these measures were seen as targeted exclusively against republicans/IRA supporters, a group who became increasingly marginalised and isolated - at least partly because of some of the activities of the IRA - and so further measures were introduced without resistance.

In fact the effect of the emergency measures has been felt by a wider section of the population in the Republic and they have contributed to a climate of opinion that has accepted inroads on the right to silence and new powers to detain for questioning about ordinary offences. And the censorship of the electronic media under Section 31 of the Broadcasting Act has led to a climate of fear and self-censorship that has seriously curtailed reporting of human rights abuses in Northern Ireland or Britain and has tended to exclude from the airwaves those who are critical of Britain's role in Northern Ireland without in any way supporting the IRA.

The case of the Irish Republic is relevant to the rest of Europe because it shows how the corrosive effects of the Northern Ireland conflict can gradually contaminate the legal system in a neighbouring state, even a democratic one. And although the Republic is something of a special case vis à vis the Northern Ireland conflict, nevertheless the spread of IRA attacks and activists to Continental Europe could well lead to new coercive measures in other countries as well. And while those measures might be targeted against the Irish initially, they could just as easily be turned against other unwelcome visitors as well.

In addition, the Republic, like Britain, is also something of a laboratory for testing out new 'anti-terrorist' techniques and measures, which may then be applied in other countries - or there may even be attempts to have them made general throughout

Europe. And the sheer volume of repressive legislation that has built up in the Republic over the last 20 years serves to reinforce the old message that failure to resist harsh measures directed against an unpopular minority can allow the power of the state to grow to such a degree that it begins to oppress the majority as well.

The new Europe: immigration and asylum[1]

Frances Webber

The 'Fortress Europe' which refugee and immigrant groups have long been warning about is virtually complete. Over the past few years, by means of conventions and agreements, laws and procedures, detention camps and soldiers, nearly all EC and EFTA states have set out to make it impossible for immigrants and asylum-seekers to enter Europe.

Historical context
The post-war reconstruction of industrial Europe depended on cheap migrant labour from Turkey, Yugoslavia, north Africa, southern Europe, south Asia and the Caribbean. All major industrial countries had the benefits of this labour; most had it without the burden of health, education and social service needed to rear these workers. They achieved this by the 'gastarbeiter' system of short contracts which gave no rights of settlement to those whose labour they used. (The UK was an exception, allowing the free entry of ex-colonial citizens until 1962, but thereafter learned quickly from its European neighbours; at the same time, however, by means of campaigns, many of the guest-workers of Holland, Belgium and Germany won settlement rights.)

With the decline in manufacturing industry from the late 1960s and early 1970s, and the coming of the technological revolutions of the late 1970s and 1980s, the labour needs of the industrialised countries of northern Europe changed radically. They no longer required the large numbers of skilled workers used to build their economies after the war. Instead, as Sivanandan has argued, they needed, on the one hand, a small, highly skilled group of core workers, and on the other, a mass of ad hoc, casual, unskilled, flexible, mobile and easily dispensable 'peripheral' workers.

Thus, in the seventies, immigration for work was effectively banned in northern Europe. Those who came thereafter did so at their peril: with no authority to work, they were confined to invisibility and super-exploitation, in danger of deportation if they complained of low pay, illegal deductions, unsafe conditions of work. Factories in which workers tried to unionise tended to receive a visit from immigration officers, and the workforce was replaced with a more compliant one. Apart from highly skilled workers, students and visitors, the only lawful immigrants became the families of those who had settled earlier, and refugees.

---

1. This is an abridged version of a piece that will appear in the annual report of the Institute of Race Relations *European Race Audit*. For details contact: IRR, 2-6 Leeke Street, London WC1X 9HS.

Until the mid-1980s, control of immigration in continental Europe was largely internal, because of the ease with which land borders are crossed. In several countries a residence permit or equivalent authorisation to stay from central or local municipal authorities, was (and still is) the passport to all social services, health care, welfare benefits, education and housing. Random passport checks and workplace raids kept the irregular sector of the workforce in check. But in the early 1980s refugees, who henceforth had been confined to Communist bloc defectors, wealthy deposed leaders or pre-arranged quotas of Chilean or Vietnamese, began to arrive in (relatively) larger numbers. All northern European countries were signatories of the Geneva Convention of 1951, which prevented the return of refugees to the country of persecution, while not granting an express right to seek asylum. Efforts were begun to see how the refugees could be prevented from entering. Visa controls began to be imposed (and, since the Geneva Convention definition of a refugee demands that he (sic) be outside his own country, it was logically impossible for refugees to be granted visas while they remained in their own countries). When asylum seekers continued to arrive without visas, some countries (Germany, UK, Belgium, Denmark) introduced legislation to impose fines on the airlines which brought them. A huge black market in forged travel documents sprang up; some host countries responded by declaring passengers with such documents to be illegal entrants, not asylum-seekers at all. Measures taken by one country provoke similar measures in others, all anxious not to become the European safe haven for asylum-seekers. Thus, the percentage of asylum-seekers accepted as refugees in Europe as a whole went down from around 65% in 1980 to 10% in 1990.

At the same time that European governments became concerned with keeping out asylum-seekers, negotiations were in train with the EC to remove all its internal borders. This would complete the free market in goods, capital, services and labour which the Treaty of Rome had contemplated but which the protectionist response to the recession of the 1970s had halted. With the signing of the Single European Act in 1986, whose aim was to complete the internal market by 1 January 1993, it was felt necessary to ensure that external borders were strengthened to keep strict control on the admission of non-EC nationals. It was also felt necessary to set up European-wide mechanisms of control, to ensure the 'fortress' was not breached by a country with lax immigration controls.

The countries of southern Europe - Italy, Portugal, Spain and Greece - were (and still are in part) countries of emigration. Workers from these countries, and from Ireland, the north's anomalous 'south' country, helped build northern Europe. At the same time, however, they - or at least Italy, Spain and Portugal - are heavily dependent on migrant labour, particularly during the harvesting season. This combination of economic pressures produced immigration controls which were honoured in the breach; Spain and Italy were both reckoned in the late 1980s to have over a million or more undocumented workers, who were tolerated for the work they did. But for these countries membership of the EC had its costs. One of these was Spain, lying only miles from Africa - having to seal its porous borders and act as Europe's immigration police on its southern edge. Immigrant groups in Portugal, Spain and Italy have all accused their authorities of turning the country into 'one vast detention centre', so great has been the change. In each country, an 'amnesty' or regularisation for undocumented workers - from which only those with employers willing to go legal and start paying taxes and improving conditions, can benefit - has been followed by strict immigration laws and a crackdown on illegal immigrants.

The opening up of eastern Europe brought with it opportunities - for investment, for replacing the 'alien' Third World labour in western Europe with less problematic but equally cheap European labour. But it also brought the spectre of millions of refugees, a spectre made flesh in Yugoslavia and Romania and Albania. The response of western Europe, formalised through EC agreements, has been to divide eastern Europe into partner-countries and problem-countries. The EC has entered association agreements with Poland and Hungary and is to do so with the Czech republic and Slovakia, freeing trade and investment with those countries, and allowing their nationals visa-free travel and work opportunities in western Europe. Part of the price for those countries, as for the EFTA countries whose nationals are shortly to benefit from favourable status in the EC, is to guard the frontiers of western Europe to prevent the entry of nationals from 'problem countries' such as Romania, Albania, Russia and the CIS.

Nuts and bolts

The EC has declined community competence in immigration and asylum matters, with the recent exception (in the Maastricht treaty) of coordination of visa controls among member states. But agreements between EC states have resulted in the setting up of comprehensive information exchange systems for the control of immigrants - legal and illegal - and asylum-seekers within EC territory. The estimated 16 million lawfully settled non-EC citizens in the EC do not benefit from the opening of Europe's borders (whenever that will be) except to the extent that they will be able to enjoy 3-month visa-free holidays in other member states. In addition to a common list of 'undesirables' - immigrants refused entry to or expelled from any member state, or suspected of being up to no good - will be compiled and drawn up by immigration and police authorities throughout the EC. A computerised fingerprint-matching system (EURODAC) will be able to detect 'multiple claimants' - asylum-seekers who try to claim asylum in one member state after being refused in another - so that they can be detected and expelled. An expulsion from one country will effectively mean an expulsion from all. In addition to EC countries, this will apply in those EFTA and central or east European states which have agreements with the EC.

The Schengen countries (all the EC member states save the UK, Ireland and Denmark) have a common list of 120 countries whose nationals require visas to enter. Non-Schengen countries have similar lists. All EC countries except Ireland, which has no formal refugee procedures, now have in place (or going through parliament) measures for turning back refugees who come via another EC country, and for 'accelerated processing' of 'manifestly unfounded' refugees. (Some processes are less formal than others, such as Greece's expulsion of 350,000 Albanians in 1992 without recourse to any procedures at all, or Italy's similar expulsion of Albanians the previous year). All countries now have a form of detention for some (though not all) asylum-seekers, particularly those subject to the new 'manifestly unfounded' procedures, in prisons, barracks, camps, reception centres and ships. Most have instituted lower levels of welfare benefits for asylum-seekers (some in kind rather than cash), together with a ban on working for all or part of the assessment procedure. Such measures together with other deterrents such as carrier sanctions and fingerprinting, have halved the number of asylum-seekers arriving in several European countries in 1992, and would have done so in all but for the reception of refugees from the former Yugoslavia, notably in Germany which took in 250,000. But Germany too closed its doors in May 1993, capitulating to the racists with the 'modification' of the constitutional right to asylum. Asylum-seekers can now be sent back to countries deemed 'safe'.

Family reunion rights are being squeezed, too, with the maximum age for the entry of dependent children moving steadily downwards, and the 'right' made subject, in more and more countries, to stiff financial maintenance and accommodation criteria. Those countries which still need migrant workers - the southern countries, Switzerland and Austria - have firm quotas for seasonal, short-term and border workers only, with no rights of settlement. In many countries, even for those long settled, citizenship is hard to come by in many countries. In the UK, the right to citizenship by birth in the territory (ius soli) was severely undermined in 1981, while in France, it is to be replaced by discretionary naturalisation for those born of foreign parents. The European model for citizenship is moving towards the blood right (ius sanguinis) of Germany, where even third-generation settlers have no citizenship rights, so that loss of accommodation or work, or conflict with the authorities, or changes in the law, can lead to deportation.

The future

The 'harmonisation' process whereby European states have built the accords, agreements and practices comprising 'Fortress Europe' are described in the next chapter (Conventions). It is enough to delineate here the next stage of the process, which is the creation of buffer zones outside the EC which will bear the brunt of Europe's immigration policing. The association agreements with Poland and Hungary have already been mentioned; under parallel agreements these countries are now obliged to take back people who get through their countries to western Europe. Poland and Hungary have detention camps housing thousands of suspected would-be illegal entrants to the west. Under an agreement between Spain and Morocco, Africans suspected of wanting to attempt the dangerous sea-crossing to Spain are held in prisons in Morocco, and 2,500 Moroccan troops patrol the Moroccan coastline to prevent the 'illegal' departure of the little people-smuggling boats. Soon, non-EC European states will sign a Convention which will oblige them to take back immigrants and asylum-seekers who passed through on their way to an EC state. And EC immigration ministers have made it clear, at their November meeting in London, that their aim in the slightly longer term is to declare all asylum-seekers from outside Europe ineligible for asylum in Europe.

COUNTRY SUMMARIES

Austria (EFTA):

16,200 asylum-seekers 1992 (40% less than in 1991, but this figure excludes 60,000 Bosnians); 9.75% recognised. 75% came from central and eastern Europe. Some asylum-seekers kept in closed camps; new detention centres were built in 1992.

June 1992: A new asylum law provided that asylum seekers with no identification, and those who had travelled through a 'safe' country, would be summarily rejected by border police. Appeal against expulsion would not prevent removal. Amnesty International estimated that under the new provisions, 90% of all asylum-seekers would be rejected.

October 1992: Immigration bill introduced setting quota of 20-25,000 limit on all immigration including family reunion, workers and asylum-seekers.

January 1993: Jorg Haider's neo-nazi Liberals got 417,000 signatures for petition for new law declaring that Austria is not a country of immigration, that illegal immigration will be combated, and that foreigners will not get voting or citizenship rights. The petition forced a debate in parliament on the issue.

Belgium (EC, Schengen):
13,000 asylum-seekers 1990; 17% recognised. Expulsions doubled in 1992 to 974; there were 11,720 arrests of undocumented immigrants (up 25% on 1991). The total number of immigration prisoners was 4,000.

1987: automatic rights of asylum-seekers to enter Belgium were abolished. Accelerated procedures were introduced to deal with asylum claims.

1991: a new Asylum law provided that applications submitted over 8 days after arrival, or unsupported by valid documents, or from people who had been expelled from Belgium in the last 10 years were to be refused. A 'double 5%' criteria for 'manifestly unfounded' claims was also adopted. This meant that asylum-seekers from countries where fewer than 5% of asylum-seekers came, and of whom fewer than 5% were accepted, were to be rejected unless they had compelling evidence that they were refugees.

1992: A new detention centre was opened at Zaventem airport (Brussels). Parliamentary Bills were introduced to force asylum-seekers to live in 'designated accommodation centres'; and to increase period of lawful detention of deportees from one to two months and to reverse burden of proof from those coming from 'safe' countries; measures to cut off social assistance to asylum-seekers automatically once their asylum claim was rejected; new measures to make family visits conditional on host's earnings; and another measure to combat illegal entrants including provisions for house arrest.

April 1993: A new bill provides for long prison sentences, heavy fines and other sanctions for those employing illegal workers, and for three new detention centres. The Employment Minister is considering introducing 'occupational ID card' in all sectors to combat illegal workers. The Interior Ministry plans to have all asylum applications screened within one week by October, when fingerprint retrieval system will come into operation.

Denmark (EC, Nordic Union)
13,884 asylum-seekers 1992 (4,000 from the former Yugoslavia).
The Nordic Union Passport Agreement 1957 was a Treaty between Denmark, Finland, Iceland, Norway and Sweden abolishing internal controls between these states. Asylum-seekers entering one country from another to be returned.

1986: Danish/German border agreement allowed mutual expulsion of immigrants including asylum-seekers crossing border illegally.

A new law allowing asylum-seekers arriving without visas to be expelled to safe country; accelerated procedure for 'manifestly unfounded' cases (affecting about 10% of cases); detention for those who could not prove their identity, reception centres for other asylum-seekers.

1988/9: the Justice minister deliberately delayed processing of applications for family reunion from relatives of Tamil refugees. Several family members died in Sri Lanka waiting for permission to go to Denmark.

1989: Carriers' liability introduced.

1991: Proposal for fast-track procedure at border allowing faster expulsion for 'manifestly unfounded' asylum-seekers.

Removal of rejected asylum-seekers before appeal. Anchored ships were brought into service as reception/detention centres.

1992: New laws restricted family reunion rights of non-Danish citizens; extended the probationary period before spouse of Danish citizen given residence rights; and adopted more stringent criteria for naturalisation (currently no automatic right to citizenship by birth in Denmark: naturalisation is based on 7 years' residence, perfect Danish and no debts to state). Also allowed detention of asylum-seekers who fail to attend police interviews, and fingerprinting of all asylum-seekers whose identity is in doubt.

1993: Prime minister resigned in 'Tamilgate' scandal; new coalition government pledges more positive asylum policy. Proposals are to include increased financial help to refugees who agree to be repatriated.

Finland (EFTA, Nordic Union)
3,634 asylum-seekers 1992 (half from former Yugoslavia). Restrictive aliens law. Tension between law and demand for migrant labour.

1990: army reinforced along border with Soviet Union and stringent passport checks to check immigration from there. 1993: Feb: following arrival of 108 Kurdish asylum-seekers by fishing boat via Estonia, draft Bill submitted to penalise refugee-smugglers, to allow border police to refuse asylum, and allow expulsion before appeal.

France (EC, Schengen)
26,600 asylum-seekers 1992 (4,200 from Yugoslavia) (less than half 1990 figure). In 1990 15% of applications were accepted. There is no automatic right to citizenship by birth in France. Strict immigration laws since 1970s. Visa controls on virtually all non-EC citizens.

1986: Pasqua law allowed 'urgent' expulsions on public order grounds; resulted in 17,000 deportations in following year, including 101 Malians chained together on special charter. Repealed in 1988.

1989: accelerated treatment for asylum-seekers with 'manifestly unfounded' claims introduced.

1990: 18,000 expulsion orders issued. New accelerated procedure for irregular asylum-seekers introduced, with no right of appeal before removal.

1991: stricter conditions for entry visas. Tough law on illegal entrants provided that foreigners must carry documents with them at all times to prove their lawful status. People facing expulsion who refused to leave or destroy documents to prevent deportation faced 6 months to 3 years' imprisonment and 10-year ban on re-entry.

Prohibition on work for asylum-seekers introduced.

1992: Law authorising detention of asylum-seekers for up to 30 days in so-called 'international zone' of airports rejected by Constitutional court; new law introduced allowing detention of asylum-seekers for up to 20 days in 'waiting zone' at airports, if claim 'manifestly unfounded', accepted by court. Law providing for carrier sanctions passed. 7 stowaways died when they were thrown off ship before it docked in France. Family reunion: refusals up to 50% in Paris region after tough new criteria applied.

Franco-Spanish agreement reached on mutual control of clandestine immigration.

April 1993: the new right wing government announces a package of laws: to combat 'illegal immigration and Islamic fundamentalism' by abolishing right of citizenship by birth in France; giving police stronger powers for random ID checks on 'immigrants'; sanctions on immigrant marriages.

Germany (EC, Schengen)

440,000 asylum-seekers 1992 (123,000 from Yugoslavia, 104,000 Romania, 31,000 Bulgaria). 4.3% accepted.

No right to German citizenship for second- or third-generation 'immigrants' born in Germany. Naturalisation conditional on adequate accommodation, language, orientation to German culture, integration into German society, way of life.

1973 on: no immigration for non-EC citizens except ethnic Germans, 'privileged foreigners' and refugees.

1980 on: restrictions on asylum-seekers including visa requirements, 8-year delay on applications, no right to work for first 5 years (later reduced), reduced social security entitlement, restrictions on freedom of movement.

1986: agreement with east Germany to stop passengers from coming through east Berlin.

1987: carrier sanctions introduced. Airline staff protest at role in expulsion of rejected asylum-seekers.

1987-9: large numbers of Aus and Übersiedler from eastern Germany and Europe admitted.

1990: Foreigners' law required all non-EC and non 'special agreement' countries' nationals to have visas.

1991: new law setting up 'collection camps' for asylum-seekers with 'manifestly unfounded' claims, accelerated procedures to cut down processing time to six weeks.

1992: new law providing for fingerprinting of all asylum-seekers; centralisation of procedure of asylum claim processing under Federal authorities; military personnel used to process claims. Thousands of Romanian gypsies deported under repatriation agreement with Romania.

April 1993: new computer system assigns asylum-seekers to 46 central camps and speeds up processing. 'Auxiliary force' of 1,600 begins patrolling Polish and Czech borders together with 3,000 frontier police.

May 1993: constitutional right of asylum modified to allow refugees to be returned to 'safe' countries of origin/transit. List includes Bulgaria, Romania, Slovakia, Senegal and Ghana. Law in force 1 July 1993.

Pilot test of military radar and night vision devices to monitor eastern borders. If successful, paramilitaries (including volunteers) will patrol borders and help guards at Czech and Polish borders.

Greece (EC, Schengen)

1,990 asylum-seekers allowed to register 1992 (77% Iraqi), excluding 350,000 Albanians refused/expelled. 29% of asylum-seekers accepted (1990). UNHCR complains that many asylum-seekers are not being allowed to register applications. Detention for immigrants and asylum-seekers with forged documents. From end of 1980s, police and military patrols have guarded Albanian border, surveillance of Adriatic coast with helicopters and boats to prevent clandestine immigration.

Under pressure from European partners, Greece attempting to seal borders (37,000 miles of coastline) and combat irregular immigration.

1991 onwards: 'exceptional measures' for policing of borders; 'crackdowns' on illegal immigrants have resulted in expulsion of thousands of foreigners, mainly Albanians.

1992: Greece became 9th member of Schengen group; passed new Aliens, Immigrants and Refugees law (the first since 1929), which set up 'anti-clandestine immigrant patrols', lists of 'undesirable aliens' and strict criteria for the issue of visas. Several Iraqi refugees drowned attempting to reach Greece in small boats.

1993: February: national police sweep to arrest and deport illegal immigrants; 500 Albanians detained, deported.

Hungary:

As a 'waiting room for western Europe' (according to head of border police) Hungary has since 1989 strengthened border patrols and entry laws to prevent entry of illegal immigrants 'in transit' for Germany, Austria, and set up detention centres. Simultaneously, in attempt to attract investment, in 1990 Hungary offered rights of residence and nationality to any Hong Kong citizen willing to invest $US 100,000.

1991: over 24,000 people detained as illegal aliens, 15,000 residence permits withdrawn. After new law October 1991 imposing conditions of minimum funds or transit visa on entry into country, 100,000 per month refused entry at borders.

1992: government announced further restrictions on entry and residence so as to allow foreigners to live in Hungary only exceptionally. Renewal of residence permits not to be routine. 1,000 suspected illegal immigrants detained immediately (mainly African, Arab, Chinese, Romanian), 740 expelled, 400 detained in camp.

January-April 1993: 10,000 people (mainly Romanian and Turkish) detained as illegal entrants.

Ireland (EC)

Immigration still dictated by very strict 1935 Aliens Act, giving unlimited powers of detention, deportation. Visa requirements imposed in line with UK. No formal refugee policy: 1991, 35 applications, one granted. One in four detained in prison. Ban on work for asylum-seekers. 1991/2: 200 refugees accepted from former Yugoslavia.

Italy (EC, Schengen)

2,650 admitted to asylum procedures 1992. 16,000 from former Yugoslavia 1991-2. Estimated 750,000 non-EC nationals in Italy of whom 80,000 Moroccan, 14,000

Somali.
The authorities tolerated a large number (over 1 million) undocumented or illegal entrants until pressure from Schengen partners to tighten up. Amnesty in 1989 was followed by tough immigration laws 1990, providing for deportation of irregular immigrants and those with no means of support, visa requirements, computerised registration of immigrants, quota system to tie immigration to labour market needs. *1991*: mass repatriation of 24,000 Albanians and agreement with Albania for cooperation in policing and patrolling coastline. Decree that all clandestine arrivals by sea would be regarded as illegal and returned.
1992: decree that other than family members and refugees, only temporary workers would be admitted, to 'retain the benefit of northern and sub-Saharan African labour without allowing for settlement'. Minister of Justice proposed lower wage levels for non-EC migrant labour. Hundreds of illegal expulsions under decree providing immediate expulsion for foreigners committing crimes, later declared unconstitutional. Many complaints that Somali, Ethiopian and Eritrean war refugees were being returned without being allowed to claim asylum.
1993: April: New decree to 'reduce numbers in jail' allows for expulsion of foreign remand prisoners. After protests Justice Ministry agreed to amend the decree to allow foreign prisoners to choose between expulsion and serving their sentence in Italy.

Luxembourg (EC, Schengen)
160 asylum-seekers 1991.
Strict immigration controls except for EFTA citizens.
Asylum-seekers coming through territory of other 'safe' countries returned. Family reunion for foreigners settled in country conditional on income and housing conditions.

Netherlands (EC, Schengen)
17,600 asylum-seekers 1992 (25% down from 1991).
Restrictive immigration policies since 1974 (family reunion only); visas required from most countries since 1980.
1991: military police begin handling asylum applications at ports. Number of asylum-seekers summarily rejected and removed (sometimes by force) increased.Fingerprinting and photographing of asylum-seekers.
1992: 12 new 'investigation and reception centres' set up, with high fences, barred windows, electronic surveillance, where asylum-seekers obliged to stay. Accelerated procedures for 'manifestly unfounded' claims. Bill provided for carrier sanctions, and for immediate expulsion of rejected asylum-seekers proposed abolition of 'tolerated status' and appeal rights. Justice minister proposed to make family reunion rights of non-EC nationals conditional on income 'to curb inflow of west Indian youths'. Agreement with Dutch Caribbean islands to deport west Indian youths convicted of crime. Detention of foreigners in police stations pending expulsion approved.
Computerised aliens' administrative system set up, with identity, residence and status of all foreigners. Linked to local registers. Police, tax authorities and social services have access. Bill to make it compulsory for foreigners to carry ID cards.
1993: April: Clampdown on illegal workers announced, with steeper fines for employers in horticulture and garment industry.

Norway (EFTA, Nordic Union)
5,238 asylum-seekers 1992 (half from former Yugoslavia).
Third World workers arrived in numbers in early 1970s to work in oil industry North Sea, after immigration of workers to Denmark and Germany stopped. Ban on primary immigration imposed 1975, further restrictions in Aliens Law 1989.
Asylum-seekers in Red Cross reception centres until 1989, when these taken over by Directorate of Immigration. Centralised registration of asylum-seekers, with photographs and fingerprints.

Poland
Another 'waiting room for western Europe'.
March 1991: signed agreement with (then six) Schengen states which obliged it to take back those illegally crossing from Poland into Schengen territory. New Bill on detention and expulsion of unwanted foreigners, allowing detention of those caught trying to cross into Germany for up to 90 days (previously 2 days). The number of unsuccessful attempts to cross into Poland has risen dramatically from 1990: 200, 1991: 11,800, to 1992: 25,000 (over the first eight months). By end of 1992, estimated 100,000 Romanians waiting in Poland for opportunity to cross to the west.
March 1993: 2,000 people arrested for illegal entry.
May 1993: Romanians visiting Poland must have a minimum of $100 to enter, under reciprocal arrangement. Poland agrees to accept responsibility for asylum-seekers entering Germany after the German constitutional amendment.

Portugal (EC, Schengen)
163 applications for asylum registered 1991 ('manifestly unfounded' applications excluded). Screening procedure in place since 1983.
From 1 January 1992 free movement provisions apply, legalising hundreds of thousands of Portuguese workers in other EC countries. About 100,000 irregular workers in Portugal 1992, mainly from Cape Verde, Guinea-Bissau, Angola.
Signing of Schengen convention in 1991 followed by amnesty for irregular workers October 1992-January 1993. New Aliens Law 1992 provided for setting up of detention centres for illegal immigrants, visa requirements. No permanent settlement to be allowed except for refugees.
Border police (Service of Foreigners and Frontiers, SEF) accused of turning back half Angolans who arrive with visas, on grounds that they were suspected of being from Zaire; using violence to expel alleged illegal immigrants. SEF admitted Africans targeted for most stringent checks at airports because of their 'incentive to migrate', but denied racism: 'We are not responsible for the fact that African passengers are black.' TAP, the main Portuguese airline, admitted that since 1991, officials have photocopied passports of all non-white transit passengers, since they were all 'potential clandestine immigrants'.
January 1993: 11 Brazilians detained in airport for three days with no beds, bathing facilities, then returned to Brazil.

Spain (EC, Schengen)
11,708 asylum-seekers 1992. 5% accepted 1991.
From 1989 on, Spain has become a 'gendarme of Europe' to keep out immigrants

and refugees from Africa. Put in place 'implacable and systematic' policy of expulsion of rejected asylum-seekers; set up marine guard to patrol coastline; fortified frontiers of north African enclaves with barbed wire, closed-circuit TV, electronic monitoring equipment; entered bilateral agreements with France to control illegal entry of Turks and Africans.

1991: Amnesty for illegal immigrants followed by crackdown on illegal immigration, particularly from north Africa, described as 'the key problem facing Spain and the EC'. Detention centres set up for those without papers or lacking means of subsistence. Complaints of the illegal expulsion of asylum-seekers and illegal detention in airports.

1992: Thousands of people crossing straits of Gibraltar in small boats arrested and expelled. Dozens drowned trying to make passage. Five new ships with electronic detection facilities patrolled Spanish coast; under agreement with Morocco, 2,500 men patrolled its coast to prevent departure of boats; detention centres set up in Morocco to hold Africans 'suspected of wanting to cross into Spain'.

April 1993: Permanent work permits for Moroccans replaced by temporary ones valid for 1 year only.

Sweden (EFTA, Nordic Union)
83,188 asylum-seekers 1992 (two-thirds from former Yugoslavia).
Seen as country of refuge during 1970s and 1980s; new rules introduced 1989 limited asylum to those within terms of Geneva Convention. Deportations of asylum-seekers not considered political refugees led to mass protests and occupations of churches in 1990, and government forced to retain 'de facto' status on compassionate grounds.

1992: proposal to expel asylum-seekers accused of petty crime and to refuse entry to those who were suspected of intending to commit crime. Refugee reception centres 'function like open prisons' according to report; asylum-seekers' living allowances cut by 5-10%. Proposal to privatise reception centres and introduce a system of loans and workfare, and to limit 'de facto' refugees by strict quota dependent on demands of labour market.

January 1993: asylum law to be revised. Abolition of 'de facto' status proposed. Doctors complain that traumatised refugees are being deported against their advice.

Switzerland (EFTA)
Foreign population 1,200,000, of whom 67% are from EC/EFTA. 18,000 asylum-seekers 1992 (drop of 57% from 1991), of whom 35% from former Yugoslavia.
Immigration limited to temporary, seasonal and border workers (with EC and EFTA workers favoured) and to refugees. Strict conditions for naturalisation of second generation 'immigrants'. No freedom of movement between cantons for asylum-seekers.

1990: new laws speeded up screening of asylum-seekers, centralised decisions, banned work for first 3 months.

1991: army deployed to help border police on eastern border for trial period. Deductions imposed from wages of asylum-seekers in work to pay for their possible deportation.

1992: Reception centre staff instructed to demand ID documents from asylum-seekers; those without ID documents not registered and in some cases refused asylum. New plans to deter asylum-seekers included repatriation assistance and information campaigns in countries of origin.

United Kingdom (EC)

24,000 asylum-seekers 1992 (50% drop from 1991). Under 10% accepted, further 65% granted 'exceptional leave to remain'.

Strict laws since 1971 limited immigration largely to family reunion, removed British citizenship from ex-colonies citizens and abolished right of citizenship by birth in UK. Rules have imposed income and accommodation conditions, strict criteria about motives of marriage (for entry of spouses), and made deportation easier. Visas, required since 1973 for most non-Commonwealth citizens, were extended to most Commonwealth citizens in 1985, 1986 and 1991 to prevent entry of asylum-seekers and others from Sri Lanka, India, Pakistan, Ghana, Nigeria, Uganda.

1987: Carriers liability law passed. Asylum-seekers detained in detention centres, prisons, floating prison off Harwich.

1990 on: asylum-seekers returned to countries they came through en route to UK.

1991: first Asylum Bill fails through lack of time before general election. Fines under carriers' liability provisions doubled to £2,000 per passenger. SAL (ID document with photograph) introduced for asylum-seekers. Home Secretary held to be in contempt of court for unlawful removal of Zairois asylum-seeker.

1992: Asylum and Immigration Appeals Bill introduced, proposes fingerprinting of all asylum-seekers and dependants, reduced housing provision, accelerated procedures for 'manifestly unfounded' claims, abolition of visitors' appeal rights. Damages paid to Kurds illegally removed without being allowed to claim asylum.

May 1993: Department of the Environment orders local authorities to carry out passport checks on housing applicants and to report 'illegal immigrants' to the Home Office.

European conventions on immigration and asylum[1]

Frances Webber

As an economic entity, the EC has been concerned since its inception with employers' needs for labour. Under the 1957 Treaty of Rome establishing the European Economic Community, freedom of movement and settlement throughout the community was guaranteed to EC workers and their families, to allow labour to move to where the jobs were. The Single European Act, signed in 1986, envisaged the completion of a single European market comprising 330 million EC nationals with full free movement and settlement rights as of 1 January 1993. There are in addition long-standing Association Agreements between the EC and Turkey, Morocco, Tunisia and Algeria, regulating, for example, labour imported from those countries.

Until recently, however, the EC has not been concerned with the immigration of third country nationals as such, which has been seen as a matter for individual member states to regulate. Common immigration and asylum policies therefore developed on an ad hoc basis as a response to the perceived common need to ensure that the opening of Europe's internal borders did not result in the free entry and free movement of those who did not belong there.

The need for some coordination was first acknowledged in 1976, when the Trevi group of Interior Ministers was set up at the instigation of the UK government to enable European countries to cooperate on issues of terrorism. The group expanded its brief in the mid-1980s to embrace all the policing and security aspects of free movement, including immigration, visas, asylum-seekers and border controls. It has worked on shared information systems on migratory flows, clandestine immigration networks and forged documents. With its informal discussions and secret agreements, far from the scrutiny of the European parliament or even national parliaments, the Trevi group served as a model for the development of common immigration and asylum policies (see Chapter 1 on the Trevi group and below for the Ad Hoc Group on Immigration).

The Schengen group
For decades, Belgium, the Netherlands and Luxembourg had an agreement allowing their nationals to move freely between their territories. In 1985 France and Germany joined the Benelux countries to sign the Schengen agreement, extending the Benelux

---

1. This is an abridged version of a piece that will appear in the annual report of the Institute of Race Relations *European Race Audit*. For details contact: IRR, 2-6 Leeke Street, London WC1X 9HS.

border-free zone. Under Schengen, border controls between the five countries were to be abolished from 1 January 1990, and working groups were set up to draw up coordinated measures on policing Schengen's external borders to keep out undesirables, by visa controls, asylum and deportation policies and information exchange. The working group drafted detailed measures which become the Schengen Supplementary Agreement in June 1990.

The Commission of the EC has always had observer status at Schengen meetings, and regarded the drafts produced by the working groups as a 'laboratory of what the Twelve (the EC) will have to implement by the end of 1992, since the Five are confronted by the same problems as those facing the Community' (in fact, the five Schengen countries shortly became six, when Italy signed in the autumn of 1990, and are now nine, with the addition of Spain and Portugal in 1991 and Greece in 1992).

The EC: Commission and Council

The EC Commission steered clear of drafting its own measures on immigration and asylum - partly because the work has already been done by the Schengen group from 1985 onwards, and partly because of the dispute among the EC states as to whether the EC had competence to draft laws in this area. The UK government in particular was adamant that matters of immigration and asylum were for national governments, not for the EC, and refused to give up its sovereign right to retain border controls even on travellers from the EC, not trusting continental immigration officers to keep the illegal immigrants out. Another reason for the resort to intergovernmental agreements in immigration and asylum has been to avoid accountability in the European Parliament, which has shown itself to be considerably more liberal than either the Commission or the Council of Ministers.

This does not mean, however, that the EC institutions have played no role in the coordination of policies among the Twelve. The Council of Ministers set up a 'Group of Coordinators' whose proposals for measures to be implemented by 1 January 1993, known as the Palma document, were adopted at the Madrid summit in June 1989. Measures the group described as 'essential' included:

* a common negative list (countries whose nationals require a visa to enter the EC), to be updated every six months, and harmonisation of the criteria and procedures for visas;
* a common list of inadmissible persons and procedures for dealing with them;
* a procedure for preventing asylum-seekers from applying for asylum in more than one member state;
* accelerated procedures for handling 'manifestly unfounded' asylum claims;
* acceptance of identical international commitments on refugees;
* definition of common measures for checks on external borders, and system of surveillance, with improved cooperation and exchange of information between police, customs etc;
* combating illegal immigration networks;
* establishing information exchange system on wanted and inadmissible persons;
* deciding which state is responsible for removing immigrants and rejected asylum-seekers from EC territory, and establishing a financing system for expulsions.

In October 1991 the Commission sent its own 'Communications' on immigration and asylum to the Council of Ministers. The communication on asylum recommended that all member states introduce accelerated procedures and common criteria for dealing with what it called 'manifestly unfounded' applications for asylum. It called for the effective deportation of rejected asylum-seekers, and the examination of asylum requests at the borders, so that removal could take effect speedily, and indicated that asylum-seekers coming from or through safe countries should be refused. A common list of countries deemed 'first countries of asylum' was to be a priority, and agreements were to be signed with third countries to ensure that they would take back rejected asylum-seekers. An effective information exchange system, and faster administrative and judicial procedures, were also required.

The Commission pointed approvingly to measures taken by member states to deter asylum-seekers, including measures 'aimed at making the material situation of asylum-seekers less attractive while their case is being considered: withholding of certain social security benefits, restrictions on employment and freedom of movement', and registration and fingerprinting of asylum-seekers to 'aid identification and combat multiple applications'. It also noted with approval restrictive visa policies and carrier sanctions adopted by some member states, and urged harmonisation of treatment throughout the community so as to avoid 'uneven distribution', with too many asylum-seekers going to states which allowed them to live and work freely. Its communication on immigration was no less repressive in its terms, concentrating on the need for measures to combat clandestine immigration, for the deportation of immigrants to third countries, and for the monitoring of 'migratory flows'.

The Ad Hoc Group on Immigration

The work required to draw up these measures - or adapt the equivalent measures drawn up by the Schengen group - has been largely undertaken by the Ad Hoc Group on Immigration. The group, comprising interior ministers of the EC states, was set up at the UK's suggestion in October 1986 to 'end abuses of the asylum process' (by asylum-seekers rather than governments). In April 1987, it proposed sanctions on airlines bringing in undocumented asylum-seekers and those with false documents (and since visa requirements had by then been imposed on most refugee-producing countries, and refugees could not get visas, this applied to most of them). Then, in 1990, it produced a draft convention to prevent asylum-seekers making more than one application in the EC: the Dublin convention. In the same year it produced a draft convention on harmonisation of controls at external borders. In 1991 it set out proposals for fingerprinting asylum-seekers, and set up a 'rapid consultation centre' on immigration problems, composed of the Troika of the Ad Hoc Group (ie immigration ministers from the countries holding the past, present and next presidency of the EC). It refused UNHCR access to its activities. In 1992 it produced draft resolutions on criteria and procedures for so-called 'manifestly unfounded' asylum claims, and, extending its brief, on policies for family reunion for non-EC nationals settled in the EC; on the admission of non-EC nationals for employment; and on expulsion from the EC.

While the Ad Hoc Group operates under international, not EC law, and produces conventions and resolutions for inter-governmental agreement rather than EC directives, it has a permanent secretariat based at the Council of Ministers of the EC, and the EC Commission sits on the group as a member. The group presents its proposals initially to the meetings of ministers responsible for immigration in the EC member states (the same people as the Council of Ministers, but meeting within the framework of 'European Political Cooperation' (EPC) rather than within a formal EC framework).

The immigration ministers, meeting in Lisbon in June 1992, for example, approved the Group's preliminary draft of a parallel Dublin convention, eventually to be signed by EFTA and other non-EC European countries. They called for joint reports, from information collected by EC member states' embassies, on countries of origin of asylum-seekers, starting with Angola, Ethiopia, Romania, Albania and Sri Lanka.

At their November 1992 meeting in London, the ministers adopted the draft resolutions prepared by the Ad Hoc group on 'manifestly unfounded' applications and 'host third countries' and approved its report on 'countries in which there is generally no serious risk of persecution'. They asked the group to expedite work on EURODAC, the automated fingerprint matching system at the feasibility study stage, which will be used to check all asylum-seekers to ensure that they have not claimed asylum before or elsewhere in Europe. They asked the Ad Hoc Group to prepare final texts of the draft resolutions on harmonisation of national policies on family reunification and admission for employment, and approved recommendations on expulsion.

The Centre for information, discussion and exchange on asylum (CIREA) was set up under the auspices of the Ad Hoc group with the approval of the Council of Ministers at the end of 1991, and has already attracted criticism for its secrecy and unaccountability. NGOs complain that they have no access to the information held by CIREA on countries of origin of asylum-seekers, and have no way of knowing if the information is up to date, comprehensive and accurate. Since CIREA is to be charged with the task of informing member states on the safety of countries from which asylum-seekers come, it is vital that the information they hold is, and is seen to be, full, accurate, and not distorted by political or diplomatic considerations. In November 1992, however, oblivious to such criticism, immigration ministers approved the setting up of another such centre, the Centre for information, discussion and exchange on the crossing of borders and immigration (CIREFI).

As the EC has had no recognised competence to deal with immigration and asylum issues, the work done by the Ad Hoc group and the agreements between immigration ministers with the approval of the Commission and the Council of ministers cannot be checked by the European Parliament. The Parliament monitors developments, particularly through its Committee for Legal Affairs and Citizens' Rights, the Committee on Development and Cooperation, and, since Maastricht, the Committee on Civil Liberties and Internal Affairs, which have been extremely critical of the anti-immigrant and anti-refugee thinking informing the work of the Commission and the Council, and of the creation of the inter-governmental framework which deprives it of any jurisdiction in the area.

Maastricht
The Treaty on European Union agreed at Maastricht in December 1991 gave the EC competence for the first time in immigration and asylum, albeit in the limited field

of visa controls. Article 100c of the Treaty gives the Council the authority to draw up a list of third countries whose nationals need a visa to enter the EC, on a proposal from the Commission and after consultation with the European Parliament. In what is described as an emergency, where there is a 'threat of a sudden inflow of nationals from a particular third country', the Council can impose visa controls for six months without input from the Commission or consultation with parliament. The Council has also been empowered to introduce a uniform model visa for use throughout the EC.

Other immigration and asylum matters come under what is known as the Third Pillar of the Treaty. They are at present to be dealt with by means of inter-governmental cooperation, within the framework of European Political Cooperation (EPC). Under Title VI Article K of the Treaty, the Council may adopt joint positions or joint actions, or draw up conventions, on asylum policy, rules on the crossing of external borders, the exercise of controls there, and on immigration policy. But it is envisaged that such joint measures may be taken in to community competence (that is to say, conventions signed by all member states could eventually become EC laws), and the Treaty envisages a conference to take these decisions in 1996. In the meantime, groups such as the Ad Hoc and TREVI groups are to be replaced by more formal structures set up under Article K of the Treaty.

THE CONVENTIONS and RESOLUTIONS:

The Dublin Convention
The primary function of the convention was to stop asylum-seekers from (a) choosing their country of asylum, or (b) making consecutive or multiple applications. The idea was that if an asylum-seeker was refused asylum in one EC country, the refusal was good for the whole of the EC.

If there was to be just one application, rules had to be laid down as to which country should deal with it, and bear the costs of keeping the asylum-seeker in the meanwhile. Before the Dublin Convention, the phenomenon known as RIO ('Refugees in Orbit') was becoming increasingly common. Anxious to accept as few refugees as possible, member states were 'bouncing' those who arrived via another European country back to that country, applying the principle that asylum should be claimed as soon as the refugee is on safe territory. In December 1988, for example, three Romanian asylum-seekers who sought asylum in Copenhagen, having transited through Austria but not claimed asylum there, were returned to Austria, where immigration officials returned them to Copenhagen. There, they were detained 24 hours before being returned to Austria once more. The Austrian authorities this time sent them to Paris, where they were detained for 12 days before being returned to Austria.

The full title of the Dublin Convention, signed in June 1990 by all the member states, is the *Convention determining the state responsible for examining applications for asylum lodged in one of the member states of the European Communities*. Its content was lifted wholesale from Chapter 7 of the Supplementary Schengen Agreement (signed at the same time). After re-affirming the commitment of the member states to the Geneva Convention on Refugees, and the right of any member state to examine any asylum application or to remove asylum-seekers to countries outside the Community, the Convention then defines the state having responsibility for an asylum claim as the one which has allowed the asylum-seeker in to the Community, either by granting a visa, or by permitting his or her illegal entry into the Community. If, however, the asylum-seeker has a husband or wife or children with refugee status in an EC country, or is a child with parents who have refugee status in an EC state, that state must deal with the claim. Measures are then set out for the receiving state to notify the responsible state and send the asylum-seeker back there. Finally, there are provisions for the exchange of information, both general (on the situation in refugee-producing countries, on 'migratory movements', new laws, procedures and cases in the member states), and particular to the asylum-seeker concerned, to check whether the applicant is known or has made a previous application in another member state.

The so-called family unity clause of the convention is deceptive. While at first glance it seems to guarantee that family members will be able to get together in the same state, in reality it is far more limited. While most asylum-seekers heading for a particular country do so in order to join relatives, the relatives very rarely have refugee status. More often they have 'exceptional leave to remain', or 'tolerated' or 'B' status. In the UK for example, 65% of asylum-seekers are granted exceptional leave to remain (ELR), while around 7.5% get full refugee status. Those granted ELR include the overwhelming majority of people often called refugees - Somalis, Tamils, Ethiopians, Kurds from Turkey and Iraq - since those fleeing civil war are not defined as Geneva Convention refugees, as they are not being persecuted, merely bombed or shelled. In addition, adults cannot join siblings or cousins.

An example or two illustrates the way the Convention works. A 17-year old Somali boy arrived in the UK to join his adult sister here. She was his only close living relative left; his brothers had been killed in the fighting, or had disappeared, his father was dead, and he had fled Somalia when his mother was killed in front of him. He had flown to Italy, using a false passport, and changed planes there for the UK. He was sent back to Italy, as the country which has permitted his illegal entry into the EC. He was too old to benefit from the family reunion provisions of the Convention, and besides, his sister only had ELR, she was not a 'refugee'.

A Ugandan woman arrived in the UK with her young child, having transited through France. At Dover she was told she would be returned to France. Her husband had been killed and she had been raped and tortured by the military in Uganda, and her UK-resident sister was her only relative. Solicitors only prevented her removal by obtaining three psychiatric reports which all insisted that she had to have her sister's care to prevent complete breakdown.

An example of the way the information exchange system might be used comes from another UK case, involving Switzerland. A Zairois applied for asylum in the UK and gave various details about himself. He said he had been in prison for a number of years in Zaire. His claim was investigated, and it transpired that the Swiss authorities had records of a man with his name living in Switzerland at the time the asylum-seeker said he had been in prison in Zaire, with a woman whose name was similar (though not identical) to that of his wife. The couple in Switzerland had claimed a different nationality. The Swiss authorities faxed the British a photo of 'their' man. On the basis of the faxed photo, the British Home Office declared that it was indeed the same man. His claim was rejected.

The Convention has been ratified by only four member states so far, including the

UK, and is not yet in force, but is generally followed in practice. Although intended to halt the 'refugee in orbit' phenomenon, if anything it has increased it, as states squabble over whether a passenger in transit through an airport lounge was 'admitted' into their territory. In 1993 another Somali refugee who transited through Italy to the UK was returned promptly to Italy, who just as promptly returned him to the UK. The British immigration authorities were only prevented from sending him back, like a ping-pong ball, to Italy, by court action.

The Ad Hoc Group has now prepared a *Parallel Convention*, for non-EC member states who want to take advantage of the first safe country principle. The wording of this convention is virtually identical with that of the Dublin convention. Those signing will include the EFTA countries and perhaps some of the east European 'buffer zone' states like Hungary, Poland and the Czech republic.

Countries like Denmark and the UK have managed by means of the Dublin convention to offload a large part of their responsibility towards refugees, by sending away anyone who did not come on a direct flight from their country of persecution. The British Home Secretary tried to apply this principle to Bosnian refugees in the summer of 1992, until outraged public opinion forced him to make a concession that the UK would not turn away those who had 'only transited' through other European countries - but the principle is still applied in all its severity to all other refugees. Until recently, Germany has not used the Convention, but the recent modification of the constitutional right to asylum now allows the German authorities to turn back those arriving through other EC countries, and - if the Parallel Convention is signed - through other signatory countries too - which will cut the number of asylum-seekers allowed to submit a claim in Germany by up to 90%. The Convention will be used to push back asylum-seekers who have travelled overland to the countries of eastern and southern Europe through which they have travelled - the least able to bear the burden.

The Resolutions on manifestly unfounded asylum claims

Another important aspect of the Ad Hoc Group's work has been to attempt to shorten asylum determination procedures. The public rationale behind this was the idea that most asylum-seekers are not refugees but 'economic migrants' who should be processed and removed as quickly as possible, both to save costs and to prevent de facto settlement in the EC. However, when a draft of the confidential resolution was leaked in October 1992, it became clear that the underlying motive was a desire to rid Europe of non-European refugees. 'Intercontinental movements are seldom necessary for protection', it said, and warned that those who feared human rights violations should 'stay in their own country and seek protection or redress from their own authorities'. If such protection was unavailable, they should move to a 'safe' part of their own country; or, if absolutely necessary, to a neighbouring country. Refugee status should not be granted in Europe 'merely because levels of security, economic opportunity or individual liberty are below European ones'. The draft proposed that only those refugees fleeing persecution should be granted protection in Europe, excluding those fleeing war or civil war who are currently granted tolerated status.

The leaking of the draft caused problems of 'presentational impact', and two new, sanitised draft resolutions were presented at the Ad Hoc group meeting in London in November 1992, and adopted by the ministers responsible for immigration, who expressed their wish that their principles be effected in binding conventions.

The *Resolution on manifestly unfounded applications for asylum* sets out criteria and procedures for dealing with so-called manifestly unfounded claims. An accelerated procedure is set out in which the processing of the claim should take no more than a month. An application can be deemed manifestly unfounded because the applicant does not fear persecution, or the claim contains no details or is inconsistent or 'fundamentally improbable'; or if the applicant could safely go to another part of his or her own country; or if false documents have been used or documents have been destroyed; or if the applicant has been refused asylum in another member state; or has made the application to forestall impending expulsion; or has failed to comply with obligations such as fingerprinting. An application can also be dealt with under the accelerated procedure if the state processing it wishes to deal with it urgently for other reasons, for example if the applicant has committed a serious criminal offence or the authorities wish to expel the asylum-seeker on public security grounds as quickly as possible.

To assist member states in assessing claims, the Ad Hoc group submitted some *Conclusions on countries in which there is generally no serious risk of persecution*, which sets out factors such as previous numbers of refugees and recognition rates, observance of human rights, the existence of democratic institutions, and the perceived stability of the country. It is claimed that there is at present no plan to draw up a 'master list' of countries deemed 'safe', although the work of CIREA, and the Immigration Ministers' call in June 1992 for joint assessment of countries such as Ethiopia, Angola and Sri Lanka belies this claim. Some countries have such lists already, and Germany is in the process of drawing one up for its own accelerated assessment procedures.

The accompanying *Resolution on a harmonised approach to questions concerning host third countries* is a unilateral extension of the Dublin convention principle to all other countries. If an asylum-seeker has come through what is called a 'host third country' which is itself deemed 'safe', or is admissible there, an attempt to seek asylum in the EC is deemed 'unlawful', so that the asylum claim need not be determined at all and the applicant can be sent straight away to that country.

Many of the criteria for assessing an application as 'manifestly unfounded', as well as the procedures, have already been taken up by member states. They are incorporated in the Asylum and Immigration Appeals Bill in the UK, which is set to become law by early summer 1993. They will result in the return of many asylum-seekers to countries deemed safe but in reality life-threatening. Kenya, for example, is likely to be considered a 'safe' country to which most Somalis can be returned (they all have to come through Kenya to get out). But Somalis are routinely robbed and beaten in the camps and by the police and military in Kenya; most are illegally there and are at constant risk of repatriation to Somalia; illness and malnutrition rage through the camps and the prospects of survival are slim.

For the first time, the Resolutions assert that an asylum-seeker who has protection in another country is acting unlawfully by leaving that country for Europe. This gives an indication of the way that measures to deal with asylum-seekers are increasingly being seen as part of the Community's battle against illegal immigrants. Those asylum-seekers who arrive in Europe with no documents, or who have had to resort to buying forged passports to get on to an aircraft, will get short shrift under this regime, as will those who have applied in another EC country (which will be ascertained by compulsory fingerprinting of all asylum-seekers and the EURODAC fingerprint matching system).

External borders convention

The Ad Hoc Group drafted the external borders convention in 1990, and it was expected to be signed in 1991 at the latest. This convention is central to the opening up of the internal market, since it puts in place the external controls and the information system needed to secure the EC's borders, without which the internal borders cannot be removed. No mention is made in it of the lifting of internal border controls, because the inclusion of such a clause would prevent the UK, Ireland and Denmark from signing it, as it has prevented them from signing the Schengen Accord on which this convention is based.

Even without such a controversial clause, the convention has still not been signed, however, because of the dispute between Spain and the UK over Gibraltar, and at their meeting in November 1992 in London, the immigration ministers of the member states expressed their 'profound regret' that no solution had yet been found.

The full title of the convention is the *Draft Convention of the Member States of the European Communities on the crossing of external frontiers*. It has not yet been officially published. Its main premise is that third country nationals have no right to enter the EC, and have to satisfy very stringent conditions to be allowed entry. There will be a common list of countries whose nationals require visas, and a uniform EC visa will be developed, based on common conditions and criteria. Visas will be granted for three months only, and passengers with visas will be admitted only if they have sufficient means to support themselves and to pay for a return ticket, and can show documents substantiating the purpose and conditions of the planned visit. They can still be refused entry if they have been reported as 'not to be permitted entry' or are considered a threat to public order, national security or international relations of any member state. There are to be thorough checks on entry and exit, and those breaching the conditions of their stay could be listed as persons to be refused entry in the future. A joint computerised list of inadmissible third country nationals is to be developed, by reference to the commission of immigration or other offences, or a reasonable belief that the person concerned is planning to commit a serious offence. The list will be contained in the European Information System (EIS) to be set up under the convention (see Chapter 1).

Third country nationals legally settled in one EC country are not to have the rights of free movement and settlement across the EC territory. Instead, the convention authorises visa-free travel for three months for them, subject to registration in the host country within three days of arrival.

The external borders of the EC can be crossed, under the convention, only at specific points and specific hours, and member states are to introduce penalties for the unauthorised crossing of external borders. Member states have a duty of cooperation in the effective surveillance of the external borders. Carrier sanctions are to be imposed by all member states on airlines, shipping and other transport companies carrying passengers with false documents or no documents.

Article 25 of the Draft convention provides for the setting up of an intergovernmental Executive Committee, to be serviced by the Council of Ministers' general secretariat but not under the jurisdiction of the EC, although the Commission will be allowed to participate in the Committee's work.

Draft resolution on family reunification

This draft was prepared for the meeting of immigration ministers in November 1992. The final text, entitled *Draft resolution on harmonisation of national policies on admission for family reunion*, is due to be presented to the meeting in May/June 1993 in Denmark. Its aim is to limit the dependants who can be brought in by non-EC workers who are living in the EC, and impose conditions on their admission. It is not known whether it will also apply to refugees. The principles set out in the draft include:

* limitation of family reunion to spouses and children aged up to sixteen or eighteen, with the exclusion of other family members. (This contrasts with the family rights of EC nationals working in another EC state, who are allowed to bring in spouse, children under 21 or in full-time education, elderly parents and other dependent relatives, and is significantly more stringent than current UK law, which allows for the admission of elderly parents, and of other relatives in compassionate circumstances).

* admission of spouses and adopted children only where the marriage or adoption is recognised by the state. (This cuts out cohabitees, and all 'de facto' adoptions, or adoptions from eg the Indian sub-continent).

* Member states will be free to impose 'waiting periods' before family reunion can be exercised. (In UK law, family reunion can be exercised immediately a person is settled or accepted for settlement here. People granted exceptional leave to remain have to wait four years before they can have family members join them).

* Member states may require spouses to prove that the primary purpose of their marriage was not to obtain admission to the territory before admitting them. (The UK led the way with the infamous 'primary purpose' rule, adopted in 1982).

* Adopted children can be excluded if the primary purpose of the adoption appears to be admission for the child. (Again, this follows UK rules on 'adoptions of convenience').

* Family reunion will not be permissible if the sponsor is in receipt of welfare benefits. (Most EC member states already have rules to this or similar effect, including the UK).

Human rights groups are concerned that the principles violate international human rights obligations such as the European Convention on Human Rights (ECHR), Article 8 of which guarantees respect for family life, and other human rights and migrant workers conventions. This despite the fact that the Maastricht Treaty declares that the Union shall respect fundamental rights as guaranteed by the ECHR.

Draft resolution on admission for employment

Another draft resolution, prepared by the Ad Hoc Group for submission to the immigration ministers in November 1992, defines the limited and temporary nature of immigration for employment which the EC will allow to non-EC nationals. The draft was not complete, and the meeting requested the Ad Hoc Group to complete its work for the June 1993 meeting.

The draft resolution, entitled *Draft resolution on harmonisation of national policies on admission for employment*, proposes that member states may admit migrant workers on a temporary basis, for six months without a special permit (this will fill the need for seasonal workers in eg Spain, Italy, Portugal and Switzerland); for up to three years as a trainee, and as a contract worker for five years maximum in the first instance. The only category which could lead to settlement is the last, but it envisages five years' tied employment with the same employer before any opportunity for permanent residence arises. There is no guarantee of equal treatment with EC workers. Family reunion rights are very limited.

The draft has been forcefully criticised for its apparently complete lack of awareness of the rights given to certain categories of workers - non-EC employees of EC companies, and those whose rights are protected by Association Agreements. If the resolution were applied as it stands all these rights, protected by EC law, would be swept away. In addition the draft ignores the ILO Conventions dealing with the rights of migrant workers. Critics accuse the Ad Hoc group of trying to re-introduce the 'gastarbeiter' system of the post-war period.

Recommendations on expulsion
The other area which the EC is attempting to tighten is practice on expulsions. Many mainland EC countries have traditionally issued far more expulsion orders than they have carried out, or have merely expelled people to a neighbouring state, allowing them to remain unlawfully or to return. But in the past few years, most EC states have begun to remove large numbers of rejected asylum-seekers back to the countries from which they fled. Further provisions for the removal of asylum-seekers are set out in the *Dublin* and *parallel Dublin* conventions and the *manifestly unfounded* and *third host country* resolutions. The *Recommendation concerning checks on expulsion of third country nationals residing or working without authorisation* agreed at the Ministers' meeting in Copenhagen on 1 June 1993, expressed the commitment to vigorously detect and expel those breaching immigration rules. Visitors, students, those entering an EC country for marriage, and those joining other family members are to be targeted for strict monitoring, and sanctions against those 'harbouring' or employing illegal entrants are to be stiffened. The *Recommendation on transit for the purposes of expulsion* has not yet been seen, but it is believed that it provides a Dublin-like system for defining the state responsible for expelling illegal entrants from the EC. Responsibility for their expulsion will rest with the country which let them in to the EC or the state in which they are found. These recommendations are expressed to be without prejudice to Community law or to provisions of international conventions on extradition.

Implementation
So far, of these conventions and resolutions, none is yet in force. The Dublin Convention is likely to be the first. It does not need formal incorporation into UK law to be followed; in 1990 the Home Secretary announced to Parliament his policy of returning asylum-seekers to countries through which they had come, and the UK authorities have been following the practice of the Dublin Convention ever since, with no debate on the subject in Parliament. The External Borders Convention, once

agreed, will need changes in UK immigration rules for its full implementation here. Third country nationals requiring visas are listed in the Appendix to the immigration rules, and the conditions for the issue of visas will need to be incorporated. Matters such as the setting up of the EDS, or the exchange of information, or the entry of names of inadmissible persons on a common list, can be done without reference to Parliament.

The Resolutions on manifestly unfounded applications for asylum and third host countries are the subject of current legislation in the UK and elsewhere (see Chapter 8: Immigration and Asylum: country summaries), as are the Ad Hoc Group's recommendation for universal fingerprinting for asylum-seekers, and the Commission's suggestions on harmonisation of conditions of reception for asylum-seekers (limiting housing rights and the increased use of detention, for example).

Aspects of the draft resolution on family reunion have been or are being legislated in member states, although there are as yet no hints of rule changes by the British government to remove rights of 'de facto' adopted children or distressed relatives to join families in the UK, or to introduce generalised waiting periods for family reunion.

Migration for work is already extremely limited throughout the EC, and is regulated by the Association Agreements with specific countries mentioned above (to which Poland and Hungary have recently been added), by bilateral agreements, and by restrictive conditions for the issue of work permits. The draft resolution in this area is still at its early stages. It is not known to what extent if at all the recommendations on expulsion would impact on national laws; monitoring of visitors and students, and detection and removal of unauthorised workers, is already vigorous in the UK, and a further 300 detention places are being provided in 1993-4.

The danger of the Maastricht process is that, once the transitional period of intergovernmental cooperation comes to an end, these extremely illiberal conventions and resolutions, drafted solely from the perspective of policing and with no regard to the rights of immigrants and refugees, will be incorporated into EC law. Already they have resulted in dramatic changes to the practice of European states, and in appalling treatment of asylum-seekers becoming the norm throughout the EC.

Inside racist Europe[1]

Liz Fekete

1992 saw an upsurge in racist violence across Europe - bomb attacks on refugee centres and murders on the streets being only the most dramatic indicators of a more widespread disease. The governments of Europe, even as they move towards a 'common, market, racism', are concerned about the dislocating aspects of this violence. But their solutions are cosmetic, based as they are on the premise that racial violence is either a manifestation of 'xenophobia', or of growing extremism. The answer to the former is (at best) the strengthening of laws against incitement to racial hatred, while the solution to the latter is the use of the state apparatus to outlaw and/or place under surveillance 'extremists' of both Left and Right. And, even as the governments of Europe seek to manage the fall-out of racial violence, they use that same violence to justify more immigration controls and anti-refugee measures. This has been seen not only in the political campaign in Germany to remove Article 16 of the constitution, but in the statements of other European politicians, like UK Prime Minister, John Major, who told the Luxembourg Summit in 1991 that 'if we fail in our control efforts we risk fuelling the far-Right.'

But there has also been a failure in our own movements to understand the rise of racism and fascism today, or to see the violence in its entirety. And this weakness is due in no small part to our tendency to prioritise anti-fascism over anti-racism, and to treat racial violence as a by-product of fascism. This, in turn, is linked to our inability to see how the racism of the post-war period differs from that of the fascism of the 1930s, or, indeed, from that of colonialism, even as we recognise that the legacy of both the fascist and the colonial periods is strongly ingrained in Europe's culture and institutions.

Identifying trends
We need only to sift through the empirical evidence before us to see that far-Right violence is just one part of a wider pattern of violence against 'minorities' that is, on the one hand, institutional (ie: carried out in prisons, through the police, etc) and, on the other, 'popular' (ie: carried out by ordinary citizens, as opposed to fascist gangs).

Far-Right terror tactics
Sweden, France, Belgium, Germany, Italy and Norway, all have racist electoral parties of the far-Right and in all these countries racist violence inclines more towards neo-nazi terror tactics than it does in Denmark, UK, Greece, Portugal and Spain where the far Right is not so strong. In the case of Germany, far-Right electoral success and neo-nazi violence draw succour from the overweening sense of

---

1. This an abridged version of a longer piece that will appear in the annual report of the Institute of Race Relations *European Race Audit*. For details contact: IRR, 2-6 Leeke Street, London WC1X 9HS.

'ethnic homogeneity' which informs political and cultural life, and is related to that aspect of German society and culture that has never fully purged itself of its fascist orientation. In Germany, where the 'foreigners law' dates back ultimately to nazi legislation, and clause 116 of the German constitution links German nationality to blood, it is small wonder that what links those who died in far-Right violence in 1992 is that they were not 'full Germans'. Hence, a Turkish family, Third World refugees, a Vietnamese worker, and the homeless, disabled people, people mistaken for Gypsies, known socialists, all rank amongst the dead.

Deeper patterns of racial harassment

France and Italy, and to a lesser extent Belgium, all have a racist party of the far-Right entrenched in the mainstream system, but here patterns of racist violence are more complex. In both Belgium and France, racial violence, it is true, is at its worst in those parts of the country where the Front National or the Vlaams Blok are strongest. But whereas in Belgium, racist violence tends currently to be more confined to the activities of the far-Right (and the police), in France patterns of racial harassment have more in common with the UK. Neither in France nor the UK is racial violence a new phenomenon, but dates rather dates from the 1950s and 1960s, when workers from the ex-colonies came to take up employment. The targets of racist violence in both the UK and France are (predominantly) those from the former colonies - hence 'Paki-bashing' in the UK and 'Arabicide' in France.

In attempting to understand why racial harassment has become so much more diffused in both France and the UK, we need to look in particular at the attitude of the police. Not only do they usually fail to see racial harassment as a crime, and thus fail to afford the victims proper protection, but they tend also to adopt a colonial style of policing towards second and third generation black communities; they assume the role of an army of occupation in the UK 'inner cities' or the French 'banlieues' (see below).

In Italy, racist violence in the post-war period is a relatively new phenomenon (although fascist violence is not) and Italy stands slightly apart from the other countries where the racist right is strong. Whereas in France the Front National has succeeded in pushing the political centre towards the Right, thus making racism respectable, in Italy, the racist Northern League has moved more to exploit the political vacuum at the centre, and used racism as a means of drawing support from the centre to its ranks. Hence, Italy seems to be at the moment experiencing an escalation of patterns of racial harassment sometimes, but not always, manipulated by the Northern League. For instance, in Come, north Italy, in the summer of 1992, 50% of voters turned out to support a referendum, organised by the Northern League, against the opening of a refugee centre in the area.

Institutional violence against refugees

In Germany, after the events in August 1992 in Rostock, international attention has focused on the failure of the police to provide basic protection for refugees. But there is disturbing evidence from Germany, that the police are themselves using violence against refugees who are housed in what are officially described, with all its nazi connotations, as 'concentrated camps'. In other parts of Europe too, most notably the Netherlands (but there are also examples from Italy and Denmark), police and prison officials are alleged to have beaten and even tortured refugees. For instance, in November 1992 riot police were deployed at the Grenshospitium, a closed-off area for asylum seekers at Amsterdam's Schiphol airport, to remove ten refugees who had attempted to organise a protest. In Germany, at the time of writing, refugee protests against the withdrawal of cash subsistence payments and their replacement by food parcels are being violently broken up by the police.

The increasing number of attacks, highlighted by international human rights groups like Amnesty International, add a poignant dimension to the call made by the Institute of Race Relations and other concerned groups across Europe, that no persons seeking asylum should be held in prisons, camps or detention centres across Europe whilst awaiting decisions on their applications.

Police racism

At least three tendencies within policing need to be commented upon: (a) the increased harassment of 'black' or 'immigrant' communities due to perpetual identity checks and increased paramilitary-style policing across Europe; (b.) the existence of colonial patterns of policing, most notably in France, the UK and Belgium; (c) the persistence of authoritarian and undemocratic police methods in many of the countries of southern Europe which have a history of dictatorship.

In relation to (a), the increase in paramilitary style police raids to hunt out 'illegal workers' is a direct result of the Single European market, the removal of borders, and the internalisation of immigration controls. It has added yet another layer of friction to that which already exists, in the form of persistent identity checks on black people across Europe. In the countries of southern Europe, paramilitary style police raids to track down illegal workers are a relatively new phenomenon, since hitherto previously undocumented workers were a necessary and tolerated part of the national economy which in certain sections relied heavily on seasonal and temporary workers. It is not hard to see that the policing of 'immigrant' communities in this way (itself brought in to satisfy their other European partners of Southern Europe's 'firmness' on immigration controls) when combined with long-standing traditions of police violence - the residue of long periods of dictatorship in the region - make for an explosive mix of racism and brutality.

In Belgium, France and the UK, the policing legacy is not that of authoritarianism, but colonialism. In France, the memory of 1961, when French police killed between 140-200 Algerians, demonstrating in support of Algerian independence on the streets of Paris, is still alive amongst second and third generation North African youth. And France was the first country to introduce in the early 1970s internal controls via its notorious street checks.

In Britain, the saturation style policing of black areas and wide-scale random stops of black individuals, are both redolent of colonial measures. The infamous 'sus' laws, under which a person could be arrested simply on the suspicion that they were about to commit an offence, and which were widely used against at the black community, were abolished in 1981, but replaced by a more intensive and sophisticated style of paramilitary policing, within the framework of special powers (Police and Criminal Evidence Act 1984, Public Order Act, 1986, and the Prevention of Terrorism Act already existed). In Belgium, where the level of internal, bureaucratic control over every aspect of a 'foreign workers' experience is unprecedented in the rest of Europe, and where a blatantly raw brutality is - as it was under Belgian colonialism - an acceptable part of police practice, special police squads, the 'brigades canines', were set up in the 1980s in areas with large 'foreign' communities. In each of these countries there has been a large number of unexplained black deaths in police custody (in Belgium, four 'immigrant' youth died in unexplained circumstances in 1992 alone) which has reinforced the belief amongst second and third generation 'immigrants' that they are second class citizens and that police crimes against them will go unpunished. Not surprisingly, both countries have also witnessed 'uprisings' among youth as a direct consequence of police harassment.

Some notes on popular racism

The specifics of racism and fascism vary from country to country, in accordance with each country's own internal logic and historical development. But what unites these variations on the theme of racism is the European dimension. What obtains across Europe today is a new pan-European common, market, racism, being implemented, harmonised and regularised at state-to-state level.

The mechanics of how this new Euro-state racism has been institutionalised in each of the member states has been described by Frances Webber in a previous chapter. But this new institutionalised racism is, in turn, producing its own popular culture that 'derives its sanction and its sustenance from state racism'. Below are notes intended to indicate the various levels at which this new popular racism is operating.

1. IDEOLOGY

(a) *The numbers game*

As each country has brought in asylum and immigration legislation in accordance with the dictates of Euro-state racism, politicians have sought to discuss the refugee and immigration issue in terms of numbers and not need, using arguments such as 'the boat is full' (Germany) or we have reached the 'threshold of tolerance' (Belgium). What we witnessed in the UK in the late 1960s and 1970s (termed 'Powellism' after the Conservative MP Enoch Powell) is now part of common sense thinking all over Europe.

(b) *Blaming the victim*

If the upsurge in racism and fascism is not placed in the context of state and popular racism, it is inevitable that a 'blaming the victim' syndrome emerges. Just as the argument before was that 'fewer numbers make for better race relations' (ie: the presence of black people was the cause of race conflict), the argument today is that 'less refugees makes for less fascism'. The logical conclusion of this, as Sivanandan has argued, is 'no refugees, no fascism', which is not far from the 'final solution'.

This argument has, of course, reached its zenith in Germany where politicians orchestrated the campaign to remove Article 16 of the Constitution. But it also present throughout Europe. In Austria, for instance, after an attack on a refugee centre in Gutenstein, near Vienna, in September 1992, the Mayors of Salzburg and Vienna responded to this outrage by announcing that they would take in no more refugees, as though the very presence of refugees was an incitement to the fascists. The fascist violence was not condemned.

(c) *Immigrants* = *crime*

Racist ideas are made popular by the press who often act as a mouthpiece for the police, or for other arms of the state apparatus. The myth that 'immigrants' cause crime is also becoming part of common sense thinking across Europe. There are various aspects to this stereotypical equation that deserve further comment.

(i) In Germany, Greece and the Netherlands, 1992/3 saw the release of racialised crime statistics which seek to identify immigrants with certain crimes. Previously, in the 1980s in the UK, the release of such statistics had led to an outcry in the black community, and social scientists and lawyers had successfully demonstrated the unscientific and prejudiced nature of the police 'data'. In the Netherlands, following the release of such crime statistics in January 1993, and subsequent statements by the police commissioner of Amsterdam linking Surinamese and Dutch Antillean youth to street crime, the Antillean government made strong protests and warned of the danger of employing stereotypes, particularly at a time of growing racism.

(ii) In the Netherlands, too, the decision of the Dutch Home Secretary, Ms Dales, in September 1991 to inaugurate a 'national debate on minorities' has served to strengthen the 'immigrants = crime' equation, which seems to have been the main framework in which the national debate took place. For instance, in a series of public statements, again by the police commissioner of Amsterdam, Ghanaian illegal workers were said to be responsible for crime in the city. The 'national debate' has also focused attention on 'ethnic conflict'. And a Dutch Secret Service working paper, published in the context of the debate, warned of the 'tribal wars of rival Muslim organisations'.

In Denmark, the media debate centres both on refugees as 'freeloaders' on the welfare state (Denmark prides itself on having the most generous welfare provisions in Europe) and as thieves and criminals taking (liberal) Danish society for a ride. Youth who threw a petrol bomb at a refugee centre in Gram justified their actions by saying they did it to 'punish shoplifters'.

(iii) The equation 'immigrants=terrorism' is becoming popular in Switzerland and Italy. In Italy, in October 1992, MEP Eugenio Melandri warned against the 'criminalisation of the struggle for immigrant rights' after an Italian daily, *Il Giornale*, carried a series of speculative stories based on police briefings, which expressed 'grave worries' about the likelihood of a renewed wave of terrorist attacks in Italy and warned that poor Third World immigrants are the most likely recruits for far-Left terrorist organisations.

In Switzerland, the source for this popular stereotype is more obviously the state. In 1992, a report on extremism, commissioned following skinhead attacks on refugee centres, was published. But the Federal Department of Justice in Berne concluded that the main threat to state security was not from far-Right violence but from the Left, particularly from foreign and exile groups. Subsequently, the state issued directives to put all 'foreign' groups, including refugees, under surveillance.

(iv) 'Gypsies = crime' is an equation, drawing on popular stereotypes of Gypsies, that dates back centuries. The stereotype is familiar across Europe, but more pronounced (and more deadly) in the former eastern bloc countries. And the new refugee and Roma communities, thrown up by the pogroms in Romania and the migrations from Slovakia, for instance, are the most vulnerable of all. Following a popular campaign against the presence of Slovakian Gypsies in Northern Bohemia, the Prosecutor General of the Czech Republic has called for new police powers to search private premises, impose a five-day limit on visits other than to relatives, and oblige would-be visitors to obtain approval from local authorities.

2. POLITICS

Popular racism does not only exist in terms of ideas and stereotypes; politicians have sought to mobilise popular racism from below. In Italy, as mentioned previously, neighbourhood campaigns have grown up to oppose the opening of refugee centres or Gypsy camps, sometimes with the backing of politicians. In Denmark, politicians have failed to condemn the activities of local people who have reacted to the presence of refugee centres in their areas by banning refugees from shops and meeting places. In Northern Spain, the (Socialist) municipality of Santa Colomba de Somoza backed a petition against a new housing project for refugees which was to have been built in an abandoned village. Also in Spain, in October 1992, the Mayor of Mancha Real and ten members of the ruling council were jailed after it was revealed that they took part in an attack on six houses belonging to Gypsies burnt down by an angry mob.

And in the summer of 1992, in Hautmont, a small town in the Nord Pas de Calais region of France, close to the Belgian border, a local Mayor organised a referendum calling for the neighbourhood to introduce its own form of immigration control. 87.1% of local residents who voted, backed the Mayor's call (the administrative court in Lille later declared the referendum invalid on technical grounds). Previously, in 1988, a referendum had been held in Sjobo, a small town in northern Sweden. In this case, the referendum, organised by the local chair (later expelled) of the mainstream Centre party, was based around the demand that Sjobo should no longer provide shelter for political refugees.

What is disturbing about these incidents is the way in which politicians are using racism and adopting themes and tactics previously associated with the far-Right, in order to gain electoral support. And when politicians start to mobilise racist constituencies to gain, or stay in, public office, and thereby institutionalise racism into the electoral processes. then we really are on the 'democratic road to fascism'.

Country by country survey of far-right parties and racist violence

AUSTRIA

Electoral parties: FREIHEITLICHE PARTEI OSTERREICHS (FPO). Founded 1955. Led by Jorg Haider. Austria's third largest party, the Freedom Party stands for pan--German nationalism, anti-immigration, and a denial of Austria's nazi past. It had, until February 1993, 33 seats in parliament (16.6% of vote), but now 5 MPs have left, claiming the FPO is too extreme, to form rival party.

In winter 1992 FPO launched its 'Austria First Petition', a 12 point programme that called for, amongst other things, tightening of Austria's refugee laws, identity cards for foreigners, and quotas on the numbers of foreign children in classrooms. 417,000 people signed the petition which, although less than anticipated, means that there will be a parliamentary debate. In January 1993, the FPO won 20% of vote in municipal elections in Graz, Austria's second largest city.

Other parties: Small neo-nazi parties include the NATIONALISTISCHE FRONT said to be 'assembling the nucleus of a highly-centralised terror organisation called the NATIONALES EINSATZKOMMANDO (NEK).' In 1986, the Austrian constitutional court ruled against the formation of nazi parties, but in February 1992 the laws were relaxed so as to make penalties less severe.

Racial violence: Throughout 1992, refugee hostels were firebombed. After an attack on one centre in Gutenstein, near Vienna, in September, the Mayors of Salzburg and Vienna did not condemn the violence but announced instead that they would take in no more refugees.

BELGIUM

Electoral parties: VLAAMS BLOK (VB). Founded 1979. Led by Karel Dillen. Stands for Flemish nationalism, anti-immigration (popular slogan used 'Our own people first') and an amnesty for second world war nazi collaborators. In 1991 elections, won 12 seats in the Chamber of Representatives and 5 seats in the senate (6.6% of vote). One MEP on the European Parliament's Technical Group of the European Right. In 1992, published 'Immigration: the solutions', a 70 point strategy based on Le Pen's programme of 'National Preference'.

FRONT NATIONAL (FN). Founded 1983. Led by Daniel Feret. The FN, which campaigns against immigration and for strong law and order policies, is a sister organisation to the French NF. Has 1 seat in the Chamber of Representatives.

Other parties: Many small, neo-nazi and skinhead groups involved in attacks on left and immigrant targets. In March 1993, 3 members of L'ASSAUT (Attack) were prosecuted for paramilitary activities after being found in possession of a stockpile of weapons.

Racial violence: Seems to be linked to areas where far-Right are influential, particularly Antwerp, where, in November 1992, 3 Moroccans were injured after an attack at a cafe.

Police: In 1992, four 'immigrant' youths died in situations arising out of contact with the police. In December 1992 public disquiet after three plainclothes police officers were sentenced to just six months imprisonment for a violent assault on a Pakistani man who did not produce his identity papers 'quickly' enough.

CZECH REPUBLIC /SLOVAKIA

Electoral parties: REPUBLICAN PARTY. Czech party. Led by Dr Miroslav Sladek. Inspired by German party of the same name, the RP calls for expulsion of Vietnamese and Cuban guestworkers, more law and order, and the resettlement of Gypsies. In June 1992 elections gained 6% of Czech vote.

Rise in Slovak nationalism has led to demonstrations nostalgic for the collaborationist regime of Tiso (Tiso was executed for nazi war crimes in 1945).

Other parties: Skinhead activity increasing, particularly around neo-nazi music scene.

Racist violence: At least 12 Roma known to have died in racist violence in 1992 in former Czechoslovakia. Vietnamese workers and African students also complain of constant harassment.

DENMARK

Electoral parties: FREMSKRIDT PARTEIT (Progress Party). Founded 1972. Led by Mogens Glistrup. Proposals include the expulsion of all Muslims and refugees.

Since 1988, when the Progress Party had 16 seats in parliament, its influence has declined rapidly and they are no longer represented in parliament.

Other parties: Several small neo-nazi organisations, most notably PARTIET DE NATIONALE, led by Albert Larsen, known to have been involved in attacks on refugee centres and Left targets. In 1992, Danish Socialist Henrik Christensen was killed at the offices of the Danish branch of the Socialist Workers Party (previously firebombed in 1988) when he opened a parcel bomb.

Racial violence: Bomb attacks on asylum centres in 1992. After attack in October 1992 in Gram, the two youths who threw the petrol bomb said it was to 'punish shoplifters'.

Institutional violence: A judicial inquiry presently underway into allegations made by two prison nurses in 1988 that asylum seekers, then detained with ordinary prisoners, had been strapped down in special cells where bright lights were kept on continuously.

FRANCE

Electoral parties: FRONT NATIONAL. Founded 1972- Led by Jean Marie Le Pen. Anti-Arab and anti-Semitic, the FN calls for an end to the 'Islamification of France', the repatriation of 'immigrants' and claims that the gas chambers were a mere detail of the second world war. In November 1991, FN launched its campaign of 'National Preference', outlining '50 measures against immigration' (said to resemble the 1933 Nuremburg laws) which includes proposals to create an apartheid system of education, compulsory aids tests for immigrants, a programme of deportation for all those who gained entry after 1974, and nationality rights based on blood. Although the FN disassociates itself from skinhead violence, FN stewards are known to have been involved in physical attacks, including the shooting of an anti-racist protestor in Nimes in March 1992.

Although the FN gained 12.5% of the vote in the March 1993 general election, the electoral system is such that they do not have any seats in parliament. Since the 1992 local elections, the FN have had 239 councillors across France.

Racial violence: New word 'Arabicide' coined to describe widespread violence against North African youth. Regions where the highest number of attacks take place are those where FN has most support. Many acts of anti-Semitic violence, including desecration of cemeteries, widely attributed to neo-nazi organisations.

At least 8 North Africans, including a young girl shot by a sniper, died in 1992 as a result of incidents with a racial element. But courts and police 'deracialise' these attacks. In November 1992 riot police were deployed outside a court after angry North African youths protested at decision that a baker, who killed a North African youth, acted in self-defence.

Police: In 1992, the Federation Internationals des Droits des Hommes accused police of 'endemic and most shocking behaviour', mostly in their abuse of identity-check powers. In January 1993, Council of Europe Commission on the Prevention of Torture urges French government to tighten procedures to protect suspects after hearing numerous allegations of police brutality.

Two North African youths died in 1992 after confrontations with police. Use of specialist French riot police to break Kurdish sanctuary and in October 1992 against the Malian squatter camp at Vincennes also cause for concern.

GERMANY

Electoral parties: REPUBLIKANER (REP). Founded 1983. Led by Franz Schönhuber. Stands for pan-German nationalism, anti-immigration and claims to have growing support in armed forces. Schönhuber himself denounces 'immigrants' collectively as 'criminals'. Following April 1992 elections, has 15 seats in state government (11% of vote). In March 1993 local elections in Hesse won 8% of vote. Their best result was in Frankfurt where they won ten seats on the city council (9.3% of vote).

DEUTSCHE VOLKSUNION. DVU(1987). Led by Dr. Gerhard Frey.
Neo-fascist, the DVU is linked to the British revisionist historian, David Irving. Gained only 0.2% of the vote in March 1993 local elections.

Other parties: 77 right wing extremist organisations are being kept under observation, say Federal Office of Criminal Investigation. These groups have a total membership of 41,400. Four organisations the Nationalist Front, German Comradeship League, National Offensive and German Alternative - banned in January 1993.

Racist violence: Attacks by 200 neo-nazis on refugee hostels in Rostock in August 1992 start of a nationwide pogrom against refugees. Violence not confined to the east. Statistics released by the Federal Criminal Police Office in 1992 show that of 2400 acts of racist violence carried out in 1991, 70% took place in the West. In May elections, 10% of West Berliners compared to 5% of East Berliners voted for the far-Right REP. At least 22 people died in 1992 in far-Right inspired killings, including Turks, refugees, left-wing activists, the homeless, disabled, and people mistaken for Gypsies. German soldiers known to have been responsible for at least three of these deaths. In the first three months of 1993 alone, twelve people died in

incidents that can either be proved to be racially motivated or where a racial motive cannot be ruled out.
Disquiet over failure of criminal justice system to recognise or penalise racism. In September 1992, gang who viciously beat Angolan to death in Eberswalde given two/three and a half year sentences for 'grievous bodily harm causing deaths'; in October 1992, member of the DVU who killed a Vietnamese guestworker given four and a half year sentence for manslaughter with judge calling it a case of 'reprehensible arbitrary law'.

Police/Army: Police, as proved by a parliamentary investigative committee into the events of Rostock, unwilling to afford refugees protection against racist attacks, and have also been accused of violent behaviour. For instance, Amnesty International are investigating allegations of police brutality at Granitz refugee camp after raid by riot police, as well as at a refugee hostel in Bremen where a 14-year-old Turkish Kurd had his arm broken during a police raid. Other asylum seekers in Bremen allege they were kicked, beaten and given electric shocks at the police station. Most recently, in February '93, police have broken up refugee protests in hostels throughout Germany. In 1993, reports of racism and criminality in Berlin's auxiliary police force. Also, German television programme exposed maltreatment in police stations. German parliament military ombudsmen reveals in February 1993 that prosecutors are investigating 48 right-wing incidents involving soldiers.

GREECE

Electoral parties: GREEK NATIONAL POLITICAL SOCIETY. (EPEN). Founded 1984, as a vehicle for the ultra-right, authoritarian, imprisoned ex-dictator Giorgios Papadopolous. It has little influence and has now lost its only seat in the national and European parliaments. Generally, Greek nationalism is on the increase particularly focusing on the situation in Macedonia and the former Yugoslavia.

Police: In February 1993 Greece's Public Order Minister announces major police round-up of illegal immigrants whom he blames collectively for crime. Crime statistics broken down to show crime rate amongst 'foreigners' greater than rest of population. Amnesty International allege that Athens Anti-Narcotics police have tortured refugees. Suleyman Akyar, a Turkish refugee, died in hospital eight days after his arrest in January 1991. Sehmus Ukus, a Turkish Kurd, arrested in 1990 was, it is alleged, beaten whilst interrogated, his feet and genitals burned with a cigarette lighter.

HUNGARY

Electoral parties: HUNGARIAN DEMOCRATIC FORUM, the largest party in the coalition government, represents an extreme form of right-wing nationalism. Increasing concern that anti-Semitism in the Democratic Forum following numerous anti-Semitic outbursts by leader Istvan Csurka in 1992 (Csurka has since been expelled from the party and has now formed the HUNGARIAN WAY).

Other parties: Growing concern about skinhead violence. In October 1992, skinheads dressed in Arrow Cross (the post-war indigenous nazi party) uniform disrupt a ceremony commemorating the Hungarian uprising of 1956; in November 1992, group of skinheads convicted of 21 acts of violence against Gypsies and foreigners; and in December 1992 members of the HUNGARIAN NATIONAL SOCIALIST ACTION GROUP led by Istvan Gyorkos, convicted of incitement and possession of weapons following police raid.

Racial violence: Three Gypsies killed in 1992 but government denies racial motivation. In September 1992 arson attacks on Gypsy homes in Ketegyhaza, on the Hungarian plain, described as the first pogrom against Hungarian Gypsies since the second world war. In November 1992 Martin Luther King Association documents 120 incidents, mainly against Arabs and Africans, since the beginning of 1992. 53 Sudanese university students left the country in November saying they feared physical attack. Parliament presently discussing the introduction of incitement to racial hatred law.

Institutional violence: Amnesty International concerned about the situation at Kerepestarcsa detention camp near Budapest following allegations of beatings and the use of tear-gas in confined spaces.

ITALY

Electoral parties: MOVIMENTO SOCIALE ITALIANO (MSI). Founded 1946. Led by Jianfranco Fini. Political descendants of Mussolini, the MSI is nationalist, anti-communist and against immigration. Although, since the April 1992 elections, it has 34 seats in parliament, its influence is believed to be on the decline, although it did make gains in some areas in December local elections.

NORTHERN LEAGUE. Founded 1982, (then Lombard League). Led by Umberto Bossi. Anti-foreigner, corporatist, the NL has now moved from a position of secession to unity under a federal structure. In 1992 elections won 55 seats, 8.7% of national vote (but 17.5% across the North). In December 1992 local elections the Northern League's share of the national vote rose from 10-16% (37-46% in North). Gained control of Varese, Lombardy, with the help of the ex-Communist PDS. The area from Varese to Legnano is said to be a 'hot-bed of radical right activity'.

Other parties: Other small neo-nazi parties include the Rome-based WESTERN POLITICAL MOVEMENT, known to have been involved in anti-Semitic actions. In February 1993, the police carried out a series of raids directed against neo-nazi skinhead groups who had infiltrated basketball and football supporters groups.

Racial violence: The influence of the far-Right can be seen in the two murders in 1992, one on a homeless man. Many organised neo-nazi actions against irregular workers and Gypsies as well as the desecration of Jewish cemeteries. Government presently considering proposals to strengthen laws against incitement to racial hatred.

Police: 2 immigrants shot dead by police in 1992.

Institutional violence: Amnesty International record allegations of torture at Sollicciano prison, near Florence, where half of prisoners are immigrants from outside the EC. In February 1993 security guards at a reception centre for immigrants are accused of torturing young immigrant, including burning his hands.

NETHERLANDS

Electoral parties: CENTRUM DEMOKRATEN (1986). Led by Hans Jaanmat. Extreme right, racist and anti-immigration it is developing links with the Belgian Vlaams Blok. Polls suggest that, if elections held now, it would gain 3% of national vote. In 1990 local elections, CD won 15 council seats, principally in Rotterdam, Amsterdam and the Hague. In September 1992, some members split from CD to form NEDERLANDS BLOK.

Other parties: Other small neo-nazi groups exist with a bonehead neo nazi music scene emerging in 1992 around the fanzine HOU KONTAKT (Keep in touch).

Racial violence: One racist murder in 1992, although courts officially deny racial motivation. In January 1992 there was a wave of bomb attacks against migrant organisations, mosques, and physical attacks on foreigners.

Police: In January 1993 Turkish man dies after being stopped by police. Concern about police harassment of immigrant youths during constant identity checks. In the summer of 1992, government introduces bill which will make compulsory identity cards for 'certain categories of persons and situations'.

Institutional violence: Concern at methods deployed to deport refugees and treatment of refugees in centres after woman refugee from Zaire, 7-months pregnant, dies in April 1992. In November 1992 riot police deployed at Grenshospitium, a closed off location at Schiphol airport. Refugees claim to be badly beaten and investigation is initiated. Then, in December 1992 results of police investigation into attempted deportation of a Romanian asylum seeker in 1992, which left him brain damaged, concludes that 'the norms of reasonable and measured behaviour have been exceeded'.

NORWAY

Electoral parties: FREMSKRITTSPARTEIT (Progress Party). Founded in 1973. Led by Carl Hagen. Stands for stronger immigration controls. Progress Party official recently argued that only Christian immigrants should be allowed into Norway, urging the 'return' of all refugees to their home countries. Has 22 seats in parliament (6.6% of vote), making it Norway's third largest party.

Other parties: Norway has a myriad of small neo-nazi, revisionist organisations such as the PEOPLE'S MOVEMENT AGAINST IMMIGRATION and NORWEGIANS AGAINST IMMIGRATION led by Arne Myrdal, until he was imprisoned in 1993 for a violent assault on anti-racists.

Racist violence: In 1992, terror attacks, such as a neo-nazi bombing of an immigrant school near Oslo, carried out by skinhead groups. A group called the BOOT BOYS is linked to WHITE ARYAN RESISTANCE and is believed to be behind many of the attacks.

POLAND

No electoral party, although anti-Semitism is widespread in public life. Numerous neo-nazi organisations such as the openly anti-Semitic NATIONAL PARTY and a split of the NP, the NATIONAL PARTY SZCZERBIEC that only accepts as members Poles of the Christian faith.

POLISH NATIONAL COMMUNITY - POLICE NATIONAL PARTY (Boleslaw Tejkowski) claims 4,000 members and uses skinheads as hit squads. German nazis from the NATIONALE OFFENSIVE accused of trying to agitate among the 350,000 ethnic Germans against the Polish state and for an anschluss between Germany and Upper Silesia.

Fascist violence: In October 1992, Polish nazis beat to death a German lorry driver near Cracow. Desecration of Jewish cemeteries is linked to the level of openly anti-Semitic sentiment expressed both by politicians and the Church.

PORTUGAL

Electoral parties: No parliamentary party of the extreme-Right but amongst the smaller neo nazi organisations CIRCULO EUROPEO DE AMIGOS DE EUROPEAN (CEDADE), European Circle of Friends of Europe, is probably the most important.

Racial violence: Although not noted for experiencing the same levels of racial violence as the rest of Europe, racial harassment does exist. In June 1992 Africans complained of being too frightened to go out at night because of skinhead attacks. Skinhead violence had previously, in 1990, led to a government committee to monitor and study the situation of minorities in Portugal. Concern over fascist influence at football emerged following violence at a Benfica match in January 1993.

Police: 1 police killing of immigrant in 1992 and many complaints of police authoritarianism and violence towards immigrants. In February 1993, the Brazilian government complains about the behaviour of frontier police at Lisbon's Potela airport.

Previously, in December 1991, Amnesty International took up the case of a white, Angolan Portuguese citizen, who alleged he was violently beaten in a police station and called a 'worthless piece of Angolan shit'.

SPAIN

No parliamentary extreme right party but many organisations nostalgic for the return of the Franco era like CEDADE (1965), (Spanish Circle of Friends of Europe), which organises the annual Franco parade, and, of course, the FALANGE. The

FRENTE NATIONALE (1986) led by Blas Pinar is probably the largest of the extreme-Right parties and claims to have 1,000 councillors in Spain elected as independents. Neo-nazi and skinhead violence organised by groups such as BASES AUTONOMAS. Following murder of Dominican worker, Lucrecia Perez, it emerged that three 16-year-old youths who participated in the killing were members of the Real Madrid Ultrasur supporters group (the other man arrested was a member of the civil guard). In January 1993, Football Anti-Violence Commission accused football clubs, like Real Madrid, of refusing to clamp down on neo-nazi violence.

Racial violence: 2 racist murders in 1992. Attacks on Gypsies and immigrant workers becoming more commonplace. In June 1992. Mayor of Fraga resigned after small town refused to denounce an attack by 30 right wingers on a hostel for North Africans. In October 1992, Mayor of Mancha Real and ten members of ruling council jailed for their part in an attack on six houses belonging to Gypsy families burnt down by an angry mob.

Police: Much harassment of foreigners following new security laws to deal with illegal immigrants and constant identity checks on black people. For instance, a police attack on a black American musician, who refused to produce his passport quickly enough, left him with severe facial injuries, including a broken nose, and led to the cancellation of his television appearance.

SWEDEN

Electoral parties: SVERIGE DEMOKRATERNA (Swedish Democrats). Founded in 1988. Led by Anders Klarstrom. Anti-immigration electoral party which has failed to make a significant impact at the parliamentary level. In September 1992 General Election, it won 5,000 votes which represents the largest vote for a fascist party since the second world war. NEW DEMOCRATS: Led by Ian Wachtmeister.

Other parties: VIT ARISKT MOTSTAND (VAM - White Aryan Resistance), responsible for a wave of bombings and attacks throughout Sweden. Although no official connection with Swedish Democrats, VAM members have acted as their stewards on demonstrations. Known to be involved in organised crime and to be armed, they are linked to STORM NETWORK, an informal network which binds together Sweden's top neo-nazis.

Racial violence: Towards the end of 1991, beginning of 1992, a maverick, racist gunman carried out a series of attacks against immigrants, killing 1 man and seriously injuring at least 10 others.

SWITZERLAND

Electoral parties: No far-Right electoral party as such, but the SWISS DEMOCRATS (formerly National Action), who have 5 seats on the National Council are known for their anti-immigrant stance. The anti-communist AUTOMOBILE

PARTY, who have 8 seats on the National Council, are associated with campaigns against asylum seekers.

Other parties: Many small neo-nazi parties like the PATRIOTICAL FRONT, THE NATIONALE AKTION FOR VOLK UND HEIMT and the NATIONALE SOZIALISTTSCHE PARTET known to have been involved in attacks on refugee centres.

Racial violence: In 1992, two deaths of refugees resulted from numerous attacks - including arson and petrol bombings - on refugee centres. Police deny racial motivation, putting it down to 'drunken behaviour'.

UNITED KINGDOM

No electoral party of any note, but the small, openly neo-nazi BRITISH NATIONAL PARTY put up candidates in the 1992 General Election with little success (as did the even smaller NATIONAL FRONT). The BNP has built up a base in certain areas of white discontent, most notably in east London where it gained 657 votes (20%) in a local by-election.

The BLOOD & HONOUR movement mobilises young neo-nazis, mostly skinheads, around racist music bands. The distributors of SCREWDRIVER SERVICES were recently sent to prison for incitement to racial hatred. Most recently, a group called COMBAT 18 or REDWATCH has emerged - its main aim being to harass 'left' targets.

Racial violence: Widespread racial violence across the country. In 1992, ten people died in racially motivated incidents, including two refugees. Recent research by the London Research Centre indicates that one in ten ethnic minority households in London have suffered racial harassment.

Police: Much concern over police methods of interrogation, and the failure of the criminal justice system to provide safeguards, following the release of both Irish and black prisoners who have served long sentences for crimes they did not commit. Police had to pay out record sums to the victims of miscarriages of justice in 1992.

Institutional violence: An alarming number of black deaths in police cells, prisons and special hospitals. In 1993, the inquest into the death of Zairean asylum seeker Omasese Lumumba revealed disturbing evidence of institutionalised violence at Pentonville prison.

(Additional information taken from *Migration Newssheet, the Campaign Against Racism and Fascism and Searchlight*)

Deaths in Western Europe: 1992/1993

[CODE: MN Medical Neglect; P Police; R Racism; FR Far-Right; S Suicide; UM Unsolved Murder]

BELGIUM 1992

6 July: Lafdil Madini, 19, shot by police in Schaerbeek, Brussels. (P)

8 July: Mohammed Ghaleb, 31, shot by night club bouncer, who refused to allow him and his friends entrance. (R)

Summer: Mimoun Sanhaji, 19, threw himself out of a hospital window having suffered serious head injuries following violent assault by police officer. (P/S)

Date unknown: Multapha El Hachimi, 19, in police cell in Berchem, St Agatha, Brussels. Police, who say he committed suicide, were believed to be pursuing a vendetta against him. (P/S)

DENMARK 1992

19 March: Henrik Christensen, Danish anti-fascist, after a parcel bomb exploded at Danish Socialist Workers Party offices. (FR)

Date unknown: Togolese man, 30, due for deportation for not having a valid visa, found hanged in a police cell in Copenhagen.

FRANCE 1992

January: Said Boumal, North African, shot and killed by men chasing him in a car. (R)

February: Idir Merhem, North African, shot by grocer in Montreuil during argument about purchase of beer. (R)

March: Kamel Hached, killed in Epinay, intervening in row over stolen scooter. (R) Djamel Chettouh, North African, killed by supermarket guard in Sartouville, Yvelines. (R)

May: Second generation Harki, shot at Olivieres Cite, Narbonne, (UM)

June: Rhani Zigh North African, shot during argument in Argenteuil while on military service leave. (UM)

June: Abdallali Lakdiar, 15, Moroccan, shot by neighbour in Chauny, near Saint-Quentin. (R)

14 August: Pierre Dieguifait, Haitian asylum-seeker, committed suicide in police custody at Chelles, Seine et Marne. (S/P)

8 October: Mohamed Bahri, shot by police while driving stolen car. (P)

Date unknown: Larbi Kada, North African, stabbed in St Symphonien, Rhone, while trying to calm reactions to theft of car radio. (R)

21 December: Hassan Ben Ahmed, Moroccan teenager, shot by police in the southern French town of Beziers while allegedly driving a stolen car. Police officer charged with manslaughter. (P)

29 December: North African youth, Bechir Karmous, 23, shot dead by security guards at Port-Canto whilst sitting at the water's edge with friends. (R)

31 December: Naima Bouchafna, Moroccan girl, 18, shot by snipers who fired through the window of her home in Ariane, near Nice. (R)

GERMANY 1992

31 January: Three Sri Lankans, including child, burnt to death in fire in refugee hostel in Lampertheim, Hessia (FR) 14 March: Dragomir Christinel, 18, Romanian refugee, beaten to death by neo-nazis who stormed a refugee hostel in Saal, near Rostock. (FR)

18 March: Gustav Schneeclaus, 53, beaten to death by skinheads in Buxtehude, near Hamburg, for calling Hitler a criminal. (FR)

19 March: Ingo Finnen, 31, homeless German, thrown into harbour in Flensburg, Schleswig-Holstein, after refusing to give nazi salute. (Fr)

6 April: Bulgarian asylum-seeker, 35, found with throat cut in woods near Struvenberg, Brandenburg. (UM)

24 April: Nguyen Van Tu, 29, Vietnamese guestworker, stabbed in Berlin-Marzahn by right-wing extremists. (FR)

May: North African man, died after nazis stormed African meeting place. (FR)

9 May: Torsten Lamprecht, 23, left-wing German punk, beaten to death by nazis who storm pub in Sachsen Anhalt, Magdeburg. (FR)

1 June: Emil Wendland, 60, homeless German, tortured and stabbed to death by skinheads in Neuruppin, Brandenburg. (FR)

8 June: Sadri Berisha, 55, migrant worker from former Yugoslavia, beaten to death by masked fascists in Ostfildern, Baden Wurttemberg. (FR)

1 August: Klaus Dieter Klein, 49, homeless German, stabbed to death by skinheads in Bad Breisig, Rhineland-Palatinate. (FR)

3 August: Ireneusz Szyderski, 24, beaten to death by skinhead doormen at dance hall in Stotternheim, Thuringia. (FR)

6 August: Polish man, stabbed to death in Berlin. (UM)

24 August: Frank Bonisch, 35., homeless German, shot by skinhead in Koblenz, Baden-Wurttemberg. (FR)

28 August: Gunter Schwannicke, 58, homeless German, beaten to death by two skinheads (one a KKK member) in BerlinCharlottenburg. (FR)

3 October: Iranian asylum-seeker, found buried in forest Pear Schwandorf. He had been shot. (UM)

7 November: Rolf Schulze, 52, homeless German, tortured and murdered by skinheads at Kolpin Lake, Brandenburg. (FR)

12 November: Abduraham, Ethiopian refugee, found dead on railway tracks in Bavaria. He had been badly beaten and stabbed. (UM)

21 November: Silvio Meier, 27, east German anti-fascist, stabbed by right-wing youth in Berlin-Friedrichschain. (FR)

23 November: Bahide Arslan, 51, Asye Yilmas, 14, and grandaughter Yeliz Arslan died after nazis firebombed their home in Molln, Schleswig-Holstein. (FR)

24 November: Karl Hans Rohn, 53, burnt to death by skinheads in Wuppertal after calling them 'nazi pigs' (FR)

November: Turk, 24, shot dead by a discotheque security guard in Cologne after the management refused him entry. (R)

15 December: Disabled man, 55, beaten to death by two neo-nazis in Siegen. (FR)

1993

January 1993: Lebanese man, 38, shot dead in Berlin (UM). Turkish man, 35, stabbed to death in Berlin (UM). Refugee from former Yugoslavia shot dead in Frankfurt(UM). Kwaku A, asylum seeker from Ghana, due to be deported, commits suicide(S). Italian, 55, shot dead in Hessen (UM). Unnamed man, 46, dies after being beaten up by skinheads who pulled his body onto the road and rolled two cars over him (FR). Lorin Ladu, Romanian refugee, shot dead by officer in police station in Strassfurt, Sachsen-Anhalt (P). Kerstin Winter, 24, anti-fascist, killed by a letter bomb in Frieburg (FR). Syrian man, 35, killed in Hessen (UM).

February 1993: Olaf Haydenblut, 24, anti-fascist found dead in his apartment in Suht, Turingen. Police say suicide. Friends say murder (UM/S). Mike Z, 22, Anti-fascist, killed by neo nazi youth in Hoyerswerda who beat him and buried him under the weight of a car (FR).

March 1993: Mabiala Maringa, Zairean refugee, 30, found dead in Berlin. (UH) Lamine D, taxi-driver, originally from Guinea-Bissau, found dead in Berlin. Parts of his mutilated body found in a plastic bag (UM). Turkish man, 56, dies of a heart attack after being attacked, allegedly by 2 members of the Republikaner Party in Mullheim. (FR)

ITALY 1992

21 January: North African, stabbed by masked nazi youths in Rome. (FR)

April: African, shot by police during alleged burglary. (P) June: Rakid Telane, shot by police in Bologna during armed robbery. (P)

September: Homeless man, killed by skinheads in Bassano del Grappa, near Venice. (FR)

1993

February:Algerian man killed at road block in Genoa, allegedly whilst driving stolen car. (P)

March: Five refugees from Kosovo killed in fire at refugee hostel in Trento. (UM)

NETHERLANDS 1992

2 March: Nieu Maas, 25, Ethiopian, died after jumping overboard. Having stowed away on Dutch ship, he had been locked in ship's detention room, and was to be returned to Ethiopia. (S)

April: Jacqueline Mulata, refugee from Zaire, 7 months' pregnant, died in refugee detention centre following lack of care. (MN)

9 August: Hamito Ovamar, 16, Moroccan, shot in Hilversum by local resident who said he and his friends were making too much noise. (R)

1993

January: Turkish man, Huseyin Koksal, dies after being stopped by police in Venlo (P)

PORTUGAL 1992

28 January: Angolan shot dead by a police officer in Damaia, a Lisbon suburb, after refusing to get into a police car. (P)

SPAIN 1992

13 November: Lucrecia Perez, 33, Dominican, shot by hooded gunmen who burst into her squat in Aravaca area of Madrid. (FR)

14 November: Hassan al-Yahahaqui, 25, Moroccan, killed by skinheads in Majadahonda, north-west of Madrid. (FR)

SWITZERLAND 1992

July: Pakistani refugee, 21, dies after an arson attack on a refugee centre in Biel. (FR)

UNITED KINGDOM 1992

January: Navid Sadiq, 15, Asian, shot during attempted burglary on shop where he worked. (FR)

3 January: Panchadcharam Sahitharan, Tamil refugee, died after gang attack in Newham, east London. (R)

23 January: Mohammed Sarwar, 46, taxi-driver from Manchester, dragged from his car and battered to death.(R) Siddik Dada, 60, Asian shopkeeper, died of multiple skull fractures after attack by gang armed with machetes. (R)

March: Donald Palmer, 52, African-Caribbean, stabbed to death by two men in Peckham, south London, one of whom boasted 'We are the National Front'. (FR)

July: Rohit Duggal, 16, Asian, killed during gang fight in Eltham, south-east London. (R)

31 July: Ruhullah Aramesh, 24, Afghan refugee, attacked by gang armed with iron bars in Thornton Heath, south London. (R)

September: Ashiq Hussain, 21, Asian taxi-driver, stabbed by youths after going to aid of another driver being racially abused.(R) Aziz Miah, 66, battered by racist gang in Newcastle on way to mosque.(R)

October: Sher Sagoo, Asian stallkeeper, killed by racist gang in Deptford, south London. (PI)

1993

March: Body of Fiaz Mirza, Asian taxi driver from East London, found in the River Thames. (R). William Wellman, elderly neighbour of Asian family, dies from smoke inhalation after Mrs Khanum's home is set on fire in arson attack.(R)

Death in western Europe: the toll for 1992:

Far-Right	29
Racism	20
Police	8
Suicide	3
Unsolved	6
Med. Neglect	1

TOTAL DEATHS   67

APPENDIX 1
Glossary of bodies and organisations

This glossary only briefly covers the Trevi working groups and the Ad Hoc Working Group on Immigration as these are covered in detail in specific chapters.

Ad Hoc Group on Immigration
It has the following working groups: Immigration Sub Group on External Frontiers; Immigration Sub Group on Expulsion and Admission; Immigration Sub Group on Asylum; Immigration Sub Group on Visas; Immigration Sub Group on Forged Documents. See Chapters 8 and 9.

Berlin Group
This is a group of Senior Officials set up by Ministers after a conference in Berlin on 30 October 1991: 'Ministerial Conference on European Cooperation to prevent uncontrolled migration from and through Central and Eastern Europe'. There were three meetings of the group in 1992: Berlin Group Senior Officials meetings on 14 January and 28/29 September; Berlin Group Drafting Committee 28/29 September (*The Vienna Group: Future work*, note by the UK Presidency, 3.7.92, CIRC 3652/1/92, Rev 1, Confidential). A second Conference was held in Budapest February 1993, the recommendations of this meeting included border surveillance measures against 'illegal' immigrants, criminalising the smuggling of 'illegal' immigrants, and measures to expel them. It is said to complement the work of the Vienna Group (below) and may be superseded by that group.

Carriers liability
The Immigration (Carriers Liability) Act 1987 provides for fines to be imposed on airlines and shipping companies who bring anyone into the UK without a valid passport or visa.

CELAD
CELAD ("Comité Europénne de Lutte Anti-Drogues"), the group of drug coordinators, set up in 1989. Its task is to exchange information and to coordinate cross-border inquiries. It works with the Pompidou Group and the Dublin Group (set up in 1990 to liaise with drug producing and transit countries).

CIREA
CIREA (Centre for Information, Discussion and Exchange on asylum). This was formally set up in 1992 under the ambit of intergovernmental cooperation. It is staffed by the General Secretariat of the Council. The meeting of Interior Ministers on 30 November 1992 approved the production and updating of a European asylum practice manual.

CIREFI
CIREFI (Centre for information, discussion and exchange on the crossing of borders

and immigration). The meeting of Immigration Ministers in London on 30 November 1992 approved the establishment of this Centre staffed by the General Secretariat of the Council, to monitor the common immigration policy of the 12 EC states and the crossing of borders.

It will look at: authorised immigration flows; unlawful immigration flows; unlawful immigration methods; forged documents; rejected asylum applicants and 'illegal immigrants who abuse the asylum procedure'; the expulsion of illegally present third-country nationals; inadmissible passenger arrivals and carriers' liabilities.

CIREFI will be a permanent organisation under the Article K post-Maastricht structure, taking over the work of the 'temporary' Sub Groups under the Ad Hoc Group on Immigration (such as the Sub Group on Forged Documents and that on External Frontiers). (*Setting up of a Centre for Information, Discussion and Exchange on the crossing of Borders and Immigration (CIREFI)*, Ad Hoc Group on Immigration, WGI 1277, 16.11.92, Confidential).

Club of Berne
Meeting of intelligence chief to exchange information on espionage and state security (involving at least Germany, Italy, Austria, Switzerland and France).

CIS
The Confederation of Independent States (CIS) is also referred to as the Former Soviet Union (FSU) which excludes the Baltic states.

Coordinators Group
The Coordinators Group was set up in 1988 to bring together the work on the Palma Document covering immigration, terrorism, police and customs, and judicial cooperation. It comprises high level civil servants from the 12 Interior Ministries. Sometimes referred to, misleadingly, as the 'Coordinators of Free Movement'. Its work will be taken over by the K4 Committee when the Maastricht Treaty comes into effect. (See Chapter 1).

Cross Channel Police Intelligence Conferences
Started in 1969 as a means of liaison between French and UK police, also later included Belgium and Netherlands.

CSCE
The Conference on Security and Cooperation in Europe (CSCE) was formed in Helsinki in 1975. It comprises all European states (East and West) plus Canada and the USA. It is a platform for discussing security in Europe and the protection of human rights.

Customs Information System
A new EC-wide computer system, Customs Information System (CIS) was launched in October. The UK headquarters is at Heathrow Airport. The system, which has been funded by the European Commission, will link EC customs officials through 300 terminals - with 25 in the UK. The purpose is to exchange 'intelligence' and 'information' on drugs and fraud. The CIS is based on the existing encrypted

message system called SCENT (System Customs Enforcement Network). The preparatory work was undertaken by the Mutual Assistance Group 1992 (MAG 1992).

The new, fast, system will incorporate standard messages such as 'stop and search' and will hold information in five main categories: persons, businesses, method of transport, commodities and trends. In each category there is space for 'intelligence' to be added. Phase II of the system will bring the addition of a dedicated CIS database in October 1993 holding 'intelligence' as well as 'details of individual cases'.

The UK Customs and Excise office recognises that the storage of personal data means that Phase II will need a legal basis with data protection provisions.

The effect on entry to the UK will be that instead of trying to watch every passenger or lorry suspects will be targeted if they fit the 'profile' of a likely smuggler according to intelligence reports. Special teams of customs officers have been formed into FASTS (Flexible Anti-Smuggling Teams) to search and if necessary to follow suspect individuals and vehicles.

HM Customs & Excise press release, 29.10.92; *83rd report of HM Customs & Excise for year ended 31.3.92.; Commons Hansard*, written answer 26.2.92; *Times*, 29.12.92.

Dublin Convention

The Dublin Convention, agreed in 1990, is designed to stop asylum seekers applying to more than EC country - the refusal of one holds for the whole EC. It goes in tandem with the first 'safe' country rule (ie: the return of asylum seekers to a countries considered 'safe'). A 'Parallel Convention', with the same effect, is being urged on non-EC European countries especially the 'buffer' states in Eastern Europe. See Chapters 8 and 9.

Dublin Group

The Dublin Group is a forum to discuss the coordination of policing assistance to drug producing and transit countries. Its membership is the 12 EC states, the Commission, Australia, Canada, Japan, Norway, Sweden and the USA.

EDU

The Trevi Ministers at their meeting in December 1991 formally agreed to the creation of the European Drugs Intelligence Unit (EDIU). Later its formal name was changed to the European Drugs Unit (EDU). See Chapter 1.

EPC

European Political Cooperation (EPC) describes the process for decision-making between the 12 EC states on those matters outside the competence of the EC's formal institutions. This covers defence and foreign affairs which under the Maastricht Treaty (Title V, Article J) is brought formally within the remit of the European Council (but not the Commission). See Appendix 2.

Eurodac

EURODAC, European automated fingerprint recognition system. The creation of this fingerprint system to identify refugees and asylum-seekers making multiple applications, or those who enter the EC illegally, or those who are to be excluded under the External Border Convention. The project was discussed with the Trevi framework and is being worked on by the Ad Hoc Group on Immigration.

The formal decision to establish EURODAC was taken by Immigration Ministers in December 1991 (Hague). A report presented to the Ministers at their meeting in London on 30 November 1992 concluded that there were no technical barriers to the creation of the system and that an independent consultant should be employed to complete a feasibility study. However, the report notes a number of 'legal issues which will require further consideration': incorporating existing national systems into EURODAC; does Article 15 of the Dublin Convention provide a legal basis; what legal instrument is needed; 'what specific data protection measures - if any - would be needed to accompany the system' (*EURODAC*: progress report to Ministers by the Ad Hoc Group on Immigration, WGI 1271, 16.11.92, Confidential). The admission on non-EC countries to the system, like Switzerland which expressed an interest, should the reports says be dependent on their ratifying the Convention parallel to the Dublin Convention. *Eurasyl* is the name of a project for the finger-printing of asylum seekers put forward by Switzerland at a Trevi group meeting.

European Committee on Crime Problems (CDPC)

This committee is within the Council of Europe framework. It has a Maritime Working Group to continue the work of the Pompidou Group on an Agreement on the boarding of ships at sea.

European Information System

The European Information System (EIS) is being developed under the remit of the K4 Coordinating Committee being set up under the Maastricht Treaty (Title VI: Justice and Home Affairs). It will hold data on policing, crime, and immigration (see Chapter 1). In the area of immigration:

> A joint computerised list of inadmissible third country nationals would be established, consisting of entries provided by Member States. The criteria for inclusion on the list are imprisonment for at least 12 months in a Member state, the commission of a serious crime or suspicion that a person is planning a serious crime, repeated or serious immigration offences and other cases where exclusion is necessary in the public interest. (*Migration Control at External Borders of the European Community*, Home Affairs Select Committee, 1991-2, HC 215-i, ii and iii., p62).

European Monitoring Centre for Drugs and Addiction (EMCDDA)

In February 1993 the Council agreed to set up the European Monitoring Centre for Drugs and Drug Addiction (EMCDDA). Its work includes: collection and analysis of existing data; improvement of data comparison; cooperation with European and international bodies. The EMCDDA will 'take account' of work being undertaken by Europol (EDU). It will have a computer network known as 'European Information Network on Drugs and Drug Addiction' (REITOX) for collecting and exchanging information. (*Council press release*, 4523/93 on the Council meeting on the Internal Market, 8.2.93).

European 'nervous system'

In addition to the European Information System (EIS) is the long-term development of the European 'nervous system', known as ENS. This project, which the Commission has been working on for a number of years, is intended to cover tax, insurance, customs, medical records and trade. In a speech to a Financial Times Conference in 1989 Filippo Maria Pandolfi, then the Commissioner responsible for telecommunications, said: 'This nervous system should allow the administrations of the national governments to interwork efficiently.' A commercial grouping, known as BOS, comprising Bull, Olivetti and Siemens - has been formed to bid for this project has opened an office in Brussels.

Europol

Europol is the name given to the European Police Organisation set out in the Maastricht Treaty's Title VI. At this stage it is intended to be an intelligence-gathering organisation whose first project is the European Drugs Unit (EDU). See Chapter 1.

External Borders Convention

The External Borders Convention has not been signed by the EC governments because of a disagreement between the UK and Spain over the status of Gibraltar. The Convention: 1) allows for sanctions if borders are crossed other than at authorised points; 2) a common list of countries whose nationals need visas to enter; 3) sanctions against airlines who bring in people without the required travel documents and visas; 4) provision of a uniform visas valid for a stay of up to three months; 5) the establishment of a computerised list of 'inadmissible' third country nationals.

GAFI (Groupe d'Action Financière Internationale)

deals with money laundering of drug profits.

Immigration Ministers meetings

Immigration Ministers meetings, started in December 1986, are formally held every six months prior to the EC Summit which ends each EC Presidency. 'Immigration Ministers' are the Home Office/Interior Ministers from the 12 EC states. They agree reports from the Coordinators of Free Movement whose reports in turn as based on those from the Ad Hoc (Working) Group on Immigration (WGI) and its sub-groups.

International Air Transport Association Control Working Group on Inadmissible Passengers (INADPAX)

Meets three times a year and brings together police, security service, border police and immigration officials, and airline representatives from the EC, EFTA, Canada and the USA. It deals with the practice of fining airlines for carrying non-admissible passengers.

Judicial Cooperation

Judicial cooperation between the 12 EC states takes place under the umbrella of European Political Cooperation (EPC) established under the Single European Act, which means it is run by the Council and is not accountable to the European Parliament. There are two working groups, one on criminal law, one on civil law. Its works is serviced by the Council Secretariat and the Commission is 'involved'. Reports are made to the European Council Political Committee which is composed of senior officials from Foreign Ministries, their work is 'reported' to the meetings of Justice Ministers. The working groups have been concerned with drawing up agreements and conventions, with ensuring that member states have signed appropriate Council of Europe Conventions and, most importantly, seeking amendment to these latter Conventions (eg: on extradition).

K4 Committee
The K4 Committee will come into operation when the Maastricht Treaty is put into effect. It will take over the work of all the ad hoc groups - Trevi, Ad Hoc Group on Immigration, MAG 92 etc. See Chapter 1.

Kilowatt group
The Kilowatt group was formed in 1997 and exchanges intelligence on international terrorism. The existence of this alliance was revealed in 1982 when Iranian students found material in the American embassy in Teheran.

The members of the network are the EC countries plus Canada, Norway, Sweden, Switzerland, the US (CIA and FBI), the Israeli *Mossad* and *Shin Beth*. *Kilowatt* is believed to be led by Israel because of its near monopoly of information on Arab groups and individuals in Europe and the Middle East. According to recent information from Swiss and Dutch sources the network is now functioning under another name.

Maastricht Treaty
The Maastricht Treaty was signed by the 12 EC governments in Maastricht in December 1991. The treaty is now in the process of being ratified by the parliaments of each member state. See Chapter 1.

Mutual Assistance Group (MAG)
MAG 92 was set up in 1989 and is comprised of the Directors-General of Customs. It works with the Coordinators, Trevi 92, and the Ad Hoc Group on Immigration. It remit covers drugs, computerised information systems, external borders, joint exercises and technical equipment. It meets 3-4 times a year.

National Criminal Intelligence Service (UK)
The National Criminal Intelligence Service (NCIS) was set up in April 1992. It includes specialist units such as the National Drugs Intelligence Unit (NDIU); National Football Intelligence Unit (NFIU); Interpol (ICPO); and Regional Crime Intelligence Offices. The National Intelligence Computer System (NICS) will eventually be linked to every police station in the country. One of its roles is to act as the contact point/clearing house for request from other EC police forces.

NATO
NATO was founded in 1949. It comprises: Belgium, Denmark, France, Germany,

Greece, Italy, Luxembourg, Netherlands, Portugal, Spain, UK (of the 12 EC states only Ireland is not a member of NATO), plus Canada, Iceland, Norway, Turkey, USA

Palma Document
The Palma Document, drawn up by the Coordinators' Group, was agreed at the EC Council meeting in Madrid in June 1989. The document brings together the issues of immigration,terrorism, border controls (external and internal), police and customs, and judicial cooperation. It has been an important mechanism in the construction of the European state. See Chapter 1 and Appendix 6.

Pol-Zoll
'Pol-Zoll' is Schengen's permanent consultative group of police and customs officers looking at joint problems concerning drugs, crime and technical cooperation.

Pompidou Group
The Pompidou Group, founded in 1972, is the Council of Europe's Co-operation Group to combat drug abuse and illicit trafficking in Europe (its long name is the European Group to Combat Drug Abuse and Illicit Traffic in Drugs). Its membership comprises the 12 EC states plus Austria, the Czech Republic and Slovakia, Cyprus, Finland, Hungary, Malta, Norway, Poland, San Marino, Sweden and Switzerland. The European Commission has observer status. Its programme is carried out under the supervision of Permanent Correspondents through working groups and seminars.

PWGOT
The Police Working Group on Terrorism (PWGOT) was formed in 1979. It is comprised of the Special Branches of the 12 EC states plus Finland, Norway and Sweden. See Chapter 1.

Schengen Agreement
The Schengen Agreement (1990) has been signed by nine of the 12 EC states - Germany, France, Italy, Greece, Portugal, Spain, Netherlands, Belgium, Luxembourg. It is now being ratified by each country's parliament (see Appendix 5).

Schengen Information System
The Schengen Information System (SIS) is being developed by the Schengen countries, and is based in Strasbourg. It is expected to be operational in 1994 and will hold information on policing, crime and immigration (see Appendix 5).

SIRENE
SIRENE, 'Supplementary Information Request at the National Entries'. It is an emergency communications system the central contact point in each member state, and is attached to the SIS. It is staffed by police officers and lawyers. At the meeting of Schengen Ministers in Madrid in December 1992 they approved the Sirene Manual which sets out the procedures for the information to be fed into the Schengen Information System (SIS).

'Second' and 'third' pillars
Out of the Maastricht Treaty came the concept of the 'second pillar', foreign affairs and defence (or 'security' as it is often euphemistically called), and the 'third pillar' covering justice and home affairs (immigration, asylum, policing, internal security, law and conventions). The 'first pillar' is the economic and social sphere developed by the European Community since the Treaty of Rome in 1957.

STAR group
The STAR group (Standige arbeidsgruppe Rauschgift) is a European anti-drug network, founded in 1972. It is comprised of representatives from Germany (the Bundeskriminalamt), Belgium, Netherlands, France, Austria, Switzerland and Luxembourg.
The Belgian Minister of Justice, Melchior Wathelet, has revealed that the US Drugs Enforcement Administration together with the US Customs and the US Army in Germany (SADEM) are also members of the group.

Trevi group
The Trevi group was set up in 1976. It comprises the 12 Member States of the EC. Originally started to combat terrorism its role expand later to deal generally with police cooperation. See Chapter 1.

Trevi Ministers meetings
References to 'Trevi Ministers' meetings are to meetings of the 12 EC Home/Interior Ministers considering policing and legal matters prepared for them by the Trevi Senior Officials group (see below). They usually meet twice a year prior to the six-monthly EC Summit meetings of Prime Ministers.

Trevi Senior Officials
The Trevi Senior Officials group usually meet twice a year prior to the six monthly meetings of Trevi Ministers. The group is comprised of a senior Interior Ministry official from each of the 12 EC states. Their reports are based on the conclusions of the Trevi working groups (eg: TREVI 1 on terrorism). Their reports also go to the meeting of the Coordinators.

Trevi working groups
There are currently five Trevi working groups: Trevi 1: terrorism; Trevi 2: police training, public order, football hooliganism; Trevi 3: organised crime and drug trafficking. In addition, the Ad Hoc Group on Europol and the Ad Hoc Group on International Organised Crime were created in 1992 and Trevi 92 was disbanded at the end of 1992. An Ad Hoc Group on Yugoslavia was set up at the beginning of 1993. See Chapter 1 and Appendix 3 on their meetings.

Trevi: Friends of Trevi
The 'Friends of Trevi' have observer status at Trevi meetings, they are: Sweden, Austria, Morocco, Switzerland, Canada and the USA. Three other countries are 'briefed' by EC states: Spain (Argentina), Denmark (Finland), Germany (Hungary).

Trevi: Troika

The Trevi 'Troika' comprises senior officials from the past, present and next Presidency of the EC. Its job is to advise the current Presidency. 'Troikas' meet both at Senior Officials level and around specific topics (eg: Trevi 1 on terrorism).

UCLAF

UCLAF, 'Unité de Coordination de la Lutte Anti-Fraude' (an anti-fraud unit), was set up in 1988. It is based in the European Commission and is composed of officials from several of the Commission's directorates together with representatives from each of the 12 member states. UCLAF has a computer system called IRENE (IRegularities, ENquiries, Evaluation) which also carries cases logged on the SCENT system.

Vienna Group

The Vienna Group was formed in 1978 to combat terrorism on the initiative of the Interior Ministers of Germany, Italy, Austria, Switzerland and France. It is also referred to as the 'Vienna Club'. In October 1991 the Group called together a conference to discuss 'clandestine' immigration inviting 13 Central and Eastern European states, plus the other members of the EC.

Vienna Group (Immigration)

This group was set up in early 1991 after a conference on 24-25 January entitled: Ministerial Conference on Movement of Persons from Central and Eastern European Countries held in Vienna. The group includes Scandinavian and Eastern Countries. A report in July 1992 says that:

> The main concern of the twelve is to control East-West migration and third-country migration through the new democracies by pursuing and encouraging policies and practical measures which will achieve that control (*The Vienna Group: Future Work*, op.cit.).

The different interests of the 12 EC countries and those of Eastern Europe are expressed in an exasperated note by the EC: 'Their interest to date seems to have been as much in reducing barriers between themselves and the West as in strengthening barriers against third-country nationals'.

Clear frustration is evident from the 12 EC states and the only practical move at this stage is a Visa Practices Working Party. However, the meeting of the Council of Europe Ministers in May 1992 agreed that the Vienna Group provided the basis for work in this field.

UK was represented at the following meetings in 1991/2 on: 25 January and 21/22 March 1991 Vienna Group of Senior Officials; 29/31 January and 1/2 September 1992 Vienna Group meetings; 18/20 May 1992 Visa Policy Working Party.

Western European Union

The Western European Union is a military alliance of nine EC member states set up in 1954 (excluding Ireland, Denmark and Greece). It was activated during the Iran-Iraq war and the Gulf War.

APPENDIX 2
Structure of the European Communities

The first main organisation, formed in 1951, was the **European Coal and Steel Community (ECSC)**. This comprised: Belgium, France, West Germany, Italy, Luxembourg and Netherlands.

Treaty of Rome 1957
Established the **European Economic Community** (EEC) aimed at integrating the economies of the six countries and the European Atomic Energy Community **(Euratom)** to encourage the non-military use of nuclear power. In 1967 the so-called **Merger Treaty** merged the three bodies into the European Community.

Single European Act (SEA) 1987
The Single European Act of 1987 amended and complemented the Treaties of Rome and Paris. The Act was intended to increase the efficiency of the Community and institutionalised co-operation between member states on foreign policy.

Membership
In 1973 the original six members were joined by Denmark, Ireland and the UK (making a total of nine), in January 1981 Greece joined and in January 1986 Spain and Portugal joined.

The 12 members of the EC are: Denmark, France, Germany, Belgium, Netherlands, Luxembourg, Italy, Greece, Spain, Portugal, Ireland and the UK.

Locations
The **European Parliament** (and the Council of Europe) are based in Strasbourg, France (the EP holds its committee meetings in Brussels). The **Commission** and the **Council of Ministers** are based in Brussels. The **Court of Justice** is based in Luxembourg.

The European Council
The European Council, set up in 1974, comprises the 12 heads of government and meets every six months at the end of each Presidency. It is not an institution of the Community under the Single European Act but it the highest decision-making body.
    It deals with issues concerning the EC and with intergovernmental cooperation.

The Council of Ministers
The Council is the legislative body of the EC. All proposals which are initiated by the Commission, and considered by the Parliament, have to be agreed (or not) by the Council. The Council comprises the representatives of the 12 Member States. The composition of the Council of Ministers varies according to the subject matter, eg:

agriculture, industry, finance, economic policy. The Council has a staff over 2,000 based in Brussels.

The ministerial level meetings are preceded by meetings of the *Permanent Representatives Committee*, known as COREPER (a French acronym). This committee operates at two levels: the Permanent Representatives of each state with ambassador status, work through COREPER II; the Deputy Permanent Representatives work through COREPER I. COREPER prepares the reports and decisions for the Council of Ministers.

The Commission

The Commission of the European Communities (often referred to as the 'European Commission') is the 'civil service' of the EC. It is headed by seventeen Commissioners, at least one of whom comes from each Member State (larger States, like the UK and Germany, have two). Each Commissioner is appointed for four years, renewable, by mutual agreement between the states. Each Commissioner is given a specific area of responsibility. The European Parliament has the power to force them to collectively resign.

The job of the Commission is: 1) to ensure that Community rules and principles are respected. They are the guardians of the Treaty of Rome and the Single European Act (it is this role that MEPs are critical of over the abolition of internal frontier controls). 2) The Commission has investigative powers and can impose fines on companies and individuals found in breach of Community regulations and laws. There is a right of appeal to the European Court of Justice. 3) it can make proposals to the Council of Ministers on economic, nuclear, and to a lesser degree, social matters. 4) it implements Community policies as decided by the Council.

The Commission is based in Brussels and has a staff of about 15,000 divided into 23 Directorates-General.

The European Parliament

The Treaty of Rome in 1957 provided for a parliament comprising delegates from national parliaments. It only became a democratically elected body in June 1979. The 518 Members of the European Parliament (MEPs) meet in political, not national, groups, and are elected for five years.

The powers of the European Parliament are limited as it has no power to initiate and pass legislation for the EC. It debates, in plenary sessions and committees, the proposals put forward by the Commission (which it can accept, reject or amend). It can question members of the Commission, and agrees its annual budget.

The legislative body of the EC is the Council. The normal practice is for the Commission to draw up a proposal and submit it to the parliament. The Commission usually takes into account the parliament's view before sending it to the Council for adoption. If the Council want to reject parliament's amendments they have to do so by a unanimous vote.

Types of decisions

The different types of decisions taken by the EC are:

Regulations: apply directly to all Member States

Decisions: binding on all Member states, companies or individuals to whom they are

addressed.
Directives: lay down compulsory objectives, but leave it to each states to translate them into national legislation.
Recommendations and opinions: are not binding

The Court of Justice

The Court of Justice meets in Luxembourg and comprises 13 judges, assisted by six advocates-general. They are appointed for six years by mutual consent of Member States. In 1988 a Court of First Instance was attached to it. The role of the Court is to: overturn any measure adopted by the Commission which is incompatible with the Treaties; to pass judgement on the interpretation of Community law; and to give opinions, which are binding, on agreements with third countries (ie: non-EC countries). In practice most of the cases referred to it do not come from governments or Community institutions but from private companies and individuals.

The role of the Court is however limited to Community institutional arrangements which are predominantly economic. The provisions under the Maastricht Treaty covering justice, law, policing and immigration will not come under its remit.

Other bodies

There are a number of other EC institutions: the Court of Auditors, Euratom, and the European Investment Bank.

Intergovernmental agreements

In the fields of immigration, policing, drugs, legal changes and terrorism the EC governments have been working through *intergovernmental agreements* rather than through the formal structures of the EC (namely, the Commission and the European Parliament).

By this mechanism draft agreements are drawn up by the Trevi or Immigration working groups in secret. Ministers then sign an intergovernmental agreement which is usually then made public. These agreements then are either presented to national parliaments as Conventions for ratification or are intended to lead to amendments in each country's laws on the subject matter.

The second (defence and foreign policy) and third (justice and internal affairs) 'pillars' of the Maastricht Treaty are to remain intergovernmental even though they will be paid for by the EC budget. The policy-making initiative will lie with the Council, its Secretariat, Steering Committees and working parties. The effect is to move from the ad hoc mechanism for reaching decisions between the governments by institutionalising their present practice, thus maintaining secrecy in the development of policy.

In addition, there are a number of organisations which are outside the EC:

Council of Europe

The Council of Europe was set up in 1949 and is based in Strasbourg. In 1990 there were 23 member states including all 12 EC states, the 5 EFTA states, plus Cyprus, Malta, San Marino and Turkey up to 1991. By 1992 there were 26 member states.

The Council of Europe has adopted a number of legal Conventions, the best known of which is the European Convention on Human Rights (ECHR), adopted in 1950. The Council of Europe is not part of the EC.

European Court of Human Rights
There are two bodies which adjudicate the European Convention on Human Rights, the European Commission of Human Rights (considers cases brought under the ECHR) and the European Court of Human Rights (hands down binding decisions on cases).

EFTA
The European Free Trade Area (EFTA) was set up in 1960. The original members of EFTA included Denmark, Portugal and the UK all of whom have since joined the EC. Seven countries are now in EFTA: Austria, Finland, Iceland, Norway, Finland, Sweden and Switzerland. In March 1993 the EC and six EFTA countries signed the European Economic Area agreement allowing the 18 countries to proceed without Switzerland (which rejected the EEA in a referendum; but it will have observer status).

Nordic Council
The Nordic Council was founded in 1952 and is now based on the Helsinki Treaty of 1962. It comprises: Iceland, Denmark, Sweden, Norway, Finland and the autonomous territories of the Faroes, Greenland (Denmark) and the Aland Islands. The aim is to further economic and political cooperation between the countries.

APPENDIX 3
Secret Europe

A total of 227 meetings of ad hoc groups and working parties took place over the two years 1991 and 1992 during the Presidencies of the UK, Portugal, Netherlands, Luxembourg (a full chronological listing of these meetings is available from Statewatch, see Preface for contact address).

Trevi group
There were a total of 41 meetings over the two years of the Trevi Ministers (Interior Ministers), their officials, police officers and internal security agencies (MI5 from the UK). In addition the various working parties sponsored an unspecified number of conferences and seminars (see Chapter 1 on the work of the Trevi group).

Trevi Ministers meeting
4 main meetings; one during each Presidency prior to the EC Summits

Informal TREVI Ministers
4 meetings, one during each Presidency prior to main meeting above

TREVI Senior Officials

5 meetings: 1 each Presidency except 2 during Netherlands Presidency

TREVI Working Group I
4 meetings; 1 during each Presidency

TREVI Working Group II
4 meetings; 1 during each Presidency

TREVI Working Group III
6 meetings; 2 each during UK & Portuguese Presidencies in 1992

TREVI 92
9 meetings; 2 UK; 2 Portugal; 3 Netherlands; 2 Luxembourg

Ad Hoc Group on Europol
2 meetings both during the UK Presidency (the UK permanently chair this group) (Only two meetings are included on the listing. However, this Working Group was set up at the beginning of 1992).

Ad Hoc Working Group on International Organised Crime
3 meetings during UK Presidency, set up in September 1992.

TREVI Troika
The UK joined the Trevi Troika during the Portuguese Presidency and took the lead during its own Presidency.

Immigration

By far the largest number of meetings concerned immigration, asylum and refugees. There were a total of 100 meetings of Immigration ministers (Interior ministers), officials, police and immigration officers.

Immigration Ministers meeting
4 main meetings; one during each Presidency prior to the EC Summits

Informal Immigration Ministers
4 meetings, one during each Presidency prior to main meeting above

Coordinators of Free Movement
15 meetings; 4 UK, 7 Portugal, 2 Netherlands, 2 Luxembourg

Ad Hoc Working Group on Immigration (WGI)
11 meetings; 4 UK, 3 Portugal, 2 Netherlands, 2 Luxembourg

Immigration Sub Group on External Frontiers
12 meetings; 2 UK, 4 Portugal, 3 Netherlands, 3 Luxembourg

Immigration Sub Group on Expulsion and Admission
12 meetings; 6 UK, 6 Portugal - first meeting of Sub Group February 1992

Immigration Sub Group on Asylum
17 meetings; 5 UK, 7 Portugal, 5 Netherlands - first meeting October 1991

Immigration Sub Group on Forged Documents
5 meetings; 2 UK, 2 Netherlands, 1 Luxembourg

Immigration Sub Group on Visas
7 meetings; 3 UK, 3 Portugal, 1 Netherlands - first meeting December 1991

Immigration Sub Group CIREA (Asylum Clearing House)
First meeting 11 December 1992.

Immigration Sub Group on Information
only 3 meetings in 1991; 1 Netherlands, 2 Luxembourg

Vienna Group
5 meetings plus the first meeting, a Ministerial Conference in January 1991.

Berlin Group
4 meetings plus the first meeting, a Ministerial Conference in October 1991.

Drug trafficking

The third major area concerned drug trafficking with a total of 37 recorded meetings (although this is certainly an under-estimate).

CELAD
20 meetings: UK Presidency: 4 meetings plus CELAD/Pompidou Troika and 1 Coordinators Group on Drugs; 4 during Portugal Presidency plus CELAD/Pompidou Group: Troika; 3 during Netherlands Presidency; 6 during Luxembourg Presidency

EDMC Ad Hoc Working Group
7 meetings; 1 UK, 6 Portugal. First meeting January 1992

Pompidou Group
6 meetings plus one joint meeting with CELAD (All these meetings occurred during the UK Presidency, it is therefore an under-estimate).

Dublin Group
4 meetings; 2 UK, 1 Portugal, 1 Netherlands - started November 1991

Law - changes and harmonisation

There are two main groupings looking a legal changes. The Judicial Cooperation working party and the Horizontal Group on Data Protection.

Judicial Cooperation (Civil) & Judicial Cooperation (Criminal)
13 meetings in all; 4 Civil; 4 Criminal; 4 general; 1 on Europe. The first recorded meeting took place in September 1991.

Horizontal Group on Data Protection
10 meetings; 5 UK Presidency, 2 Portugal, 2 Netherlands. Group's first meeting in October 1991.

Ad Hoc Group on Community & Criminal Law
2 meetings in October 1992

Other meetings

MAG 92 (Customs)
3 meetings during UK Presidency.

Political Committee
6 meetings; 3 each year; 2 Presidencies had two meetings, two Presidencies had one.

Other sporadic meetings include: *Committee on European Crime Problems*: only 2 meetings June and April 1991; *Ad Hoc Committee on International Law*, 8 October 1991; *Commission Precursors Working Group*, 19-20 October 1992; *European Political Cooperation Working Group*, January 1991 & February 1992.

APPENDIX 4
European Convention on Human Rights

The European Convention on the Protection of Human Rights and Fundamental Freedoms was signed on 4 November 1950 by the member states of the Council of Europe, a 'peaceful association of democratic States which proclaim their faith in the rule of law and their devotion to the spiritual and moral values which are the common heritage of their peoples'. In fact, as Gareth Peirce has remarked, the Convention was a recognition that never again could any European government be trusted to protect its people from its own human rights abuses. The right of individual petition, allowing anyone to take the government of his or her own country to court, was a significant innovation which prevented the Convention from becoming a dead letter like its sister, the Social Charter of 1953.

The United Kingdom was the first country to ratify the Convention, in March 1951. By 1992 there were 26 signatory states (27 when the Czech Republic and Slovakia re-sign as separate states, and 28 when Poland signs). The UK has also had more cases taken against it, and has been condemned for more violations, than any other ratifying state.

The institutions set up by the Council of Europe to monitor the Convention are the Commission, the Committee of Ministers and the European Court of Human Rights. The aggrieved individual must first exhaust domestic remedies, which can take years. Then a petition goes to the Commission, which declares it admissible or inadmissible and, if admissible, decides whether there has been a violation. If so, the case goes either to the Committee of Ministers or to the European Court, depending on the response of the respondent state. Many cases are the subject of a 'friendly settlement' negotiated by the Committee of Ministers and result in no definitive ruling.

Seventeen of the Council of Europe states have incorporated the Convention into their domestic law. The United Kingdom has refused to do so, although it has usually changed laws or administrative practices after adverse rulings from the European Court of Human Rights (with the notable exception of the Prevention of Terrorism Act).

The UK has also refused to sign the 4th, 6th and 7th Protocols to the Convention, which guarantee rights in relation to immigration and residence, appeals and miscarriages of justice and abolish the death penalty.

The Convention is not incorporated into EC law, although it is acknowledged in the preamble to the Single European Act, and is taken into account by the European Court of Justice in its interpretation of member states' obligations.

Convention

Art 2: Right to life
Art 3: Freedom from torture or inhuman or degrading treatment or punishment
Art 4: Freedom from slavery, servitude and forced labour
Art 5: Right to liberty and security of person
Art 6: Right to a fair hearing within a reasonable time by an independent and impartial tribunal established by law
Art 7: Freedom from retroactive criminal law
Art 8: Right to respect for private and family life, home and correspondence
Art 9: Freedom of thought, conscience and religion
Art 10: Freedom of expression
Art 11: Freedom of assembly and association
Art 12: Right to marry and found a family
Art 13: Right to an effective remedy before a national authority
Art 14: Freedom from discrimination
Art 15: Power of state to derogate (except from Arts 2, 3, 4(1), 7) in time of war or public emergency threatening the life of the nation
Art 16: Power of state to impose restrictions on political activity of aliens
Art 25: Right of individual petition
Art 46: Recognition of compulsory jurisdiction of Court

Protocol No 1
Art 1: Protection of property
Art 2: Right to education
Art 3: Free elections

Protocol No 4
Art 1: Freedom from imprisonment for debt
Art 2: Freedom of movement of persons
Art 3: Right to enter and remain in one's own country
Art 4: Freedom from collective expulsion

Protocol No 6
Art 1: Abolition of death penalty

Protocol No 7
Art 1: Procedural rights of aliens
Art 2: Right of appeal
Art 3: Compensation for miscarriage of justice
Art 4: Right not to be tried or punished twice
Art 5: Equality of spouses

Ratifications and acceptances
by member states of the Council of Europe

	Conv	A25	A46	P1	P2	P4	P6	P7
Austria	x	x	x	x	x	x	x	x
Belgium♦	x	x	x	x	x	x		
Cyprus♦	x	x	x	x	x	x		
Czech & Slovak FR*								
Denmark	x	x	x	x	x	x	x	x
Finland	x	x	x	x	x	x	x	x
France♦	x	x	x	x	x	x	x	x
Germany♦	x	x	x	x	x	x	x	
Greece♦	x	x	x	x	x			x
Hungary*								
Iceland	x	x	x	x	x	x	x	x
Ireland	x	x	x	x	x	x		
Italy♦	x	x	x	x	x	x	x	x
Liechtenstein♦	x	x	x		x		x	
Luxembourg♦	x	x	x	x	x	x	x	x
Malta♦	x	x	x	x	x		x	
Netherlands♦	x	x	x	x	x	x	x	
Norway	x	x	x	x	x	x	x	x
Portugal♦	x	x	x	x	x	x	x	
San Marino♦	x	x	x	x	x	x	x	x
Spain♦	x	x	x	x	x		x	
Sweden	x	x	x	x	x	x	x	x
Switzerland♦	x	x	x		x		x	x
Turkey♦	x	x	x	x	x			
United Kingdom	x	x	x	x	x			

As at 1 January 1992
Conv = Convention
A25 = Art 25 (right to individual petition)
A46 = Art 46 (acceptance of Court jurisdiction)
P = Protocol
♦ countries which have incorporated ECHR into domestic law
* Czech & Slovak Federal Republic signed the Convention in 1991, and will have to re-sign as separate states. Hungary also signed in 1991.

Some issues dealt with by the Convention

Art 2: killings by security forces in Northern Ireland 1971-2: *Ireland v UK*, *Stewart v UK*; by invading Turkish forces in Cyprus 1974: *Cyprus v Turkey.*

Art 3: torture in Greece after coup 1967: *Denmark, Norway, Sweden, Netherlands v Greece*; techniques of interrogation in Northern Ireland: *Ireland v UK*; torture and physical punishment by the British administration in Cyprus: *Greece v UK*; corporal punishment of juveniles: *Tyrer v UK*; refusal of entry to UK of citizens expelled from Africa: *East African Asians cases*; extradition to death row in USA: *Soering v UK.*

Art 5: internment of IRA suspects: *Lawless v Ireland*; under emergency provisions: *Fox, Campbell and Hartley v UK*; under PTA: *Brogan* (followed by UK derogation under Art 15); length of pre-trial detention: *Stoegmuller, Neumeister, Matzneller v Austria*; indeterminate detention: *Thynne, Wilson, Gunnell v UK* (discretionary lifers); *X v UK* (mental patient); of vagrants: *Vagrancy cases v Belgium.*

Art 6: right of access to courts: *Golder v UK*; *Campbell v Fell* (prison: communication with lawyers); length of criminal process: many cases, large number against Italy. Right to interpreters, free legal aid. Fair trial procedures: *Lüdi v Switzerland.*

Art 8: criminalisation of homosexuality: *Klass v Germany, Norris v Ireland*; discrimination against illegitimate children: *Marckx v Belgium*; care proceedings and parental rights: *Eriksson v Sweden*; *O, H, W, B and R v UK*; separation from spouse and children by expulsion or refusal of admission: *Abdulaziz v UK, Berrehab v Netherlands*; right to privacy of correspondence: *Malone v UK, Golder v UK*; telephone tapping: *Kruslin v France, Huvig v France.*

Art 9: does not protect conscientious objectors if substitute civic service possible: *Grandrath v Germany.*

Art 10: publication in public interest: *Sunday Times v UK, Observer v UK*; information about abortion: *Open Door Counselling and Dublin Well Woman Centre v Ireland*; use of defamation proceedings to silence political opponents: *Thorgeron v Iceland*; *Demicoli v Malta.* Does not protect access to employment (eg *Berufsverbot* in Germany).

Art 11: right of peaceful demonstration: *Ezelin v France*; *Platform Arzte fur das Leben v Germany*. Does not protect right to strike.

Commentary

It is an indictment of Britain's human rights record that, between 1983 and 1991, it has had more cases taken against it under the European Convention of Human Rights than any other country, and has had more adverse judgements made against it than any other country. It accounts for 17% of all cases taken (1983-1991), 73% of all adverse judgements by the Committee of Ministers (up to 1987) and 25% of all adverse judgements by the European Court of Human Rights (up to 1987). The numbers for selected countries are given below (*Council of Europe, Survey of Activities and Statistics* (annual).

Number of individual applications registered by reference to the member state against which the application is registered. (selected countries)(Up to 1987 only)

	1983	1984	1985	1986	1987	1988	1989	1990	1991
Austria	29	36	42	61	78	61	137	159	135
Belgium	18	41	32	44	64	46	65	94	67
Denmark	9	5	12	13	9	20	17	14	22
France	45	59	70	86	115	139	212	248	1
FRG	93	115	104	106	116	113	169	146	139
Greece	-	-	-	1	22	19	17	26	29
Ireland	9	8	5	4	7	5	11	13	7
Netherlands	29	45	34	50	56	75	107	109	98
Spain	10	15	19	17	22	34	71	69	75
Sweden	46	51	64	68	83	88	84	125	90
Switzerland	27	49	33	50	62	58	104	107	113
UK	152	128	112	140	141	145	224	236	202
All countries*	449	586	596	706	860	1,009	1,445	1,657	1,648

*Including some not listed above

The total number of applications per country is followed by the number of violations under headings A and B up to 1987: Austria: 738 (A:4 B:11); Belgium: 471 (A:3 B:10); Denmark: 121 (A:0 B:0); France: 1,374 (A:1 B:1); FRG: 1,101 ((A:1 B:7); Greece: 114 (A:1 B:0); Ireland: 69 (A:0 B:2); Netherlands: 603 (A:1 B:8); Spain: 332 (A:0 B:0); Sweden: 699 (A:1 B:2); Switzerland: 603 (A:3 B:4); UK: 1,478 (A:37 B:19). Total for all countries: 8,956 (A:51 B:76).

A: Number of cases in which the Committee of Ministers has found one or more violations of the Convention up to 1987. B: Number of cases in which the European Court of Human Rights found one or more violations of the Convention up to 1987.

APPENDIX 5
The Schengen Agreement

In July 1984 France and Germany signed an agreement in Saarbrucken to lift many of the existing frontier controls. In the October Belgium, Luxembourg and the

Netherlands countries joined the agreement. When it became clear at meetings of the Council of Ministers that there was little chance of a EC-wide agreement on internal border controls the five countries signed that Schengen Agreement in June 1985.[1]

The aim of Schengen I, 1985, was the abolition of border controls between member states by 1990. It set up working groups to deal with 'compensatory measures' in policing and security (narcotics, arms, border controls and security, information exchange, threats to public order and state security); movement of people (asylum, border controls, visa controls, exchange of information, a common deportation fund); transport (including lists of passengers carried across borders); and customs and circulation of goods. The working groups drafted further detailed measures which were agreed in the Schengen Supplementary Agreement in June 1990. Italy joined in November 1990, Portugal and Spain in June 1991 and Greece in 1992.

Schengen I was an administrative agreement requiring no parliamentary involvement. Frontier policing checks were initially reduced to visual inspections and spot checks. It was agreed to 'harmonise' policy on visas, co-ordinate crime prevention and search operations, in particular in connection with narcotics and laws governing their use, arms and explosives trade, and the registration of hotel guests (the West German Lander, which have jurisdiction for law on police matters, were excluded from this process as were the parliaments).

The Schengen Agreement (Schengen II), agreed by the governments in 1990, has been subject to parliamentary ratification in each country. It is now not expected that this process will be completed until the end of 1993.

The effect of the Schengen Agreement extends the powers of police forces and internal security agencies. Powers given to chase after a fleeing subject marks a first step towards legally sanctioning police and law enforcement activity on foreign

---

1. Hereafter referred to as the Schengen Agreement. Full treatments of the Schengen Agreement are given in the following: *a] Race & Class*, Europe: variations on a theme of racism, £4.00 from: The Institute of Race Relations, 2-6 Leeke Street, London WC1X 9HS; *b] Schengen*: internationalisation of central chapters of the law on aliens, refugees, security and the police, H Meijers et al, published by Kluwer, 1991. Paperback, 202 pages; *c] Netherlands Council of State*, opinion and critique. Hague 8.4.1991; *d] Towards the building of a Fortress Europe? The enforcement of internal and external border controls on people in the new Community "with internal borders"*, Massimo Pastore, Istituto di Scienze medico forensi, Torino, Italy. Paper presented at the 20th Annual Conference of the European Group for the Study of Deviance and Social Control, September 1992, Padua, Italy; *e] Schengen: Intergovernmental scenario for European police co-operation*, working paper 5, Monica den Boer, European Police Co-operation project group, Department of Politics, University of Edinburgh, 31 Buccleuch Place, Edinburgh EH8 9JT;*f] Schengen, Ad Hoc Immigration Group and other European intergovernmental bodies*, Antonio Cruz, Churches Committee for Migrants in Europe, Briefing paper no 12; *g] The Schengen Agreement: introduction, bibliography and full text*, Statewatch briefing paper no 2.

sovereign territory (*Schengen II*, Arts.40 and 47). What is notable is that permission to operate on foreign territory is to extend to undercover work, using such means as observation across frontiers, infiltration of drug rings, or the introduction of Europe-wide police surveillance(secret recording of movements, specific checks) (*Schengen II*, Arts. 41,75, and 100). Another clause of the Treaty deals with the need for mutual assistance between the national intelligence agencies in the interests of national state security (*Schengen II*, Art.48). This article was added to the treaty at the very last minute in November 1989.

The operation of the Schengen Agreement comes under an 'Executive Committee' of Ministers with the day-to-day operations being run by the Central Negotiating Group (CNG). Under the CNG there are a number of working parties, with sub-groups, including: Working Group 1: Police and Security: weapons, telecommunications, and legal experts; Working Group 2: Movement of persons: common manual, asylum, visas, and readmissions. There are also working groups on drug trafficking and Treaties, and a Committee on external borders.

Schengen Information System (SIS)
The Schengen Information System (SIS) is a computerised information exchange system based in Strasbourg. It is planned to come into operation in December 1993.

The creation of the SIS is set out in Articles 92-119. All the Contracting Parties (as the member countries are called) will have access to reports on 'persons and objects' through an automated search procedure. Each country will set up and maintain a 'national section'. The job of the central unit in Strasbourg will be to ensure that each national section holds identical data files, i.e. each national section will hold its own and the data from all the other countries. The purpose of the SIS is: 'to maintain public order and security, including state security, and to apply the provisions of this Convention relating to the movement of persons, in the territories of the Contracting Parties, using information transmitted by the system' (Article 93). The data to be stored can include nationality, 'any particular objective and permanent physical features' (i.e. a person's race), and the 'reason for the report' (which can include information relating to political beliefs).

The categories of information include: 1) persons wanted for arrest for extradition purposes (Article 95,lays down arrest and search powers); 2) aliens 'who are reported for the purposes of being refused entry' (Article 96.1); 3) the decision to hold data 'may be based on a threat to public order or national security and safety which the presence of an alien in national territory may pose' (96.2); 4) data on those who placed in 'provisional' custody refers to missing persons and to 'in order to prevent threats'(Article 97); witnesses (Article 98); 5) data on 'discreet surveillance' or specific checks for potential serious crime, 'prevention of threats to public safety' (Article 99.1/2) and at the request of authorities responsible for 'State security' on those who present a serious threat to 'internal or external State security'(Article 99.3); 6) data on objects wanted for evidence in criminal proceedings (Article 100). There are no criteria laid down whereby the information stored is to be directly related to a criminal offence and much will be 'intelligence' based on suspicions.

The data subject will, in principle, have the right of access and the right to correct the information held (Articles 109 and 110). These rights and the right of appeal are to be those available under each state's national law but with the following exceptions. Access is categorically denied if it: '*may* undermine the performance of the legal task specified in the report, or in order to protect the rights and freedoms of others' (Article 109.2; Italics added). Access is also to be denied in cases of 'discreet surveillance' including those relating to the security of the State (Articles 109.2 and 99.2).

Access to unprotected data held on the SIS which may be based on 'intelligence' (eg, suspicions) could have serious consequences for the individual: arrest, extradition, refusal of entry). The Agreement allows for the exchange of information for crime prevention and police surveillance purposes. Thus practices already considered dubious at the national level are given 'international currency'.

Recourse to the law will only be in the national courts, and then only in relation to respective national authorities. A person being held in another country based on information - passed on without their knowledge or agreement, which may or not be accurate - provided by their home or another country will face great difficulty in tracking down the source of the information. For example, the Treaty allows for a person who has been cautioned to be extradited without further formalities (*Schengen II*, Art.67).

Control and accountability
The Agreement sets up an 'Executive Committee', each country having one representative. It will have powers to legislate and to set up subsidiary working parties (*Schengen II*, Arts. 131-133). It combines the functions of legislature, executive and judiciary. The SIS is controlled by the Central Negotiating Group SIS (CNG.SIS), with the day-to-day work under the Steering Group (OR.SIS). A 'joint supervisory authority' to oversee the 'technical support' functions of the SIS was also created. This is comprised of two representatives from each country's data protection authority (*Schengen II*, Articles 115). No mechanisms are set out for parliamentary or judicial review. The European Parliament has passed several resolutions criticising the Schengen Agreement (and the Trevi group) because of secrecy surrounding its deliberations and its unaccountable nature. In February 1991 adopted a resolution criticising the undemocratic nature of the Schengen Agreement and its effect on immigrants and asylum-seekers (see Chapter 1 on the SIS becoming the European Information System, EIS).

APPENDIX 6

In this Appendix four documents are summarised in relation to the Trevi group and the wider development of the European state (see Chapter 1).

The Palma Document
The 'Palma Document', agreed in Madrid in June 1989, sets out areas of essential action under a number of headings.

Under the heading *Action at external frontiers* Trevi is charged, along with the Ad Hoc Group on Immigration and MAG 92, with: a system of surveillance at external frontiers; improved co-operation and exchange of information between law enforcement agencies and customs; 'combatting illegal immigration networks'; establishing a system to exchange information on people who are 'wanted' and those who are 'inadmissible' to the EC. Under *Action at internal frontiers and inside the EC*: drug trafficking, terrorism, development of a common system of search and information.

Under *Terrorism*: intensifying the exchange of information about the 'removal of citizens of third countries which represent a possible terrorist danger to security'; 'permanent targeted exchange of information' on known members of terrorist groups; establishment of a central registry of false documents, explosives, detonators; study of a common system for wanted persons (removal of third country nationals and suspects under police surveillance).

Declaration of Trevi group Ministers
The Declaration of Trevi group Ministers, agreed in Paris on 15 December 1989, sets out 'Principles' starting with the 'essential personal freedom..(of)..the freedom of movement'. While: 'We utterly reject the idea that this development would result in the creation of a Community closed to the rest of Europe and the world... At the same time we note with growing concern the development of organised crime across frontiers. Terrorists and professional criminals are increasingly adept at exploiting the limits of competence of national agencies'.

The Principles also refer to the differences in legal systems and the problems created for 'public order and internal security'. Four areas of cooperation are put forward: 1) *Communication and exchange of information*: the posting of liaison officers; setting up national intelligence units on drugs; the creation of a common information system; 2) *Frontiers*: 'to introduce at external frontiers controls which will safeguard the interests of all Member States'; in the longer term the allocation 'at a European level [of] a radio frequency common to all services responsible for public safety'; the framing of bilateral agreements for the crossing of common frontiers 'when following persons suspected of serious offences, or when in pursuit of individuals having committed flagrant violations of the law'; 3) *Technical training*: 'we will encourage our agencies to exchange information and experience on new technology and methods'; widen the knowledge of each others organisations and laws; 4) *Liaison officers*: to develop a network of liaison officers 'posted to countries which are not members of the EC', and examine the possibility of extending their work 'to other forms of crime'; 'We will keep like-minded non-member countries informed on policy developments..'

The Programme of Action
The Programme of Action, agreed by the Trevi group Ministers in Dublin in June 1990, is divided into three Chapters: Areas of Cooperation, Methods of Cooperation and Implementation of Cooperation.

Chapter 1 covers the cooperation between the police and security services on: 1) *Combating terrorism*: asks them to 'intensify' the updating of 'detailed information concerning the activity of terrorist groups, their techniques, logistics supports, their financing and the incidents they provoke' and for the provision of a permanent procedure for 'assessing terrorist threats against Member States' (see above); to improve security standards at airports, ports, railway stations, and possibly ferryboats; to 'facilitate the search for terrorists' to appoint liaison officers; to display 'wanted' posters at frontier posts; to immediately communicate information which may be of use to another state; to set up a system for encrypting documents sent through the TSFN (see above); 2) *Combating drug traffic*: to exchange information on the sources and methods of drug transportation; to ask Members States who do not have national drugs intelligence units to consider setting them up; to study the need for a European drugs intelligence unit; to conduct the 'controlled delivery' of drugs in order to locate distribution networks; 3) *Combating organised crime*: to exchange and update information on the forms of organised crime and the laundering of profits 4) *Combating illegal Immigration*: these agencies are to exchange information on: 'clandestine immigration networks, the identification of aliens reported for the purposes of refusal of entry to a member state and of aliens considered likely to compromise public order, the techniques used in the manufacture of travel documents'. 5) *Technical cooperation*: in order to combat 'illegality and criminality' especially its new forms such as credit cards and data processing; they are to contribute to a European 'central collection' of 'objects, substances, products and documents'. 6) *Training*: the exchange of officer to train them in the organisation, methods and legislative procedures in other states. 7) *Extension of co-operation*: to other subject ' concerning public order and internal security... this cooperation may include exchanges of information on methods of combatting serious disturbances of public order'. 8) *Exchange of experts and liaison officers*: these officers may 'be granted status of members of the administrative and technical personnel of their country's diplomatic mission..[and..they shall enjoy the privileges and immunities pertaining to that status'. 9) *Liaison officers outside the EC*: to create a network of officers in countries outside the EC; 10) *Control at External frontiers*: to ensure effective control members states may conclude agreements to coordinate their effects and this to include immigration officers; 11) *Police cooperation in common frontier areas*: to improve cooperation and surveillance including mobile joint control units; 12) *Common information system*: member states to study 'the development of a common information system designed to collect data and descriptions of persons and objects'.

The Palma report (1992)
The Coordinators Group report on the Palma document, December 1992, sets out the progress on the key areas of the European state. The relevant sections are as follows:
Action at External borders: Essential: Underpinning this area are the External Borders Convention and the development of the European Information System. Objective: Definition of the common control measures to be implemented after 1992 and of a surveillance system at external frontiers: *Ad Hoc Working Group on Immigration*: 1) provisions drawn up by Trevi 92 are in the External Borders Convention, 2) Common manual to be drawn up for use by external border control authorities; *MAG 92:* as part of it's External Frontier Strategy, 'a risk analysis of the Community's external frontier has been completed'. It is intended that there will be a 'continuous risk analysis'. Objective: Improvement of cooperation and of information exchange between police and customs services: *Group on Data processing*: developing this in relation to the European Information System; *Ad Hoc Group on Europol:* being attended by customs officers; and, 'An interface is being

considered between the European Information System and the Customs Information System'. Objective: Action to combat illegal immigration networks: *Ad Hoc Group on Immigration:* carried out a survey in July 1988 and is adapting the questionnaire for a follow-up; *Trevi 92:* drew up report on guiding principles which it submitted to the External Frontiers sub-group (of the Ad Hoc Working Group on Immigration); Objective: Introduction of a system for the exchange of information on (a) wanted persons (b) inadmissible persons: The main developments are of the European Information System (EIS) and the Customs Information System (launched in 1992). The report notes the delay in developing the EIS because of the planned interface with the Schengen Information System; *Trevi: European Information System sub group:* submitted report to the Horizontal Group on Data Processing; Of the 'desirable' measures under this heading the report notes that since the Palma Document was agreed to further 'items' have been added to the work on the 'harmonisation' of laws on immigration and aliens - on family reunification and admission for purpose of employment.

Action at internal frontiers: The report notes the differences between the UK, Denmark and Ireland over the issue of border controls. Objective: Compensatory measures on drug trafficking: *Trevi 3:* implementing through its work on the European Drugs Intelligence Unit; *MAG:* through its External Frontier Strategy and the Customs Information System. Objective: Cooperation between police and customs in frontier areas: *Trevi 92:* report accepted at Trevi Minsters meeting in December 1991; *MAG:* Declaration on Customs Mutual Assistance agreed between the Directors General of EC customs at Harrogate on 29 May 1992. This includes: designation of a central contact point in each Member State; the 'desirable' measure of requiring aliens to complete hotel registration forms is not being implemented.

Action to combat drug trafficking: The work in this area has mainly been implemented by Trevi 92, the Trevi 'Programme of Action', and MAG as part of its External Frontier Strategy. It also includes the creation of the European Monitoring Centre for Drugs and Drug Addiction (EMCDDA), which was formally agreed by the Council at its meeting on 8 February 1993.

Terrorism: Trevi 1: stepping up the exchange of information on the 'removal of nationals of third countries representing a potential terrorist threat'; *Trevi 1:* exchange of specific information on 'known members and activities of terrorist groups' in one Member state where 'the security interests of another Member State may be affected'; *Trevi 1:* cooperation in the case of actual wanted persons including 'the possible use of the media'; *Trevi 1:* studying the feasibility of creating 'in the wanted persons joint system' of categories covering 'removal of nationals of third countries' and 'surveillance of suspicious persons'. What constitutes a *'suspicious person'* is not defined. *Trevi 2:* creation of a central archive system for forged documents, explosives, detonators etc.

Select bibliography

Police

Anderson, Malcolm, 1991, *Working Paper I: The French Police and European Co-operation*, Edinburgh: University of Edinburgh.

Andrade, John, 1985, *World Police and Paramilitary Forces*, London: Macmillan.

Archer, Clive, 1985, 'The Police in Sweden', in Roach, John and Jürgen Thomaneck (eds) *Police and Public Order in Europe*. London: Croom Helm: 255-271.

Bannas, Günter, 'Jeder muß alles können', Die GSG 9. fünfzehn Jahre nach 'Mogadiscio' / Begleitschutz, Beobachtung, Festnahmen', Frankfurter Allgemeine Zeitung 16 October 1992

Bayley, David H. 1985 *Patterns of Policing: A Comparative International Analysis*, New Brunswick, NJ: Rutgers University Press

Busch, H. et al. 1985 *Die Polizei in der Bundesrepublik*, Frankfurt: Campus

Busch, Heiner, 'Auf dem Weg ins polizeilichen Europa - Spanien', Bürgerrechte und Polizei 1991 Nr. 3: 25-28.

Circular Letter Platform 'Fortress Europe?' Multiple issues 1992-1993

Collin, Richard O. 1985 'The Blunt Instrument: Italy and the Police', in Roach, John and Jürgen Thomaneck (eds.) *Police and Public Order in Europe*. London: Croom Helm: 185-214

Coveliers, Hugo (1989) *Securitas Belgica. De Rijkswacht is overbodig*. Antwerpen: Hadewijch.

Cullen, Peter J. 1992. Working Paper II: *The German Police and European Co-operation*, University of Edinburgh

Das, Dilip K. 1986 'Military Models of Policing: Comparative Impressions', Canadian Police College Journal Vol 4 No. 4: 267-285

Das, Dilip K. 1991 'Comparative Police Studies: An Assessment'. Police Studies Vol 14: 22-35

Engelen, J.J.F. 'De Nieuwe Politiewetgeving in België'. Tijdschrift voor de Politie September 1992: 361-364 (I) and October 1992: 399-403 (II)

European Police Summer Course, 1991: Lectures. Warnsveld: Politiestudiecentrum.

Fijnaut, C.J.C.F. 1989 'Ontwikkelingen op het gebied van de reguliere recherche in de omringende landen' in Fijnaut, C.J.C.F. en A. Heijder Recht van spreken. *Twintig jaar Recherche Advies Commissie*. Lochem: Van den Brink: 30-44

Fijnaut, Cyrille 1992. 'Politiestelsels in Europa. Democratie en structuur', in Tijdschrift voor de Politie September 1992: 350-352.

'Gendarmeries et polices à statut militaire.' Special issue of the Cahiers de la sécurité intérieure, no 11 (Novembre 92 - Janvier 93)

Hazenberg, Anita and Frans-Jan Mulschlegel (eds and compilers) 1992 *Facts, Figures, and General Information*, (revised edition). Amersfoort: European Network for Policewomen, 1992

Hudson, Robert C. 1988 'Democracy and the Spanish Police Forces Since 1975', Police Journal vol 61 no 1: 53-62

Hunter, Ronald D. 1990 'Three Models of Policing', Police Studies Vol. 13: 118-124

Kania, Richard R.E. 1989 'The French Municipal Police Experiment', Police Studies Vol. 12: 125-131

Kurian, George Thomas 1989 *World Encyclopedia of Police Forces and Penal Systems*. New York: Facts on File

Lochem, P.J.P.M. van et al (eds) 1989 *Report of the European Police Summer Course 1989*. Apeldoorn; Warnsveld: Nederlandse Politie Academie; Politie Studie Centrum

Macdonald, Ian R. 1985 'The Police System of Spain', in Roach, John and Jürgen Thomaneck (eds) *Police and Public Order in Europe*. London: Croom Helm: 215-254

Outrive, L. van et al 1991 *Les Polices en Belgique, Histoire socio-politique du système policier de 1794 à nos jours*, Bruxelles: Ed. Vie Ouvrière.

Outrive, L. van en Jan Cappelle 1991 *Twenty Years of Undercover Policing in Belgium: The Regulation of a Risky Police Practice*. Leuven: Katholieke Universiteit Leuven, Department of Criminology

Pierantoni, Umberto 1990 'The NOCS: An Elite Italian Police Squad', International Criminal Police Review July-August 1990: 18-20

PIOOM database 1992-1993 compiled by Drs. B.J. Jongman at Leiden University

Police en Europe 1991. Special issue of the *Cahiers de la Sécurité Intérieure*, No 7 (Novembre 1991 - Janvier 1992)

Roach, John, 'The French Police' in Roach, John and Jürgen Thomaneck (eds.) *Police and Public Order in Europe*. London: Croom Helm, 1985: 107-141

Schoonings, Katinka 1992 *Equal Treatment of Policewomen in the European Community*. Utrecht; Amersfoort: Justice Research Exchange; European Network for Policewomen

Semarak, Arved F. et al. 1989 *Die Polizeien in Westeuropa*. Stuttgart: Richard Boorberg Verlag

Skolnick, Jerome H. and David H. Bayley 1988 *Community Policing: Issues and Practices Around the World*. Washington, DC: U.S. Department of Justice

Statewatch Multiple issues 1991-1992

Steer, David 1990 'Policing and Police Research in Denmark', Police Requirements Support Unit Nr. 37: 6-7

Steer, David 1990 'Policing and Police Research in France', Police Requirements Support Unit Nr. 38: 7-11

Thompson, Leroy (circa 1986) *The Rescuers. The World's Top Anti-Terrorist Units*. Newton Abbot: David & Charles Publishers

Vetschera, Heinz 1992 'Terrorism in Austria: Experiences and Responses', Terrorism and Political Violence vol 4 no 4 (Winter 1992) pp. 210-233

Wieviorka, Michel 1990 'Mouvements terroristes et action antiterroriste: l'expérience française', Les cahiers de la sécurité intérieure Vol. 1 No. 1 (avril-juin 1990): 95-112

Zachtert, Hans-Ludwig 1991 'Das Bundeskriminalamt Gestern, Heute, Morgen', Kriminalistik November 1991: 682-687

Internal security services

Binnenlandse Veiligheidsdienst 1992 Ontwikkelingen op het gebied van de binnenlandse veiligheid. Taakstelling en werkwijze van de BVD. Den Haag: Ministerie van Binnenlandse Zaken

Binnenlandse Veiligheidsdienst 1992 Jaarverslag 1991. Den Haag: Ministerie van Binnenlandse zaken

Brunet, Jean-Paul, *La Police de l'ombre. Indicateurs et provocateurs dans la France contemporaine.* Paris: Seuil, 1990

Bundesamt für Verfassungsschutz 1990a *Bundesamt für Verfassungsschutz: Aufgaben - Befugnisse - Grenzen.* Bonn: Der Bundesminister des Innern

Bundesamt für Verfassungsschutz 1990b *Verfassungsschutz in der Demokratie. Beiträge aus Wissenschaft und Praxis.* Köln: Carl Heymanns Verlag

Bunyan, Tony, *The Political Police in Britain*, Quartet, 1977.

Burdan, Daniel avec Jean-Charles Deniau 1990 *DST. Neuf ans à la division antiterroriste.* Paris: Éditions Robert Laffont

Busch, Heiner 1990 *Polizeiliche Zusammenarbeit in Europa - Grenzöffnung und 'Ausgleichsmaßnahmen für den Sicherheitsverlust'.* Endbericht eines von der EG-Kommission geförderten Forschungsvorhabens. Manuscript, Berlin.

Busch, Nicholas 1992 'The New Security Police Law: Austria's "Pre Hoc" Harmonization with Schengen Policies?' Platform "Fortress Europe?' Circular Letter no 5: 1-3

Chalet, Marcel et Thierry Wolton 1990 *Les Visiteurs de l'ombre.* Paris: Grasset

Dobry, Michel 1992 *Le renseignement politique interne dans les democraties occidentales.* État de la recherche. Paris: IHESI

Dufourg, Jean-Marc 1991 *Section manipulation   De l'antiterrorisme à l'affaire Doucé.* Paris: Michel Lafon

Faligot, Roger and Pascal Krop 1989 *La Piscine: The French Secret Service since 1944.* Oxford: Basil Blackwell

Guisnel, Jean et Bernard Violet 1988 *Services secrets. Le pouvoir et les services de renseignements sous la présidence de François Mitterrand.* Paris: Éditions la Découverte

Harstrich, Jacques avec Fabrizio Calvi 1991 *R.G. 20 ans de police politique.* Paris: Calmann-Lévy

Klerks, Peter 1989 *Terreurbestrijding in Nederland.* Amsterdam: Ravijn

Klerks, Peter 1991 'Veiligheidsdiensten in verandering', in Almelo, A.E. van en P.G. Wiewel. *Politiezorg in de jaren '90.* Arnhem: Gouda Quint

Komitee Schluss mit dem Schnüffelstaat 1990 *Schnüffelstaat Schweiz: Hundert Jahre sind genug.* Zürich: Limmat Verlag

Magnusson, Erik 1989 *Maktkamp om Säpo.* Lund: Corona

Marion, Pierre 1991 *La Mission Impossible. À la tête des Services Secrets.* Paris: Calmann-Lévy

Molenaar, Fjodor/Jansen & Janssen 1991 *De vluchteling achtervolgd. De BVD en asielzoekers.* Amsterdam: Ravijn

Norton-Taylor Richard, *In Defence of the Realm? The case for accountable security services*, Civil Liberties Trust, 1990.

Ostrovsky, Victor and Claire Hoy 1990 *By Way of Deception.* London: Arrow Books

Parlementair Onderzoek 1990 Parlementair Onderzoek naar de wijze waarop de bestrijding van het banditisme en het terrorisme georganiseerd wordt. Verslag namens de onderzoekscommissie uitgebracht door de heren Van Parys en Laurent. Brussel: Handelingen Belgische parlement 59/8-10 (1988)

Parlementarischen Untersuchungskommission EMD 1990 *Vorkomnisse im EMD.*

Bericht der parlamentarischen Untersuchungskommission (PUK EMD). Bern Conference 'The Proper Role of an Intelligence Agency in a Democracy', Sofia, Bulgaria 8-10 April 1992. Minutes of the meetings.

Quadruppani, Serge 1989 *L'anti-terrorisme en France ou la terreur intégrée 1981-1989*. Paris: Éditions la Découverte

Richelson, Jeffrey T. 1988 *Foreign Intelligence Organizations*. Cambridge, MA: Ballinger

Rossigneux, Brigitte et al. 1988 *Espionnage: le polar et la manière*. Paris: les Dossiers du "Canard"

Töllborg, Dennis 1991 'Covert Policing in Sweden: The Swedish Secret Service' Report to the Joint Meeting of LSA and ISA, Amsterdam June 26-29 1991. Preliminary version.

Verdeckte Ermittler in Tübingen. Tübingen, manuscript, 1992.

Verfassungsschutzbericht 1989, 1990, 1991. Bonn: Der Bundesminister des Innern

Vié, Jean-Émile 1988 *Mémoires d'un directeur des Renseignements généraux*. Paris: Albin Michel

Willan, Philip 1991 *Puppetmasters: The Political Use of Terrorism in Italy*. London: Constable

Zeger, Hans G. et al. 1990 Alpen-Stasi. Die II. *Republik im Zerrspiegel der Staatspolizei*. Linz: agis/sandkorn

Newspapers: Guardian, International Herald Tribune, Libération, Le Monde, De Morgen, NRC Handelsblad, TAZ Volkskrant. *Weekly and monthly magazines*: Bürgerrechte und Polizei, Fichen-Fritz, Geheim, Innere Sicherheit, Intelligence Newsletter, Kriminalistik, Lobster, Le Monde Diplomatique, Security Intelligence Report (formerly Counter-Terrorism), Der Spiegel, Statewatch, WoZ, Keesing's Record of World Events

Northern Ireland

Adams J, Morgan R and Bambridge A, Ambush: *The War between the SAS and the IRA*, London: Pan Books, 1988.

Bell D, *Acts of Union: Youth Culture and Sectarianism in Northern Ireland*, London: Macmillan, 1991.

Bolton R, *Death on the Rock and Other Stories*, London: Allen, 1990.

Britain's Army for the 90s: Commitments and Resources, Defence Committee, Second Report, HC 1992/93: 306. London: HMSO, 1993.

British Intelligence, Brian Nelson and the Rearming of the Loyalist Death Squads, Belfast, 1993.

Brewer J, *Inside the RUC: Routine Policing in a Divided Society*, Oxford: Clarendon Press

Bruce S, *The Red Hand: Protestant Paramilitaries in Northern Ireland*, Oxford: Oxford University Press, 1992.

Committee on the Administration of Justice, *Inquests and Disputed Killings in Northern Ireland*, Belfast: CAJ, 1992.

Committee for the Transfer of Irish Prisoners, *Double Sentence*, Belfast, 1991.

Coughlan A, *Fooled Again? The Anglo-Irish Agreement and After*, Cork: Mercier

Press, 1986.

Coulter C, *Web of Punishment*, Dublin: Attic Press, 1991.

Dillon M, *Stone Cold: the true story of Michael Stone and the Milltown massacre*. London: Hutchinson, 1992.

Dillon M, *The Dirty War*, London: Arrow Books, 1990.

Ferrers Report, *Report of the Interdepartmental Working Group's Review of the Provisions for the Transfer of Prisoners Between UK Jurisdictions.*

Foot P, *Who Framed Colin Wallace*, London: Pan Books, 1990.

Harvey R, 'The Right of the People of the Whole of Ireland to Self-Determination, Unity, Sovereignty and Independence', New York Law School Journal of International and Comparative Law, Vol 11, pp167-206.

Hillyard P, 'Political and Social Dimensions of Emergency Law in Northern Ireland' in Jennings A (ed) *Justice Under Fire: The Abuse of Civil Liberties in Northern Ireland*, London: Pluto Press, 1988. pp191-212.

In Whose Name? Britain's Denial of Peace in Ireland, London: Troops Out Movement, 1991.

Ireland in Europe: A Shared Challenge. Economic Co-operation on the Island of Ireland in an Integrated Europe. Dublin: Stationery Office.

Jack I, 'Gibraltar', Granta, 25, 1988.

Jennings A (ed) *Justice Under Fire: The Abuse of Civil Liberties in Northern Ireland*, London: Pluto Press, 1988.

McCann E, *Bloody Sunday: What Really Happened?* Dingle: Brandon Books, 1992.

MacFarlane L, 'Human Rights and the fight against terrorism in Northern Ireland', Terrorism and Political Violence 4: 1, 1992. pp89-99.

Miller D, *Whose Truth? The Media and the Gibraltar Killings*, Glasgow University Media Group, 1989.

Murray R, *The SAS in Ireland*, Cork: Mercier Press, 1990.

O'Dowd L, 'Strengthening the Border on the Road to Maastricht', Irish Reporter, No 9, 1993, pp12-15.

Philip C and Taylor A, *Inside the SAS*, London: Bloomsbury, 1992.

The Political Vetting of Community Work Group, *The Political Vetting of Community Work in Northern Ireland*, Belfast: Northern Ireland Council for Voluntary Action, 1990.

Porter S, 'Unhealthy Surveillance: Investigating Public Health in South Armagh', Critical Public Health (forthcoming).

Report of the Public Inquiry into the Killing of Fergal Caraher and the Wounding of Michael Caraher 30th Dec. 1990, Irish National Congress/Cullyhana Justice Group, 1992.

Rolston B, 'Containment and its Failure: The British State and the Control of Conflict in Northern Ireland', Chapter 7 of George A (ed) *Western State Terrorism*, Cambridge: Polity Press, 1991.

Rolston B and Tomlinson M 'The Challenge Within: Prisons and Propaganda in Northern Ireland', in Tomlinson M et al (eds) *Whose Law and Order? Aspects of Crime and Social Control in Irish Society*, Belfast: Sociological Association of Ireland, 1988, pp167-192.

Rolston B and Tomlinson M *Unemployment in West Belfast: The Obair Report*, Belfast: Beyond the Pale Publications, 1988.

Rowthorn B and Wayne N *Northern Ireland: The Political Economy of Conflict*, Cambridge: Polity Press, 1988.
Ryder C, *The RUC: A Force Under Fire*, London: Methuen, 1989.
Ryder C, *The Ulster Defence Regiment: An Instrument of Peace?* London: Methuen, 1991.
Smith D and Chambers G, *Inequality in Northern Ireland*, Oxford: Clarendon Press, 1991.
The Ulster Defence Regiment: the Loyalist Militia, Dublin: Sinn Fein Publicity Department.
Urban M, *Big Boys' Rules: The SAS and the Secret Struggle against the IRA*, London: Faber and Faber, 1992.

Ireland (South)

Derek Dunne and Gene Kerrigan, *Round Up the Usual Suspects*, the Cosgrave Coalition and Nicky Kelly, Magill, Dublin 1984;
Michael Farrell, *Sheltering the Fugitive the Extradition of Irish Political Offenders*, Mercier, Cork 1985;
Michael Farrell, *The Apparatus of Repression*, Field Day Theatre Company, Derry 1966;
Michael Forde, *Extradition Law in Ireland*, Round Hall Press, Dublin 1987.
Gerard Hogan and Clive Walker, *Political Violence and the Law in Ireland*, Manchester University Press 1989;
M T W Robertson, *The Special Criminal Court*, Dublin University Press 1974
Bill Rolston (ed), *The Media and Northern Ireland*, Macmillan, London 1991.

Immigration, asylum, racism

Ad Hoc Group Immigration: *Draft resolution on manifestly unfounded applications for asylum*. Brussels, July 1992.
Ad Hoc Group Immigration: *Resolution on manifestly unfounded applications for asylum; Resolution on a harmonised approach to questions concerning host third countries; Conclusions on countries in which there is generally no serious risk of persecution*. London, November 1992.
Asylum and Immigration Appeals Bill. HMSO, 1992.
Berger, John and Mohr, Jean: *A seventh man*. Harmondsworth, 1975.
Böhning, W and Werquin, J: *The future status of third-country nationals in the European community*. Brussels, CCME, (1990).
CARF: Bimonthly, London, Jan 1991-. Articles on immigration, asylum and racism in Europe in all issues.
CARF/Southall Rights: *Southall: the birth of a black community*. London, 1981.
Carr, Matthew: 'The year of Spain', in Race & Class 34:4, 1993.
Castles, Stephen: 'Racism and politics in West Germany', in Race & Class 25:3, 1984.
Castles, Stephen: 'The social time bomb: the education of an underclass in West Germany', in Race & Class 21:4, 1980.
Cohen, Steve: *Imagine there's no countries: 1992 and international immigration*

controls against migrants, immigrants and refugees. Manchester, Greater Manchester Immigration Aid Unit, (1991).

Cruz, Antonio: *Carrier sanctions in five community states: incompatibilities between international civil aviation and human rights obligations.* Brussels, CCME, 1991.

Cruz, Antonio: *An insight into Schengen, Trevi and other European intergovernmental bodies.* Brussels, CCME, (1989).

David, Kenith, ed: *Europe 92: reflections from the underside.* Geneva, World Council of Churches, (1992).

Dedecker, R: *The right of asylum in Europe: some proposals on accelerated procedures for the 12 member states.* Brussels, Jan 1992.

Drüke, L: *Asylum policies in a European community without internal borders.* Brussels, CCME, 1992.

Dublin Convention, Cmnd 1623, HMSO, 1991.

EC Commission: *Communication from the Commission to the Council and the European Parliament on immigration.* Brussels, Oct 1991.

EC Commission: *Communication from the Commission to the Council and the European Parliament on the right of asylum.* Brussels, Oct 1991.

European ministers responsible for immigration: press release. London, 30 November 1992.

European Parliament Civil Liberties and Internal Affairs Committee: *Survey of the right of asylum in the Community member states.* Brussels, 1991.

European Parliament Civil Liberties and Internal Affairs Committee: Annex to notice to members (on Budapest ministerial meeting 15-16 February 1993). Brussels, March 1993.

Fekete, Liz: 'The anti-fascist movement: lessons we must learn', in Race & Class 28:1, 1986.

Fekete, Liz: 'Europe for the Europeans, East End for the East Enders', in Race & Class 32:1, 1990.

Fekete, Liz: 'Racist violence: meeting the new challenges', in Race & Class 30:2, 1988.

Ford, Glyn: *Fascist Europe: the rise of racism and xenophobia*, Pluto, 1993.

Gordon, Paul: *Passport raids and checks: Britain's internal immigration controls.* London, Runnymede Trust, 1981.

Gordon, Paul: *White law: racism in the police, courts and prisons.* London, Pluto, 1983.

Guild, Elspeth: *Protecting migrants' rights: application of EC agreements with third countries.* Brussels, CCME, 1992.

Institute of Race Relations: *Policing against black people.* London, IRR, 1987.

IRR European Race Audit: Quarterly bulletin. London, Institute of Race Relations, Nov 1992-continuing

Joint Council for the Welfare of Immigrants: *Unequal migrants: the EC's unequal treatment of migrants and refugees.* London, JCWI, 1989.

Joly, Daniele: *Refugees: asylum in Europe? London,* Minority Rights Group, 1992.

Mallet, N: 'Deterring asylum-seekers: German and Danish law on political asylum', Immigration & Nationality Law and Practice, 5:4, 1991.

Migration Newssheet. Monthly. Brussels.

Newham Monitoring Project/CARF: *Newham: the forging of a black community.*

London, 1991.

Niessen, J: *European migration policies for the nineties after the Maastricht summit.* Brussels, CCME, 1992.

Race & Class: *Europe: variations on a theme of racism,* (Special issue.) 32:3, 1991.

Read, Mel and Simpson, Alan: *Against a rising tide: racism, Europe and 1992.* Nottingham, Spokesman, 1991.

Refugee Forum/Migrants Rights Action Network: *The walls of the fortress: European agreements against immigrants, migrants and refugees.* London, 1991.

Rule, Ella: 'The Spanish law on asylum and refugees', in Immigration and nationality law and practice, 6:3, July 1992.

Sitaropoulos, Nicholas: 'The new legal framework of alien immigration in Greece', in Immigration and nationality law and practice, 6:3, July 1992.

Sivanandan, A: *Communities of resistance: writings on black struggles for socialism.* London, Verso, 1990.

Sivanandan, A: *A different hunger: writings on black resistance.* London, Pluto, 1982.

Sivanandan, A: 'The new racism', in New Statesman and Society, 4 November 1988.

Sivanandan, A: 'Racism: the road from Germany', in Race & Class, 34:3, 1993.

Webber, Frances: 'Europe 1992', in Race & Class 31:2, 1989.

Webber, F: 'If I'm sent back I'll die anyway', in Race & Class 34:2, 1992.

Human Rights

Gibson, Urban and Niessen, Jan: *The CSCE and the protection of the rights of migrants, refugees and minorities.* Brussels, CCME, 1993.

Human Rights Law Journal: monthly. Kehl am Rhein.

Immigration Law Practitioners' Association: *Application by the ECJ of the human rights obligations contained in instruments of which EC member states are parties: relevant extracts from the decisions.* London, Law Society, Aug 1992.

Immigration Law Practitioners' Association: *The case law of the European Convention on Human Rights in immigration, asylum and extradition: relevant extracts from the decisions.* London, Law Society, Sept 1992.

Robertson, A H and Merrills, J G: *Human rights in Europe: a study of the European Convention on Human Rights.* 3rd edition, Manchester, Manchester UP, 1993.

Trevi, Europol and the European state

Bunyan, Tony 'Towards an authoritarian European state', *Race & Class,* special issue: 'Europe: variations on a theme of racism', 1991.

Development of Europol, report from the Trevi Ministers to the European Council, Maastricht, December 1991.

Migration Control at External Borders of the European Community, Home Affairs Select Committee, HC 215-i, ii & iii, 1992.

Practical Police Cooperation in the European Community, Home Affairs Select Committee, HC 363-i & HC 363-II, HMSO, 1990.

Programme of Action relating to the Reinforcement of police cooperation and of endeavours to combat terrorism and other forms of organised crime, June 1990.

Progress made in implementing the Palma Report, Council, CIRC 3658/4/92, 5.11.92, Confidential.

Report on Europol, Civil Liberties and Internal Affairs Committee, European Parliament, rapporteur: Lode van Outrive MEP, November 1992.

Treaty on European Union (Maastricht Treaty), European Communities, 1992.

Weichert, Thilo, 'Freie fahrt für alle daten', Im fadenkreuz Europas, Green Party, Germany, 1993.

Subscribe to Statewatch bulletin

If you want to keep up with the developments covered in this handbook why not subscribe to Statewatch bulletin which is published six times a year.

Subscriptions: UK & Europe: £8 a year, students and unemployed; £10 a year, individuals; £15 a year, community and voluntary groups; £20 a year, institutions.

Individuals can pay by cheque or by Visa/Access card by sending: Name and address on card, card number, and expiry date. Institutions: can order by invoice. Europe: please pay by Eurocheque, international money order or with a sterling cheque drawn on a UK bank.

Send to: Statewatch, PO Box 1516, London N16 0EW, UK